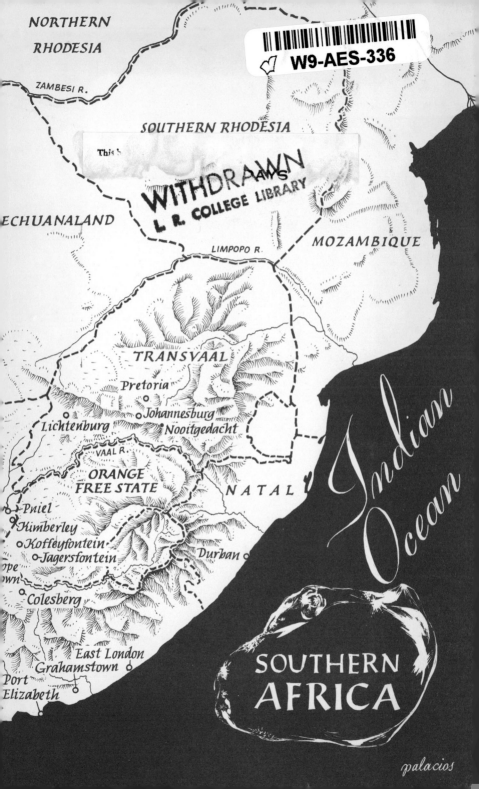

NORTHERN
RHODESIA

ZAMBESI R.

SOUTHERN RHODESIA

ECHUANALAND

MOZAMBIQUE

LIMPOPO R.

TRANSVAAL

Pretoria

Johannesburg
Lichtenburg          Nooitgedacht

VAAL R.

ORANGE
FREE STATE          NATAL

Pniel
Kimberley
Koffeyfontein
Jagersfontein          Durban

Colesberg

East London
Grahamstown
Port
Elizabeth

Indian
Ocean

SOUTHERN
AFRICA

palacios

# DIAMOND

EMILY HAHN

# Diamond

THE SPECTACULAR STORY OF EARTH'S RAREST

TREASURE AND MAN'S GREATEST GREED

*Doubleday & Company, Inc.*

*Garden City, New York, 1956*

Many thanks to Sir Ernest Oppenheimer,
chairman of De Beers Consolidated Mines, Ltd.,
and of Anglo American Corporation of South Africa, Ltd.,
and to all the officials of those companies
to whom I turned for help.

*Most of the material in this book originally appeared in* The New
Yorker, *some of it in different form.*

553.8
H12d

34353
November 1956

*Library of Congress Catalog Card Number 56–9394*

# Contents

DIAMOND

Kimberley has also diamonds

The corporation of Kimberley
was born in 1888 and I now
it is one of the most powerful
business empires on earth,
throughly dominating the world's
diamond industry

13, 4, 15

# Kimberley

A while ago, when I told a Johannesburg lady I was going to Kimberley, she said impatiently, "It will just be a waste of time. Kimberley's a dreary little place. It isn't a city at all; it's a state of mind. The people who live there are crazy about it— they're always bragging—but you couldn't induce me to spend any time there. As far as I'm concerned, it's just a backward little mining town with a terrible climate." Johannesburg is a younger city than Kimberley, and a larger one; with its sky- scrapers, department stores, and movie houses, and its popu- lation of three quarters of a million, it is South Africa's pride, and will stand comparison with the other big towns of the world. The same can't be said for Kimberley, even though, as I discovered, its fifty-five thousand inhabitants, like city people everywhere, complain of a traffic problem. Johannesburg is there because of gold, but it has developed other interests and has become the largest city in the Union of South Africa; Kimberley is there because of diamonds, and although it has acquired some urbanity and an air of permanence it still is, as my Johannesburg acquaintance said, a mining town. (As she said, too, the weather is terrible; I went there in February—midsummer in South Africa—and it was sizzling.) But Kimberley has something of its own—something, perhaps, of San Francisco's quality, which is hard to describe without using the word "history." And that sounds a little overblown, for Kimberley is only eighty-five years old.

Kimberley is not a very small city, as such things go in South Africa, but it has the atmosphere of one. It is a company town, and most of its citizens are held together by the common history of De Beers Consolidated Mines, Ltd., the great corporation that was born in Kimberley in 1888 and is now one of the most powerful business empires on earth, thoroughly dominating the world's diamond industry. Practically everybody in town works for De Beers or has worked for De Beers or has an ancestor who worked for De Beers. Many of the old mining families have dispersed, and quite a lot of the young people of Kimberley have branched out into work unconnected with diamonds—schoolteaching, shopkeeping, manufacturing, and so on—but most of the people know each other, and one hears the same names again and again. When two Kimberley residents who don't happen to know each other are introduced the conversation is apt to go something like this:

"Weren't you at school with Viljoen, or was that someone else with your name?"

"No, that was me. Viljoen and I are first cousins, you know —or, wait, is it second cousins? That's right, second cousins. We grew up together, but he started working in the washing plant here in '27, and I went to the Rand."

One thing that makes Kimberley seem small is the fact that it is pinched in by five vast gaping holes—the deepest open-pit mines ever dug by man. There is no digging in any of the pits these days, and hasn't been for half a century or more, but beneath three of them there are active mines, with shafts and tunnels and trams and all the other paraphernalia of modern mining. The most famous of the pits, the abandoned Kimberley Mine, also known as the Big Hole, which lies on the northwestern outskirts of the town, is about thirteen hundred feet deep; it is half full of water now, and even the surface of the water looks, and is, a long way down. The years have modified what must have been the supreme ugliness of the land around the Big Hole and the lesser holes, and the town is now reasonably full of tree-lined avenues, flowers, and little ornamental pools, but the greenness is of that precarious, stubborn kind familiar to people who live in the drier regions of our West. The tailings—waste rock and earth—from the enormous cavities were piled up over a wide area spreading out from their rims. Tailings are a familiar part of any mine landscape; after all, one has to put the stuff somewhere. The flat-topped mounds from the gold mines have long been a vexation to Johannesburg, but Kimberley has been luckier. Cyanide is used in the extraction of gold, and nothing will grow on gold tailings until it is leached out—an arduous and expensive process—but diamond tailings aren't barren, and the ground around the Kimberley mine has been taken over by camel's-thorn trees and scrubby grass. It is a pleasant, parklike region of small hills that you can drive through without ever suspecting that every cubic inch of earth for many feet down was hauled out of the nearby pit, and weathered, and crushed, and sifted, and scrutinized, before it was thrown aside.

The streets of central Kimberley are broad and well paved,

and lined with respectable banking houses, hotels, and shops, but they twist and turn capriciously, describing odder patterns than the streets of the oldest European cities. The Kimberley streets began as the footpaths of the mining camp, and the footpaths twisted and turned to avoid casually placed shacks, the guy ropes of tents, and other impedimenta. Kimberley residents thus have a traffic labyrinth, and they are as proud of it as Londoners are of the maze of the city. The oldest part of Kimberley, which comes to an abrupt end against the southern edge of the Big Hole, hasn't changed much since it was built or, rather, assembled. Many of the buildings that housed the town's first diamond brokers still stand—squat one-story brick structures, divided into cubbyholes of offices, with small windows at which dusty, impatient diggers would line up all day to haggle over their loot. There are also corrugated-iron houses that used to be portable but are now firmly rooted to the ground; they usually have tiny *stoeps*, or verandas, added on, and gardens. Eighty years ago, at the height of the diamond rush, one of these houses was advertised—cash and carry—in a mining-camp newspaper: "IRON HOUSE FOR SALE! An Iron House, 45 feet x 22 feet inside, two large windows with iron shutters: one pair large folding doors, with sashlights: Pitched Roof: Linen Ceiling: with Locks, Bars, and Bolts complete." In those days, iron houses were popular because they could be taken apart, loaded on an oxcart, and set down again wherever their owners felt like digging. Mr. A. J. Beet, the leading local historian, who is now seventy-four, remembers a story he heard as a child about one of those elaborate practical jokes that flourish in mining camps. A man who lived in an iron house found a good big diamond and celebrated his luck in the traditional manner, passing out before midnight. His friends picked up his house, complete with furniture and insensible host, and carried it across the road, where they set it down facing in the other direction. When he awoke in the morning, he called out to a neighbor, "I don't know what it is, but something's funny this morning. The sun just came up on the wrong side."

One of the civic peculiarities of Kimberley is the prevalence of debris-washing. Any resident who digs up his own ground to build a garage or add a wing to his house naturally wants to have the dirt washed out to see whether it contains diamonds, and there are men who make a business of debris-washing, carrying their simple gear from spot to spot, wherever a road is being laid or a building is going up. "Of course, diamonds turn up here and there," a Kimberley man told me. "Why wouldn't they? This town was the diggings. But let me warn you, if you haven't got a license to dig, it's a complicated business finding a diamond, even on your own property. First, you must report the find to the police, and then you have to make a statement, and fill out forms, and all that. Nobody without a license is supposed to have an uncut diamond in his possession. If you should happen to find one accidentally, you'd be best advised just to throw it away."

I hadn't gone to Kimberley for diamonds, or anyway not to acquire them. I had gone there for history, and history is what I got—plenty of it. Practically everybody in Kimberley is an amateur historian. The town has an excellent library, where old newspapers, diggers' licenses, and other records are carefully preserved, and it is always full of Kimberley citizens looking up things about Kimberley. It was there that I met Mr.

Beet and there, too, that he sat with me for hours, recounting
the early history of Kimberley as he gazed steadily at me with
his milky-blue eyes. Gradually, with the aid of Mr. Beet and a
multitude of books and documents, I pieced together something of the confused story of the rush and of the chaotic,
exuberant infancy of the world's most celebrated diamond-
mining town.

Before the first diamonds were discovered in the veld—no-
body knows for sure whether it was in 1866 or 1867—the region
was agricultural and, in the eyes of the world, unimportant.
Back in the seventeenth century, when the Dutch and the
British were disputing about who ruled the waves, the Dutch
East India Company planted a colony at the Cape of Good
Hope, where its ships could provision, and before long a good
many people settled there—mostly Dutch but also quite a few
British, Huguenots, Swedes, and Germans. Some founded the
city of Cape Town, and some fanned out into the surrounding
countryside, where they grew wheat and vines or raised sheep
and cattle. During the Napoleonic Wars, the Dutch were, however unwillingly, allies of the French, and in 1806 the British
took over the territory and set up two crown colonies—the Cape
Colony and, along the coast to the northeast, Natal. Not long
afterward, the Boers, or Dutch farmers (*boer* is Dutch for
"farmer"), began their famous treks, to get away from the enemy and to avoid crowding. A Boer considered himself crowded
if his farm was smaller than six thousand acres. The Voortrekkers, as the emigrants were called, pushed into the veld,
fighting off and driving out native tribes, until they had got beyond the Orange River, the northern boundary of the British
territory, and there they established an independent republic

—the Orange Free State. Some of the Voortrekkers went even farther north, beyond the Vaal River, and these established another republic—the Transvaal. As it happened, the boundaries proclaimed by both republics took in slivers of land occupied by the Griquas, a people of mixed Dutch and Hottentot blood, who lived more or less nomadically on the veld around what is now Kimberley. The Griquas were bound by treaty to the British, and the Voortrekkers let them stay where they were; there were only four or five thousand Griquas, anyway, and there was plenty of room for everybody. The real territorial arguments started later—once the rush was on.

For about a hundred years before the South African rush began, the world's chief source of diamonds had been Brazil; before that, it had been India. In 1866 diamonds were still coming out of India in a small, unsteady trickle; Brazil had produced a gush, but her mines were nearly worked out; and other sources, like Borneo, had never yielded much. Our grandparents probably thought that the world's supply of diamonds was just about exhausted, and were dazzled when they heard of the discoveries on the veld. The news didn't quite explode like a bombshell, though; in fact, it was slow-moving, retarded at the outset by people like Mr. J. R. Gregory, a geologist who scouted the area in 1868 for a London diamond firm. Gregory concluded dogmatically that the veld was not diamondiferous; the few stones that had been picked up there, he reported, were brought to the locality in the crops of ostriches. He didn't pursue the matter to the point of investigating where the ostriches had found the diamonds in the first place, and, on his recommendation, his firm dropped all interest in the veld. Nobody seems to know what happened to Mr. Gregory when the rush started, only a year later; presumably, he didn't remain on the company's payroll long.

The circumstances of the first diamond find are still hotly argued in Kimberley and other places where people are engaged in the diamond trade—New York, Amsterdam, Antwerp, London, and, for that matter, Johannesburg. Did the Boer child find the first diamond in 1866 or 1867? Was it Schalk van Niekerk who first recognized it as a diamond or was it Jack O'Reilly? What started Van Niekerk and/or O'Reilly thinking about diamonds, anyway? If you ask these questions in Kimberley, you get a variety of answers. Diamonds must have been lying around the veld in full sight of the Boers and the Griquas for many years—kicked by children, trampled into the mud by livestock, outshone by colored pebbles, perhaps even actually swallowed by ostriches—and certainly diamonds as big as eggs were used by witch doctors as part of their professional equipment. But unless you have a trained eye you are not likely to spot a diamond in a heap of gravel, although, to be sure, there is something special about some rough diamonds— the comparatively few that are formed in sharp crystals and are unfrosted. The light seems to have been caught in them and to have remained there, in a peculiarly vivid, cold, silvery gleam.

In 1932 Mr. Beet looked up the man who, as a boy, found the first South African diamond, Erasmus Stephanus Jacobs, and persuaded him to dictate an account of the event, which Jacobs did in Afrikaans, the Boer language and the only language he knew well. Until recently, people of British descent in South African industrial centers seldom went to the trouble of learning Afrikaans—a language based on seventeenth-century Dutch that over the years has borrowed words from Portu-

guese, English, and various native dialects—but on the veld
and in Kimberley everyone has spoken Afrikaans for at least a
century. Mr. Beet, whose grandparents came to Kimberley from
England during the diamond rush, had no problem communi-
cating with Jacobs, for he speaks Afrikaans fluently, but he did
have other problems. "Jacobs was an old man," Mr. Beet told
me. "He had told his story many times, but there were many
things he didn't remember. Why, he didn't even remember the
year he found his diamond! I tried to pin him down, I worked
him hard, but even so there's a lot to be desired in his account."

Mr. Beet had translated and transcribed Jacobs' account,
and he let me read it, leaning over me and breaking in frequently as I did so.

*I was born on the 23rd October, 1851 [the account started],
and at the time my life story began our family lived on the
farm "de Kalk," on the south side of the Orange River, in the
district of Hope Town . . . My parents were then well-to-do,
and my father, Daniel Jacobus Jacobs, owned the farm "de
Kalk," and also many cattle and sheep.*

"The first finds weren't made at Kimberley, of course," Mr.
Beet pointed out. "They were made along the rivers—the Vaal,
north of here, and the Orange, to the south. It was some time
before the diggers learned about what we call 'dry' mining."

*I did not herd the livestock, but used to help my father in
general work about the farm [Jacobs went on]. One day a water
pipe leading out of a dam became choked up, and my father
sent me out on the veldt to cut a long thin branch of a tree
that could be used to clear the pipe. Having secured what I*

*wanted, and feeling somewhat tired, I sat down in the shade*
*of a tree, when I suddenly noticed in the glare of the strong*
*sun a glittering pebble some yards away.*

"I remember how he described it," Mr. Beet told me. "He
said it blinked like this." He spread his fingers, closed them into
a fist, and suddenly splayed them out again. Then he let me
return to Jacobs:

*I became curious and went and picked up this mooi klip*
*[pretty pebble]. It was lying between some limestone and iron-*
*stone. The spot was quite a distance from our homestead, but*
*only about a couple of hundred yards from the bank of the*
*Orange River. I, of course, had no idea that the stone was of*
*value. I was at the time wearing a corduroy suit, and simply*
*put the pebble in my pocket. I did not feel at all excited at*
*finding such a beautiful stone. . . . After reaching home, I*
*handed the pretty pebble to my youngest sister, who simply*
*placed it aside among her playthings. . . . A month or two*
*after finding the stone, my two sisters and my brother and I*
*were playing a game known as "Five Stones"; one was the dia-*
*mond and the others ordinary river stones. Van Niekerk ar-*
*rived during the game and greatly admired the stone, and tried*
*to scratch a windowpane with it. My mother noticed that Mr.*
*van Niekerk had taken quite a fancy to this "white stone," so*
*she gave it to him.*

This was one of the parts of the Jacobs story that Mr. Beet
was unhappy about. Schalk van Niekerk, who lived in a house
on the Jacobs property, was a divisional councilor, a sort of
welfare officer appointed by the farmers of the Hope Town

district; although Jacobs considered his father well-to-do, the farmers were, from our point of view, a rather poverty-stricken lot, and they had worked out a mutual-aid system. Jacobs, Mr. Beet complained, had been known to tell the story of the find differently; according to the variant account, Van Niekerk had asked Mrs. Jacobs to keep an eye out for pretty stones, the boy had turned the pebble over to her, and she had popped it into her workbox and then given it to her neighbor as a matter of course.

"What's the difference?" I asked. "One story is as good as the other."

Mr. Beet snorted. "All the difference in the world," he said. "We don't know whether Van Niekerk was actually on the lookout for diamonds or whether a pretty stone just happened to catch his eye. And that business about scratching a window-pane—that's really exasperating. It would indicate that Van Niekerk knew he had a diamond. But if he did, why did he go and sell it to O'Reilly for only a few pounds?"

Jack O'Reilly was a peddler. He lived in the settlement of Colesberg, a hundred miles or so southeast of the De Kalk farm, and traveled a regular route, making a circuit of the farms in the district. He hunted a little on the side—mostly lions—and was a famous shot. Whether or not Van Niekerk knew he was selling a diamond, O'Reilly was convinced he was buying one. He wrote his name on a windowpane with the stone, and then he sent it to Dr. W. Guybon Atherstone, a mineralogist in Grahamstown, a town down near the coast, for an expert opinion. Atherstone, in his turn, seems to have consulted various people, including the Catholic Bishop Richards, who wrote *his* name on a windowpane with the stone. The mineralogist and the bishop next tried some jewelers' files on it, and the files were blunted while the stone remained unscratched. It looked very much as if O'Reilly had himself a diamond, and they told him so. In the end, O'Reilly sold it to the governor of the Cape Colony, Sir Philip Wodehouse, who seems to have paid him what Dr. Atherstone had said it was worth—five hundred pounds. Sir Philip had it shown at the Paris Exhibition of 1867. O'Reilly's luck was noised about, of course, and people all over the veld, from the Transvaal to the Cape Colony, began going around looking at the ground. In time, more finds were made, and by 1869 the rush was on.

The *klip* that started it all, which is still known in Kimberley as the O'Reilly diamond, was a clear blue-white stone of twenty-one and a quarter carats. Mr. Beet doesn't know what happened to it after Sir Philip's death, which means, I daresay, that nobody knows. O'Reilly's family later asked De Beers Consolidated for a reward for having initiated the whole diamond rush, but nothing came of the request, and Jacobs, in his statement, complained bitterly that his family had not received a shilling for their contribution to South Africa's development. As an adult, he tried his hand at digging, but he never had much luck; Mr. Beet collected thirty pounds from Kimberley residents for him in his old age, and that appears to be all he ever got for his find.

Many professional diggers were floating about the world in the late 1860s—men who had learned their trade among the forty-niners in California, in the Australian gold diggings, in the New Zealand gold fields, or in all three places. It is true that their specialty was gold, but they were, first and foremost, treasure hunters, not specialists, and, anyway, as far as they could make out from the reports that reached their far-flung lodginghouses, prospecting for diamonds wasn't much different from prospecting for gold. Like alluvial gold, diamonds were said to lurk in the sand and gravel under and beside running water—that was where they had always been found in India and Brazil—and the same method of extraction was used for both: the gravel was panned until the precious stuff sank, of its own weight, to the bottom. From both hemispheres, diggers sailed to South Africa and, following a host of local adventurers, made their way to the fields. It was a long, hard trip from the coastal cities—seven hundred miles from Cape Town, four hundred and fifty miles from Durban or Port Elizabeth, four hundred miles from East London, straight across country on vile roads, or no roads at all, over mountains and rocky plains, then over the high desert plateau called the Great Karroo, and, finally, onto the veld—and the diggers traveled any way they could, some on foot or muleback or horseback, some by cart or chaise. Most of them, though, went by ox wagon—the famous South African covered wagon, so like our own, drawn by as many as sixteen oxen. A wagon could carry twelve men and their gear, and it not only took the diggers where they were going but served as a dwelling place, and a comparatively comfortable one, when they got there.

Fewer of the Boers joined the rush than might have been expected. On the whole, they didn't approve of treasure hunting; all they wanted was to sit on their *stoeps*, smoke their pipes, and let their cattle graze. For a time, some Boers refused to throw their land open to diggers, though they could have made a small fortune, and perhaps a big one, by leasing out digging rights, as their neighbors condescended to do, and here

and there an embattled farmer warned diamond seekers off his
land with a shotgun. But eventually most of the Boers suc-
cumbed and began doing some digging themselves, or leased
their land, or sold it and moved away. At the height of the rush
a man who owned two farms ran an advertisement in one of
the mining-camp papers that read, significantly, "The owner,
although convinced of the diamondiferous character of these
farms, offers them for sale, knowing too well the result of a sudden rush of Diggers."

Considering what some of the diggers looked like, it is not
strange that the farmers should have been wary of them.
Gardner F. Williams, a mining engineer from Saginaw, Mich-
igan, who was the first general manager of De Beers Consolidated, describes them in his book, *The Diamond Mines of
South Africa*:

> . . . *Hardly a nation in Europe was unrepresented. Black
> grandsons of Guinea coast slaves and natives of every dusky
> shade streaked the show of white faces. Butchers, bakers, sail-
> ors, tailors, lawyers, blacksmiths, masons, doctors, carpenters,
> clerks, gamblers, sextons, laborers, loafers . . . fell into line in a
> straggling procession to the Diamond Fields. Army officers
> begged furloughs to join the motley troop, schoolboys ran away
> from school, and women even of good families could not be
> held back from joining their husbands and brothers. . . .
> There was the oddest medley of dress and equipment: shirts
> of woollen—blue, brown, gray, and red—and of linen and cot-
> ton—white, colored, checked, and striped; trim jackets, cord
> ridingbreeches and laced leggings, and "hand me downs" from
> the cheapest ready-made clothing shops; the yellow oilskins*

*and rubber boots of the sailor; the coarse, brown corduroy and*
*canvas suits, and long-legged, stiff, leather boots of the miner;*
*the ragged, greasy hats, tattered trousers or loin cloths of the*
*native tribesmen, jaunty cloth caps, broad-brimmed felt, bat-*
*tered straw, garish handkerchiefs twisted close to the roots of*
*stiff black crowns, or tufts of bright feathers stuck in a wiry*
*mat of curls; such a higgledy-piggledy as could only be massed*
*in a rush from African coast towns and native kraals to a field*
*of unknown requirements, in a land whose climate swung*
*daily between a scorch and a chill, where men in the same hour*
*were smothered in a dust and drenched in a torrent.*

The main goal of the rush was not the Orange River but the
Vaal, for word of mouth had it that diamonds were far more
numerous there. Hope Town, where Erasmus Stephanus had
picked up his diamond, was not altogether neglected, however;
the famous eighty-three-and-a-half-carat Star of South Africa
was found there in 1869—not on the ground but in the possession of a Griqua witch doctor. (It was bought from him—some
say by the same Schalk van Niekerk—for five hundred sheep,
ten oxen, and a horse.) The first sizable party to reach the Vaal
was a relatively respectable one, led by a British major. He and
his companions set out from Pietermaritzburg, in Natal, in November 1869, and made their way to a little mission settlement
called Hebron, on the north bank of the river, forty miles north
of the present site of Kimberley. There they found two Australian diggers and a Boer trader walking along the riverbank
and examining the ground like men who had dropped some
small change. The two groups teamed up and soon headed for
another mission settlement, called Pniel, twenty miles down-

stream. "Diggers have their habits," a Kimberley man told me, in the detached tone of one discussing ants or bees. Most Kimberley people today take this attitude toward the subject— interested but not involved. "They hear of a strike somewhere, and they go wherever it is and set up their camp and plant. If they'd only stay and give it a chance, they would probably do quite well, but no. They hear of a strike somewhere else, and —bing!—they're off to the new spot."

By the end of 1869, ten thousand diggers had reached the Vaal and had staked out claims along its banks for miles down- and upriver from Pniel—some on land owned by farmers and some on land owned by missionary societies but most on land owned, as far as anybody knew, by no one at all. The diggers paid rent where there was rent to pay, but they got into endless quarrels over claim jumping. What with the congestion and the chaos, the diggers soon decided they had better do some self-policing, and in various localities they established Diggers' Committees, which started by arbitrating disputes and soon were thinking up and enforcing regulations of various sorts and issuing diggers' licenses. What landowners there were gladly left such matters to the diggers, and before long a semblance of order came into the fields. The committees set a limit to the size of a claim—this varied, but ordinarily a claim could be no more than thirty-one feet square—and they ruled that no man could hold more than two claims at a time. Of course, two partners could hold four claims, and a group of men could manage to corner quite a lot of land; a map of the diggings along the Vaal or, later, in and around Kimberley was not a neat checkerboard but a patchwork of rectangular pieces of various sizes.

For a time the diggers stuck close to the banks of the Vaal, but by force of circumstance they became good amateur geologists, and before long they found that they were discovering more and bigger stones a short distance inland—in a special type of boulder-strewn, water-worn gravel, which the river had deposited at a time long gone when it was on higher ground, twisting and turning and cutting new channels. The gravel was, according to Williams, "a medley of worn and rolled chips of basalt, sandstone, quartz, and trap, intermingled with agates, garnets, peridot, jasper, and other richly colored pebbles, lying in and on a bedding of sand and clay." Indeed, when South African diamond gravel is wet, it is one of the prettiest mixtures that can be imagined—full of rich greens and reds and yellows. Following the example of the men from California and Australia, everybody shook his gravel down thoroughly in a "cradle" (a wooden trough divided by two or three screens of wire mesh), threw out the bigger pieces of rock, and washed what was left until only the heaviest stuff, in which diamonds, if there were any, would be found, remained. This concentrate, known as the "wash," was then spread out on a table and carefully searched for diamonds. At first the men did the washing on the riverbank, but as they moved inland the more prosperous of them hired natives to carry water up to the workings and to lend a hand with the digging. Soon the land for half a mile on either side of the Vaal was pocked and pitted with diggings. Eventually, fifteen or twenty feet down, the diggers reached bedrock, and off they went to stake out new claims.

The diggings at the Vaal paid off well, apparently confirming the theory that the place to look for diamonds was the banks of great, rushing rivers. But then, in August 1870, a find was made a hundred miles south of the Vaal that was to lead to an entirely new set of conceptions about diamond mining. This was on a farm called Jagersfontein. (*Fontein* is Afrikaans for "fountain" or "spring" and is encountered in South African place names as often as the word "water" is in the place names of our own country, like Sweetwater and Stillwater.) The farm was in the southern part of the Orange Free State, a good forty miles from the Orange River, and its land was altogether different from that along the banks of the Vaal; instead of gravel, there was the plain red topsoil of the veld with here and there an outcrop of another sort of soil—yellow and light and crumbly. For some years—even before the influx of Voortrekkers—Jagersfontein had belonged to a Boer family named Visser. The farm was in territory occupied by the Griquas, and the Vissers had had to make a strange arrangement with the famous Griqua leader Adam Kok III. Whenever Kok and his wife took it into their heads to visit Jagersfontein, the Visser in possession had to strip his wife of all she was wearing and present the costume to Mrs. Kok. The Widow Visser who was running the farm when the diamond fever struck the country had twice submitted to this ceremony, and then Kok had drifted off to the east and bothered her no more.

One day in 1870, the Widow Visser's foreman, Jaap de Klerk, saw some garnets in a *spruit*, or dry watercourse, and, having heard that garnets are a sign of diamonds, he began to do a little digging in his spare time. Within a month he found a fifty-carat diamond. He took it to the nearby town of Fauresmith, where he sold it for three or four pounds to a courier he met in a bar. The courier took it to more sophisticated quarters, thereby starting a rush in the direction of Jagersfontein. It was

a good strike—so good that although the Widow Visser charged
two pounds a month for digging rights, instead of the ten shillings customary along the Vaal, diggers flocked to the farm and
cheerfully paid up. At one time as many as fourteen hundred
men were working there. Twenty-eight hundred pounds a
month is a good income, and Mrs. Visser didn't have to do any
digging on her own.

North and west of Jagersfontein, on the border of the Orange
Free State, there were three farms: Bultfontein, Dorstfontein,
and Vooruitzigt (which means "forward-looking"). All were
part of the same large tract of land—just under sixty square
miles. The city of Kimberley stands on what was Vooruitzigt,
the northernmost of the farms. It was Dorstfontein, the middle
farm, that was the first to yield diamonds—in September 1870.
There, in a hollow called Du Toit's Pan, or, as it was later
spelled, Dutoitspan (a *pan* is a shallow, flat-bottomed, clay-
lined depression), they found the now familiar yellow earth,
and in the yellow earth they found diamonds thickly strewn
close to the surface and even, after a heavy rain, open to the sky,
waiting to be picked up. There was a terrific scramble for
Dutoitspan, and hundreds of diggers staked out claims. Financiers arrived on the scene, and a syndicate of them bought the
farm, for twenty-six hundred pounds, but they didn't change
the by then established rules of digging; they continued to lease
out digging rights and to leave all problems of policing to the
Diggers' Committees. Then, in November, diamonds were
found on Bultfontein, just to the south, and it quickly went
to another syndicate, for two thousand pounds.

Vooruitzigt, a sixteen-thousand-acre farm, was owned by two
Boer brothers named de Beer—or, as practically everybody ex-

cept the brothers has written it, De Beer—who had paid the
Orange Free State Government fifty pounds for it in 1860, not
thinking at the time that they were doing a good stroke of business. For some reason, Johannes Nicolaas de Beer has always
been remembered and his brother, Diederick Arnoldus, has not
—possibly because there is still a picture of Johannes Nicolaas
in the Kimberley Museum. (He was a long-jawed, whiskered,
dour-looking man.) The De Beers themselves dabbled a bit in
digging, and at first they attempted to hold down the number
of prospectors on their farm. In May 1871, a mining-camp
newspaper reported:

*An instance of Yankee ingenuity comes to us from De
Beers'. Everyone knows that it is next to impossible to procure
a claim at that place, owing to the determination of the proprietor to open it only to a few individuals. It appears that a Mr.
Bedee—a lately arrived American military man, holding high
testimonials from President Grant—was at De Beers' the other
day to see if by any means he might obtain a footing there.
He was followed about by an agent of De Beer's, who, after
some time, appeared determined to show fight. "Shame," cried
the Yankee. "Is that the way we treated you when you sent
over to the United States, requesting to have your independence recognized?" Their feelings thus adroitly appealed to, the
bystanders took up the cudgels on behalf of the American. Just
then, up came old De Beer with a subscription list for a Dopper
Church. Seeing a long list of half crowns, the American guessed
the nature of the document, although he had no conception to
what it referred. Putting his hand in his pocket, he gave the old
gentleman two-and-sixpence. "Hurrah voor de Amerikaner!"*

*thereupon resounded from all sides, and in less than five minutes the shrewd Yankee had an excellent claim marked out for him.*

Later in 1871, the De Beer farm was the goal of two great rushes—one of them the greatest rush in South Africa's history—and a small horde of financiers kept after the brothers to sell it. They held out for a while, but then gave in and sold the property, for six thousand pounds, to a Port Elizabeth syndicate, and went right out and bought another farm—one presumably not stocked with troublesome little crystals. Johannes Nicolaas doesn't seem to have commented much on the affair, though late in life he told an acquaintance he had concluded, after due consideration, that he could have got a lot more money for Vooruitzigt—perhaps ten times as much—if he had held out a little longer.

"Oh well," said his friend, "why worry? What could you have bought with more money, anyway?"

De Beer said stoutly, "A new span of oxen."

Then, having accidentally bequeathed their name to one of the most gigantic corporations in the world, the brothers dropped out of sight. The famous Vooruitzigt farmhouse still stands, a few miles from Kimberley, near a village called Homestead. It is occupied by small holders and surrounded by barbed wire and chicken houses; like most old Boer farmhouses it is a mean-looking little place, full of tiny, crowded rooms, but it is strongly built, and it looks out on beautiful rolling country, fertile enough to be conspicuous on the veld. Livingstone once "outspanned"—unyoked his oxen—and made camp there. It must have provided a very pleasant camp site.

Swarms of men were now digging the yellow earth, and
other swarms were digging the boulder-strewn gravel, and soon
what had started out as an occasional camp on the landscape
changed to the scene present-day Kimberley residents point to
in blown-up photographs on their walls—a great jumble of
tents, shacks, and iron houses, jostling one another for space.
Kimberley itself sprang up in 1871, though the settlement was
not properly christened until 1873, when it was given the name
of the British Colonial Secretary then in office. It was one settlement among many, and they were all unlovely but vivid. The
life was one of either constant dust or constant mud. The veld,
sparsely covered with scrub and an occasional camel's-thorn
tree, is flat for the most part and open to burning sun and, occasionally, pelting rain. The first diggers were in too much of a
hurry to contemplate town planning, or even to make themselves comfortable. They could not be bothered with trivialities
like hygiene; a diggers' camp stank to heaven, and if it hadn't
been for the purifying sun, epidemics would have been graver
and more frequent than they were. After all, to the prospector
a mine is a short-lived thing. There is something in the ground
that can be dug out and sold, and the idea is to dig it out as
quickly and cheaply as possible, dispose of it, and then move
on to another cache. This is not the sort of attitude that leads
to town planning; that comes later, when traders follow the
prospectors, women arrive, and men begin to wash their necks
and wonder about schooling for their children.

Very soon, traders did come to the settlements—first men
from the coast and then men from overseas. They set up shacks
and tents near those of the miners and went into business, selling gear and provisions and, in many cases, buying diamonds.

On Saturday, October 15, 1870, the first issue of the *Diamond News & Vaal Advertiser,* a weekly newspaper, was published in Pniel. (Later, following the crowd, it moved to Dutoitspan and, still later, to Kimberley.) The front page was covered with large advertisements, some in Afrikaans, some in English, and some in both, and all set up in the varied type that characterized papers of the period. A display type in which the letters look as if they were constructed of logs was a great favorite. In the biggest ad in the first issue, Mr. Wilhelm Schultz, of Lippert & Co., with offices in Hamburg, Germany, and Port Elizabeth, begged to inform the public that he had opened a general wholesale-and-retail store. "Being in connection with the above well known Firm, who have their own Establishment in Europe, he ventures to say that he will be able to DEFY ALL COMPETITION," the ad stated. Schultz would give liberal advances on diamonds for export to Europe, and would pay full market prices for wool, ivory, and ostrich feathers.

The *News's* first editorial declared, "Hasty and hot discussion on political topics, likely to interfere with the development of the great and fruitful industry which is the life of the place, the *News* will avoid. . . . Territorial questions are to be subordinated to material welfare." Yet territorial questions couldn't be suppressed; the old indifference to boundaries had disappeared as soon as the diamond rush began. The Transvaal claimed the north bank of the Vaal, and the Orange Free State claimed both the south bank and the Kimberley area. Both republics could put up a plausible case; the respective areas had for a long time been popularly regarded as part of their territories. But the Griquas—in the person of Nicholas Waterboer, Adam Kok's son—claimed both banks of the Vaal and Kimberley, basing their case on old pacts and treaties with the Boers and the British. For a time the British were reluctant to get involved in these controversies; they sent some officials up to the Vaal to keep order and to look after the interests of the British diggers, but they made no claim to any of the disputed territory, though some of the diggers were under the impression that they had. It was no easy matter to keep order, as an early letter to the *News* indicates:

> *Hebron,*
> *October 8, 1870*
>
> Sir,
>
> *The landdrost [magistrate] of the Transvaal came to me this morning and asked me to pay him the license, which I refused to do. Whereupon he threatened to send me to Potchefstroom [the capital of the Transvaal] as a spy, for what I do not know; or otherwise sell your cart, so he said, to pay. He also threatened to throw me into the river. He said, "You [the British] throw people into the river at Klip Drift, and I will throw you in here." I replied, "Clothes and all?" which made him very angry. He also said he would not allow me to go on working. Now, I want to ask you to do me a favor, and let me know what I had best do, as the British Government has proclaimed this country, and as a British subject I suppose I am entitled to protection. Will you, if there is a Civil Commissioner arrived, lodge this complaint before him. Mr. De Villiers says this proclamation is all "bosh" or something of the kind. Send me an answer, and oblige yours truly,*
>
> W. *Gillman*

No one knows whether or not the *landdrost* ever threw Mr.

Gillman into the river, but by the summer of 1871 the territorial dispute was raging so fiercely that the British felt compelled to step in. They studied the matter for a few months, and in October announced their decision: All the disputed area belonged to the Griquas. Within a few days, Nicholas Waterboer made a present of the entire territory to Queen Victoria, and in 1873 it was established as the Crown Colony of Griqualand West. The Boers grumbled, but there was nothing much they could do. The Orange Free State did not come off too badly; it still had Jagersfontein, and eventually it received ninety thousand pounds from the British by way of indemnity. The Transvaal never received a shilling.

Through all the territorial disputes and outbursts of violence, the tone of the *Diamond News* was invincibly urbane. Tough eggs though most of the diggers were, they were always referred to as "Mr.," and the stories of finds were invariably couched in very polite language:

*A Large Find:—Messrs. Vermaak and party found, yesterday morning, seven diamonds, the largest being 2½ carats.*

*Good Fortune: We have been informed by one of the party that Messrs. Coxon, Webster and others have found 27 diamonds, valued at £4000.*

*Who'll Buy?—On Tuesday three navvies, lucky fellows, were hawking about at the Klip Drift Diggings, a fine stone of 12 or 15 carats which they had obtained at the Good Hope Diggings. They were anxious to sell it to keep their party at work; they, however, refused £250.*

Even when it was reporting on lawlessness, the paper suc-

ceeded in giving an impression of leisurely understatement. A
report of a holdup began, "A curious and decidedly unpleasant incident befell Commissioner Truter last week." On the
last day of 1870 an outraged citizen wrote that something had
to be done about the mails; he said he had sent six rubies in a
letter from Pniel to a friend in Port Elizabeth, and when the
envelope arrived, three of the jewels were gone. "I trouble you
with this matter, Mr. Editor," he concluded, "believing that
you will make allusion to it in your paper and will agree with
me in thinking the affair sufficiently serious to demand en-
quiry."

From the start, there were items in the *News* indicating that
the diggers' social life was flourishing—"Another billiard table
is on its way from the colony to Pniel," and "The Music Hall
at Klip Drift is being pushed forward"—and before long there
were ladies about, enough ladies to make a ball successful. "On
Wednesday evening Upper Hebron came out strong in the
dancing line," wrote a *News* correspondent. "The *élite* of the
Fields went in for a subscription ball in the billiard room of
the Royal Oak Hotel, where the table was taken down for the
purpose. Kid gloves and satin slippers were at a premium, and
as for white satin vests and pumps, they were not to be had. A
goodly company of bright eyes were present." Six months after
the paper was started there was a sufficiently goodly company
of bright eyes in Pniel for the *News* editorial writer to begin
worrying about the effect on them of scantily clad native helpers. "May we suggest to the local authorities the desirableness
of making and enforcing some regulations with reference to the
attire of native servants?" the editorial for April 29, 1871, began, and it went on, "No one with any observation can have

failed to perceive how those natives whose practice it is to go about in a state which, for aught to the contrary, may be termed totally nude, obtrude themselves upon notice, as though they gloried in their shame—as no doubt they do. The consequence is that no respectable female can walk the streets . . . without having her sense of sight shocked in a manner for which there is no earthly excuse."

There were plenty of smaller vexations, and some larger ones. One letter writer pointed out waspishly to the editor that the English language was going to pieces in the camps. His particular grievance was neologisms—for instance, the word "jumping," for "stealing" or "sneaking in ahead," and the word "bogey," for "bad" or "faulty." Even the newspaper, he complained, had got into the habit of using the adjective "off-colored"—properly applied only to certain diamonds—to describe the pigmentation of half-caste people. But the letter writer was obviously fighting for a cause that had already been lost. The social column of the same issue reported on a diggers' party at which, after the customary toast "To the ladies!" one guest leaped up and proposed "Three cheers for the off-colored ones!" According to the paper, the cheers were vociferous.

The greatest vexation of all in the settlements was I.D.B., or illicit diamond buying. Right from the start, native employees filched diamonds that the claim owners hadn't happened to see and sold them at prices under the going one. The traders who bought these diamonds were looked upon as the real offenders (that was why the practice was called illicit diamond buying), and since nearly everybody who wasn't digging diamonds was trading in them—innkeepers, horse copers, merchants—the list of suspects was long. The situation, as a matter

of fact, was fluid; traders sometimes abandoned their stock to
go digging, and diggers who had no luck turned in disgust to
trade and made bigger fortunes than they would have if they
had found another Star of South Africa. In any case, there were
hardly enough ethics to go around, and in time illicit diamond
buying became so rife that trying to stop it was like trying to
stop Victoria Falls. In spite of many rough-and-ready preven-
tive measures devised by the Diggers' Committees, more and
more natives took to picking up and hiding diamonds, and
more and more traders bought such stones for practically nothing and then sold them for something less than the going price.
Economically, I.D.B. was a bad thing, and morally it was even
worse—these diamonds were, after all, stolen goods—but every
trader knew that if he turned down a chance the next man
would grab it, and many traders let principle go hang. What
with one thing and another, so much diamond smuggling was
going on that some people not prone to exaggeration estimated
that in the 1870s half the caratage produced at Kimberley and
in the Vaal wound up in the hands of illicit buyers.

I.D.B. infuriated the diggers, and one unfortunate Kimberley
canteen keeper, who was rumored to be seeing far too much of
furtive natives after dark, was set upon by a mob of diggers,
who burned his tent and all his stock. Apparently, the mob enjoyed this experience, for the men went on to burn down a
whole district, which they afterward virtuously described as an
undesirable haunt of native women. Then they set out along
the road to another canteen, whose owner, somebody said,
bought diamonds by night. The local magistrate rode out to in-
tercept the crowd, and made a speech urging them to desist and
go home, but, as the News reported, "he was respectfully lis-

tened to, and then loudly cheered by the mob, who, however, proceeded on their way."

Not long after this jaunt, the Kimberley diggers held a lively meeting at which they voted unanimously that natives shouldn't be allowed to hold claims. Until then, a few natives had been permitted to take out licenses and work on the diggings, but the Europeans complained that it was a bad practice; it gave the natives an alibi for any stones they might be caught selling to I.D.B. agents. Besides, as one digger pointed out, the money a native earned working his own claim wouldn't do him any good; he would only spend it foolishly. It was resolved at the meeting that every digger should have the right "to search his own niggers whenever he chose," and that the government should be urged to curb I.D.B., if necessary by means of mounted policemen. The boys probably felt better for getting all this off their chests, but I.D.B. went on. Penalties were duly increased, threats flew thick and fast, and diamonds kept slipping through. A cartoon drawn at the time to decorate the edges of a map of the Kimberley mine shows a procession of huge diamonds attached to native legs walking out past a guard stationed at a compound entrance.

Of all the mines that lie under the South African sky, yawning in their old age, the Kimberley Mine probably has the most interesting story. It was the goal of the second great rush on the De Beers' property, so it was first known as the New Rush at De Beers', or De Beers' New Rush. For a while, it was also called Colesberg Kopje. *Kopje*, or *koppie*, means "hill" in Afrikaans, and it was on a slight elevation in the flat veld, a couple of miles north of the site of the Old Rush, that the discovery that led to the New Rush was made by a group of young prospectors from Colesberg. After the naming of the town of Kimberley, the mine came to be known as the Kimberley Mine. The young men from Colesberg arrived on the spot July 16, 1871; since it was winter, they all wore red stocking caps, and they called themselves the Red-Cap Company. Their leader was Fleetwood Rawstorne—surely the prettiest name in diamond history. They camped near the little *kopje*, which was shaded by camel's-thorn trees, and for a day or so they prospected in the ordinary fashion, digging here and there or merely looking over the bare ground in the hope of finding a diamond. One evening, when they went to their leader's tent for dinner, they discovered that Damon, the Rawstorne family's old native retainer, had got drunk. This was a habit of Damon's, and to punish him, Rawstorne sent him out in the dark and set him to digging by moonlight while the party ate their dinner. Damon came back sooner than expected, grinning triumphantly, with a few small diamonds glittering in his hand. That night, at least, Fleetwood Rawstorne didn't discipline him further.

The young men were exultant and excited, but they faced an awkward problem. It was Sunday night, and the Diggers' Committee had laid down a rule that people couldn't stake out claims on Sunday. On the other hand, it would be very foolish to wait for Monday morning; whenever a find of this sort was made the news leaked out immediately, no matter how hard the discoverers tried to conceal it. Damon was sure to tell other natives soon, if he hadn't told them already. So the Red-Caps staked out their claims then and there—Rawstorne's holdings centered on the spot where Damon had made his find —and, as it turned out, they got away with it. They also sent

word of the find to a few Colesberg friends and relatives who
were camping nearby, and these started out for the *kopje* early
the next morning in what they hoped was complete secrecy. In
vain; though they "inspanned," or yoked their oxen, very
stealthily, neighboring campers spotted them. The leaders had
hardly got moving when a throng was hot on their heels. The
New Rush had begun.

By noon on Monday, hundreds of diggers had flocked to the
*kopje*, staked out thirty-one-foot-square claims, and begun digging furiously. By this time they knew something about "dry"
mining, as the digging at places like Dutoitspan and the De
Beers farm came to be called, to distinguish it from the alluvial
digging along the Vaal, but there was a great deal that they
didn't know. They knew that under the red topsoil—an inch or
two down, five feet down, ten feet down—they stood a chance
of coming to the crumbly yellow earth that contained diamonds; they also stood a chance of coming to a substratum of
rock and shale, and this, they had painfully found out, was not
diamondiferous. So the luck of the diggers varied. One man
might strike it rich right away, and the man on the next claim
might not find a thing. Since each claim was worked according
to the idiosyncrasies of its owner, not all the diggings sank at
the same rate. Some claim owners could afford to hire native
helpers, while others did everything themselves, and naturally
it took the latter much longer to get through the red soil. Two
weeks might go by before a lone digger could prepare his first
"wash" and so discover whether he had a productive claim or
had drawn a blank.

Mining experts had learned some of the hazards of open-pit
digging at Dutoitspan and the Old Rush, which by now was

known as the De Beers Mine, and from the start a special precaution was observed at the Kimberley Mine: roadways were
left straight across the digging area, north to south, forty-seven
feet apart and fifteen feet wide. This meant that each claim
owner had to sacrifice seven and a half feet on one side of his
holding. The object, of course, was to give every digger access
to his claim—some of the claims would have been left as islands
otherwise—and although the diggers grumbled, they knew the
regulation made sense. They brought their earth up to the roads
by the bucketful (some using rope hauls and some carrying it
up stairs chopped out of the earth), loaded it on wagons, and
carted it off to where they had set up their washing equipment
and their sorting tables. The system worked for a while, but
as the prospectors dug deeper and deeper it turned out that the
crumbly yellow ground was not reliable material for roads. The
roads began to give way under the weight of the carts. Moreover, the diggers could not be trusted; in spite of regulations,
they kept picking out stray bits of the roads' foundations. First
one, then another, and then a lot of accidents happened; carts,
mules, and drivers slid off the roads and tumbled into deep
claims, squashing anyone who happened to be working beneath. The diggers mended their roads with timber and rock,
and here and there they put up a shaky little bridge, but they
couldn't stave off the inevitable, and by the end of 1872 not
one of the roads across the Kimberley Mine was passable.

It didn't take the diggers long to devise a new method of
bringing the pay dirt to the surface. In 1873 they set up a bat-
tery of hauling machines on massive platforms, called "stagings," at the two ends of the crater, which was taking on the
shape of an oval. The basic apparatus was a sort of windlass,

from which a steel cable ran down into the mine. The stagings had three levels—the top one for cables going out to the middle of the pit, the middle one for cables going to intermediate diggings, and the bottom one for cables going almost straight down the cliff edge. Each claim owner had his own windlass and cable, and the buckets went up and down all day long. At first, the diggers or their employees turned the wheels by hand, but as time went on many of them began to use larger buckets, and some of them installed huge horizontal wheels, known as horse whims, which were turned by horses or mules. From a distance, the scene was fantastic—like a series of gigantic, glittering cat's cradles—but the system was far more successful than the roadways had been, and far less lethal.

No sooner had the haulage problem been solved than the diggers were confronted with another problem—that of water. Actually, water always presented a major obstacle to the open-pit miners, one way or another. At first they couldn't get enough of it to wash down the pay dirt, and in the early days enterprising peddlers would drive to the diggings in wagons loaded with drums of water. Now, as the pit went down, water became an even worse problem—indeed, a menace. The diggers had tapped the underground water table, and their claims were soon swamped. At first they pumped the water out with small hand pumps, but soon these couldn't begin to cope with the seepage. Again, though, a solution was thought up, and in this case it was thought up by a twenty-one-year-old man who was later to play the key role in the building of De Beers Consolidated and in the expansion of the British Empire in Africa. In 1874 Cecil Rhodes brought a steam-powered pump to the fields and began renting it to diggers. Within a year he had acquired enough pumps to take care of all the mines in the area.

On its fourth birthday—July 16, 1875—the Kimberley Mine was flourishing as never before. The diggers kept hauling out the yellow earth, diamond brokers and buyers, financiers, and merchants kept arriving, and the settlement, with its tents and iron shacks and brick houses, kept growing, until it merged with the settlements around the De Beers Mine, Bultfontein, and Dutoitspan. Kimberley was no longer merely a camp; it was a town. But it was like no other town on the earth—a town where, as one observer put it, "deep kaffir songs, laughter, the crowing of cocks, an occasional shot, all echoed with eerie distinctness about (an) eccentric stage on which a great play was being so inexorably enacted." And then, at the height of Kimberley's prosperity, the diggers ran into something that they had feared all along. At a depth of about seventy feet, they came to the bottom of the yellow soil. Under it was a greenish-blue ground that seemed hard, and this, they were convinced, was bedrock; as each man reached it, he packed up and moved off; if he wasn't bothered by scruples, he might cover it with yellow earth and sell his claim to an unsuspecting newcomer before departing. The days of the Kimberley Mine, Dutoitspan, Bultfontein—all of them—seemed numbered.

Then, in 1876, a tremendous discovery was made. The credit for it belongs to Dr. W. Guybon Atherstone, of Grahamstown, who had assured Jack O'Reilly that his *klip* was a diamond. Atherstone reasoned that since the yellow soil wasn't alluvial it must be of volcanic origin, and that the diamonds in it must have come from deep underground with other molten rock. Therefore, he felt, the blue ground might be worth digging into. A few diggers tried their picks on it, and it turned out not to be so hard after all; pieces of it came up, and there was a crystal embedded in one of them. It glittered only feebly, but it was the harbinger of terrific things. Excitement had never run so high, and there was a new rush over the old diggings. In time, the miners learned a lot about the blue ground; for one thing, they learned that when it was exposed to the air it weathered into the friable yellow stuff they had first encountered. But it took geologists to find out what the blue ground really was and how deep it went. Evidently, as Atherstone said, it was of igneous origin, and eventually the geologists determined that it occurred in the form of huge tubes, which appeared to be escape valves for some great reservoir of boiling material in the middle of the earth. A long time ago, the tubes, necks, pipes— the geologists use all these terms—terminated at the earth's surface as volcanoes; then the volcanoes had died down and had been eroded, leaving the supply pipes exposed just as the forces of wind and water had sliced them off. The pipe of diamond-iferous soil under the *kopje*, it was now clear, was a regular oval, about ten acres in area and, for all practical purposes, bottomless.

There was a rhythm to the early history of the Kimberley Mine—boom, disaster, boom, disaster—and it was now to be repeated again. The blue ground held out, of course, but as the mine reached its present outlines a new problem had to be faced, and this probably was ultimately to put an end to open-pit mining in Kimberley. The diamondiferous ground, the diggers had gradually discovered, was surrounded by reef, or rock and shale, and as more and more of the reef was exposed it began to break off and slide. Here it might be well to point out that in South Africa the word "reef" means two things. The

Reef, or Rand, of Johannesburg gets its name because it is a ridge, for *rand* in Afrikaans means "ridge"; but *rand,* or "reef," is also the word used for the rock surrounding diamondiferous ground—the stony wall around a diamond pit. In the late 1870s the reef around the Kimberley Mine was falling into the pit in great slabs, and before long there was no stopping it. The harder the harassed diggers worked to haul the rubble out of the way, the more landslides there were. It was like trying to dig a hole in a sandbank beyond the depth that the laws of gravity permit. Digging had become not only pointless but perilous, and by 1882 the diggers were again moving off and it again looked as if South African diamond mining was doomed.

Once more the Kimberley Mine's obituary was premature. This time, engineering and big business came to the rescue. Once and for all, the new men—the capitalists and the engineers—threw out the concept of diamond mines as surface phenomena. The pipes obviously went down a long way, and they obviously had to be worked as any other deep mines were— underground. This meant sinking shafts and digging tunnels. Capital was required—a lot of it. Claims were amalgamated. Companies were formed. Companies ate each other up. The great consolidation that was to be known all over the world simply as De Beers came into being. But that is another story. The story of the rush ends with the birth of De Beers, though the people of Kimberley haven't forgotten it. How could they, with those great pits gaping at the sky?

Today, the Kimberley Mine is surrounded by a high wire fence. The fence has been there ever since late in the last century, when a man committed suicide by throwing himself into the crater. The city authorities were never able to retrieve his body, and some people say that every now and then it rises to the surface and floats about. Ducks and other waterfowl have adopted the gloomy artificial lake as a retreat, and they can often be seen swimming on it. Standing behind the fence and peering down at the tiny birds, one finds it difficult to believe that all this was dug either by hand or by the most primitive machinery. In comparison, the Pyramids don't seem so wonderful, after all.

One day, Winston Churchill's father, Lord Randolph Churchill, and a group of friends, men and women, were staring down into that pit. Lord Randolph grew philosophical. "All for the vanity of woman," he said.

"And the depravity of man," added one of the ladies.

# CHAPTER TWO

# Old Digger, Old Fool

What started out as a diamond rush in South Africa is now a system of corporations that are piled up on each other, to form an inverted pyramid, in a relationship fantastically close and complex. Diamonds financed the development of gold mines. Gold mines led to the recent uranium discoveries. African finance in general underwrites a considerable part of the world's banking activities. To an ordinary unfinancial brain like mine it is all so deep and mysterious that it came as a considerable shock to discover that the map of Africa is still dotted, close to the cradle of the whole thing, with diamond diggings of the earliest pattern. Private diggers still wield their picks and shovels (anyway steam shovels) and scratch away at the surface of the same earth that is pierced by shafts, practically next door —shafts that go down thousands of feet into diamond-bearing volcanic stocks.

The private diggers see nothing out of the ordinary in this. To them, digging is a natural, sensible proceeding, and underground mining seems prosaic and rather decadent. They see no reason why they should give up time-honored, respectable habits or relinquish ancient hopes. Wasn't the famous Jonker diamond found by a digger like themselves—only a few years back, in 1934—practically picked up from the sand, lying there like a common pebble near the deep Premier Mine of Pretoria? The Cullinan was a deep-mine stone, but the Jonker is different; it has become the diggers' talisman.

Most directors of the De Beers Consolidated Mines Company don't care very much nowadays for the idea of digging as these hopeful men are doing for water-deposited diamonds. They feel that the practice is small-scale, archaic, and bothersome to a system that has been painfully built up to produce, market, and uphold the price of diamonds. Digging is picturesque; that they do not deny, but it is anachronistic. However, nobody with experience of life in diamondiferous country has any illusions about the hold it takes on the human imagination. A digger is a gambler of a special sort, as confirmed an addict to chance as is any regular horse player. The company when it tries to discourage the digging habit is up against something of the same sort of problem faced by Nationalist China's government some years ago when it outlawed opium smoking. Addiction cannot be cured simply by decree, as the Chinese authorities soon discovered, and so they decided upon slow withdrawal of the drug instead. Not even that could be called an unqualified success. What really licked the opium habit in China was the fact that it ultimately became *démodé*. Young Chinese rather scorned the "Big Smoke" because it was so old-fashioned compared with getting drunk, and something of this sort may overtake diamond digging in South Africa. At any rate De Beers hopes so. In the meantime the company has devised a system of licensing that will in time, presumably, kill the whole dizzy dream.

To get a De Beers license, for instance, for digging on Nooitgedacht Farm, about twenty miles from Kimberley where the biggest diamond mines used to be worked, the applicant must produce satisfactory evidence that he is a bona fide digger who has been employed personally in digging operations in the mining district of Barkly West for a minimum period of ten years, and that he has held a digger's certificate prior to 1940. Barkly West, where Nooitgedacht is located, was formerly called Klip Drift, which is Afrikaans for Stony Ford; it was one of the best-known and most boisterous diggers' settlements in the old days. Many of the phrases printed on a digger's license recall those old days. No one license holder may peg more than four claims at a time. Each claim measures forty-five feet square except in the river bed, where it can be thirty by sixty feet instead. The license costs five shillings a month for each claim. All diamonds found on company property like Nooitgedacht must be handed in to the company's offices more or less within a week of the find, or anyway before the end of the month—De Beers drive their diggers on a loose rein—for registration, valuation, and, if the digger wishes, for sale as well, but he is not obliged to sell his diamonds to the company. He can take them outside and sell to some other licensed agent if he feels he can get a better price. Whatever he gets, however, he must pay 10 per cent of the value, based on the company's estimate, to De Beers as royalty. De Beers doesn't hold a monopoly of all diggings. There are others in the vicinity under government control, and there the diggers who hold licenses do not have to pay a royalty on their findings to anybody. Most

of them prefer to make an arrangement with De Beers nevertheless, for the company makes things easier in certain ways:
water is supplied on order by De Beers at fourpence per sixty
gallons, and water is vitally necessary to digging and very expensive to acquire privately.

One Thursday morning in March, which means in autumn
in South Africa, I set out from Kimberley for Nooitgedacht with
two De Beers officials whose work it is to keep an eye on the
diggings there. We drove over the veld, which was uncom-
monly green after one of the wettest summers in this genera-
tion's memory: even so the dirt road was becoming powdery
after two dry days, and our car was soon pinkish with dust. It
is very red ground at Kimberley. Bright red anthills stood in
solid, steep little mountains one or two feet high among the
scrubby gorselike plants that kept the ground from being out-
and-out desert. The car bounced between gullies exactly like
New Mexican arroyos; the land looked flat but was not; we had
to twist and turn among shallow hills for a long time before we
entered an opening in the barbed-wire fence that surrounds the
farm. (Though strictly speaking, of course, Nooitgedacht, an
area of five thousand acres, has long since ceased to be a farm.)
It was ten-thirty in the morning when we got there. The sun
glared down on three or four iron shacks and a gasoline pump,
with one big and several small thorn trees shading the front
doors of the little house. Nearby was a big water tank on stilts,
with a native caretaker drowsing in its shadow. There was no
other shade anywhere in sight.

Three of the shacks were part of the same building and com-
prised the De Beers offices. The door on the left bore an enamel
plaque announcing that Mr. Cohen, licensed De Beers valuer

and buyer of diamonds, visited the place every Friday. We unlocked and entered the middle shack, where there were a table,
a desk, and two or three chairs. In the corner of the window sill
was one of the small scales I had learned to recognize in my
travels through diamond country; tiny units of weight, like
scraps of tin foil, measure carats and fractions of carats. One of
the men went into the left-hand room and set to work brewing
tea. South Africans are tremendous tea drinkers. They outdo
the British and even the Chinese at this exercise; they drink tea
almost as often as they light cigarettes. While the water
heated and the men went through papers I amused myself
studying some records of diamond finds which were written out
and hanging on the wall. All finds of stones weighing more than
a hundred carats had been noted there according to the dates
of discovery, exact weights, and the names of the men who had
found them.

"Most of the diggers are colored people," explained the
younger of the company men, meaning that they were people
of mixed blood. "But we have some native diggers too, and a
few Europeans. You'll notice that most of the names are Afrikaner, but some are English. One of the oldest diggers here
is an Englishman, Mr. Field; he was interviewed for one of the
local magazines the other day and I believe he's quite set up
about it—Mr. Field's been on the diggings longer than anybody. He claims to be ninety years old. I wouldn't know, myself."

"Could be. It's a healthy life," said the other man, Mr. Van
der Westhuizen. He looked as if he knew what he was talking
about; he was himself a big, strong man, sunburned and vigor-
ous. "I felt fine when I was digging," he continued. "I was out

here in the old days; I've bought more than one license. Never had any luck, though, and I gave it up when I took this job with De Beers. It *is* a healthy life; you're out in the open all day and you get plenty of exercise." He drained his teacup and put it down on the tray. "Well, are you ready to go and see some of the boys?" he asked.

I was, so we went out again to the car, leaving the other man in charge. Mr. Van der Westhuizen stopped short just before we got there and picked up something from the sandy ground. He grinned reminiscently as he looked at it, and handed it over to me. "Digger's peg," he said. "It's what they use when they peg out a claim; one of these is put in each corner."

It was an oblong piece of metal with a name inked on it— "Van Rensburg"—and a date, fixed onto a short, stubby piece of wood that was sharpened at the lower end. Stirred to memory, Mr. Van der Westhuizen, backing the car out from under the shade tree, began telling me what a rush was like. The opening of new grounds was announced first, and the diggers would congregate to look over the area. On the appointed day, well before the hour, they lined up at the starting tape, ready with their pegs. At the starting gun off they went, each making for some particular plot of land he had already sized up as likely to pay well. There were always several claimants for each promising bit, so the race was terribly fast and a lot of cheating went on. Some gangs arranged a sort of secret relay race, with fresh runners lying concealed under bushes and leaping out to take the place of their tired partners. There were always disputes about such matters after the races, and there had to be professional surveyors standing ready to measure the claims properly when the pegs had been put in. The last big rush was at Lichtenburg, about seventy miles away, in 1927. Twenty thousand people participated, and at least hundreds, so it was said, cheated: some hired college athletes to run for them, and the whole thing was such a shambles that public opinion turned against rushes from that day on. As in the case of the older diamond fields of Klip Drift and Colesberg Kopje, fortunes were sometimes made by tradespeople and hotelkeepers who never dug a spadeful in their lives or handled a diamond except as a side line. The proprietor of the Langrish Hotel, which was the only rooming house in Lichtenburg at the beginning, put up two hundred iron bedsteads in his back yard to accommodate the people who flooded in. He hung numbers on them and assigned them to the lodgers, and that is where they slept for weeks and weeks. When it rained, as it often does in South Africa with suddenness and ferocity, the alfresco sleepers were just out of luck; they had nowhere else to go.

"Those were the days," said Mr. Van der Westhuizen nostalgically.

We were driving over what I took at first to be pathless desert, but there was an inconspicuous road among the dunes. Here and there we passed even fainter tracks leading away from ours, to outlying shacks where diggers lived.

"Not that they don't have busy diggings today," continued Mr. Van der Westhuizen. "It was very busy for a long time at Gong Gong at the river. We'll run over and see that later; perhaps somebody's working on a breakwater. I haven't had a look at that part of the world for some time." I didn't know just what he meant by "breakwater." I had heard of *the* Breakwater, the big one down at Cape Town, where I.D.B.—illicit diamond buying—convicts used to be sentenced to seven-year

stretches. But that had been built and used for years, and
I.D.B. people don't drag down quite such long sentences any
more; it was obviously not what Mr. Van der Westhuizen
meant. I decided to wait and not interrupt him. He was still
talking about digging.

"It's a good, healthy life, as you'll see for yourself," he said,
"and there's always a chance of making a find. That's the exciting thing about digging; there's always a chance. Remember
the Jonker diamond? That was found by a digger."

We were approaching a strange setup near the road; in fact,
it was so near that it would have stood in our way if we had
gone straight ahead. The road obligingly deflected, however,
and swung around it in a wide detour.

"That's the way it is in the fields," said Mr. Van der Westhuizen, stopping the car where the road started to turn. "You
turn around a minute and take your eye off the path you came
in by, and ten to one you find a ditch there when you start
back."

We got out and stepped over various piles of rubble, and
made our way to the edge of a pit in the bare red earth. Three
natives were busily employed in it, digging deeper with a small
mechanical shovel, swinging it around by hand and cranking
the arm. As the shovel's jaws bit into the ground it encountered
a boulder too large to shift. Shouting at each other, the men
stopped cranking and began to wrestle bodily with the rock. It
all seemed to go rather slowly and inefficiently in the baking
sun, and I looked with mild wonder at a great heap of similar
boulders that had been piled up around the diggings. The excavation was already six or seven feet deep and clearly represented a vast amount of toil.

About ten feet away on a trampled little knoll stood a four-legged contraption where two more natives were working, shaking a big rectangular sieve that fitted on the legs like a loose tabletop. This was one of the famous "Baby" machines that used to be an important part of a digger's outfit in earlier days. It was invented by an American engineer named J. L. Babe, but it might have wound up with the name Baby anyway: it took the place of the old-fashioned cradle in which miners washed their earth when they did placer mining in California as well as South Africa. One of the old, mildly smutty jokes of the digging profession is of the angry woman who was told by her husband's companions that he couldn't meet her when she arrived; he was too busy making a Baby.

On another knoll a European was overseeing a process in which another native stooped down by a rotating affair like a giant saucepan, full of thickly dirty, swirling water. This was the wash, which by gravity and centrifugal force sends the heavy gravel to the bottom outside edge, with whatever diamonds might be among the pebbles. The native was tapping the concentrate there at the bottom, letting it slide out into a shallow sieve, through which the water drained off.

Mr. Van der Westhuizen introduced me to the European, who was named Mr. Bishop, an elderly man who wore a khaki topee. The only men I ever saw in topees, anywhere in Africa, were these diggers who had to work in the glare of the veld. Mr. Bishop looked very healthy, as sunburned people usually do, and his blue eyes were clear.

"The lady would like to see you do some sorting. Is your wash ready?" asked Mr. Van der Westhuizen.

Mr. Bishop said it was ready and he was just on the verge

of trying out the first sample. Things had been very slow lately,
but he'd do his best to find something for my benefit, he said,
and both men laughed. He called to the native with the sieve
of concentrate, and the two walked over to a little table nearby
that was covered with damp sacking, pulled taut, shaded by a
canopy so that the light was just right. The boy deftly turned
over his sieve, like a child making a mud pie, and lifted it off,
leaving a cake-shaped heap of wet gravel in the middle of the
sacking. Water trickled out of it towards us, down a slight incline.

"Ever seen any sorting?" asked Mr. Bishop. "I'll show you
how it's done. You've got to look sharp to see the small stuff."

He picked up a tool something like a putty knife, and cut out
a portion of the cake and with a sweeping motion flattened out
the gravel so that it was only about one pebble thick on the
burlap. We all bent over to study it carefully. The gravel shone,
wet and multicolored. I let out a yip of discovery and picked
up a grain that looked clear and glittery. Mr. Bishop shook his
head and smiled wearily.

"Crystal," he said. I dropped the thing and went on looking.
Mr. Van der Westhuizen picked out a red sphere about an
eighth of an inch across and told me that was a good sign of
diamondiferous earth. It was garnet, but there is so much garnet
in diamond wash that we didn't bother to keep it. Finally Mr.
Bishop scraped the searched gravel off the table and cut out
another lot. Again we all hunched over it. I tried to hunt me-
thodically, portion by portion, but it was he who found something, long before my eyes had got to it. It was a dark lump
that looked to me like smoke-blackened bottle glass.

"Bort," he said, handing it over to me. Bort, as I already

knew, has some value for industrial purposes; it is badly discolored diamond. When I looked at this one closely I could see
that it was crystalline in a close-grained way. No light came
through it at all.

"Worth a few shillings," said Mr. Bishop. He pulled from
his pocket a small receptacle that proved to be the outside shell
of a Benzedrine inhaler; he unscrewed the top of this and
dropped in the piece of bort and returned it to his pocket. "Better than nothing," he said cheerfully.

"About a carat, I should think," said Mr. Van der Westhuizen. "Anybody found anything very big lately, do you
know?"

Mr. Bishop took off his topee and wiped his head. He considered and said he hadn't heard of anything good for quite a
while. "There aren't enough men around here to make much of
a record. They've mostly gone off to the new diggings," he said,
"but I didn't; it called for too much investment. That's not
real digging there. They're *dynamiting* the stuff, man; that's a
mine, that is. It's not exactly a pipe, but it's a fissure full of
blue ground. I couldn't afford the gear."

Mr. Van der Westhuizen nodded gravely. We worked our
way through the rest of the batch on the table without making
further discoveries. The discarded gravel lay at the foot of the
table where I eyed it dubiously. Had we really looked through
it carefully enough? Mr. Van der Westhuizen read my mind
and replied: "They have another go at that stuff, you know,
before it gets thrown out. We call it 'bantam.' On every field
you'll find special people—children or women or native boys—
who go through the bantam to pick up diamonds that might

have been overlooked. You'd be surprised what they find sometimes."

Mr. Bishop had started on a new batch of gravel. "You might
bring me luck," he said jocosely, "a newcomer like you. I could
use a good find."

Mr. Van der Westhuizen remarked that it wasn't like the
good old days. Mr. Bishop said, "Ah well, it wasn't always so
easy then either." Straightening up, he went on, "I've been at
this the best part of my life. Stopped once in a while—altogether, I've stopped digging three times, for good each time.
Once I really did stay out of it for a long time. I brought up the
children in Durban so as to be well away from all this. I wasn't
going to let them waste their lives like the old man if I could
help it. And I'm glad to say not one of them has followed my
example. But as soon as they were grown up and settled in life
—why——" He made a gesture to show what he meant: there
he was, back at it again. "Old digger, old fool, you know," he
said cheerfully. Actually, he didn't seem to me to be doing too
badly. He had a lot of equipment, and six boys working for him,
and in the background I noticed a nice-looking car. Mr. Bishop
wasn't poverty-stricken, though I could appreciate the fact that
it was an uncertain kind of existence. I asked him if he lived at
Nooitgedacht.

"Not any longer," he said. "I live in Kimberley. I used to
stay out here except for weekends, but my wife's nervous about
being alone in the house nowadays. There've been a few bur-
glaries at Kimberley. So I go home every night. It means getting up pretty early in the morning, before five, but I'm used
to it."

"It's a healthy life," said Mr. Van der Westhuizen, "and you don't look your age."

Mr. Bishop said, "Did you see that newspaper interview with Mr. Field?"

"I did," said Mr. Van der Westhuizen. They looked at each other.

"If he's ninety, so am I," said Mr. Bishop irritably and with what might have been a touch of jealousy. "Two years ago he was seventy-eight. That's all I know about it."

The next excavation we visited was not far away; this digger, Mr. Van der Westhuizen explained before we got out of the car, was a colored man who had been working on the diggings for a good long time and had a nice little outfit. He was a nice fellow altogether, I understood; the sort of fellow who deserved a lucky break. We found him sorting gravel at his table, with his partner looking on, but he willingly paused to show us around his pit. He was working on a bigger scale than Mr. Bishop, and I observed with considerable awe the rubble his boys' industry had extracted from the claim. What held the work up, he said, was the immense size of the boulders they had to pull out in order to collect the material in between: the river must have been a raging torrent that rolled this stuff into position in ages past. The boulders were piled up outside the pit in quantity sufficient, I decided, to build at least two cottages. They were really of various colors but they were red from the dust—red like the diggers' clothes and boots: red as my handkerchief with which I mopped my wet face. The dust got into my nose and I sneezed.

"Like to try your hand at sorting?" asked the digger. "A new hand brings luck, they say."

Eagerly I accepted, and took my place at the sack-covered table. As I had seen the others do I cut out a wedge-shaped slice from the heap and scraped it toward me. Immediately something exciting came into view—a tiny drop of light, light with edges, as clear as a bit of ice, coldly gleaming.

"There!" said the digger in gratified tones as I grabbed it. "What did I tell you?"

This time it wasn't quartz. The digger held it up to the light. "Nice little stone," he said, and his partner took it and rolled it around in the palm of his hand and said, "More than a carat." Two or three boys came over to look, and then it was popped into its Benzedrine-inhaler case. Glowing with pride, I went back to scraping and searching, but it was soon obvious that I had brought all the luck I was going to bring that day.

We spent the rest of a long morning on the fields. I remembered best a very tall old man with one of the most expensive English public-school accents I had ever heard. He said, "The last lady who came out to look at the diggings, as I remember, was the Honorable Mrs. Cuffe. That would have been back around 1925."

"How long's he been at it?" I asked as we drove away through the barbed-wire opening.

"All his life, one way or another," said Mr. Van der Westhuizen. "Mr. Anthony must be close to seventy-five. It's a——"

"Oh, it's obviously a healthy life, but not, on the whole, a profitable one, is it?" I said.

Mr. Van der Westhuizen was a romantic type, and this hurt his feelings. "That old man has made a packet in his day," he said defensively. "The trouble with all of them is just one

thing: they always put it back into digging. When a man finds
a big stone and earns eight, ten thousand pounds on it,
ten to one he just branches out instead of retiring. Sometimes he goes in for breakwater work. I'd like to show you a
breakwater if I knew where there was one going on. A breakwater is when you take and dam the river and turn it out of its
bed, and dig where the water's been. That's where you find the
very best stones—big and clear and beautiful. But it costs a lot
of money. A lot of money." His voice trailed off and he concentrated on the road, which was growing worse as we drove down-
hill towards a river. At the best of times South African driving
is pretty rugged, but this was worse than usual. It was not only
the road, either, that was getting more bumpy; the land on
either side of it had undergone a lot of upheaval. Red rock, red
dust, red rubble lay tumbled about, showing that hundreds of
diggers had been hard at work over all of it for incredible distances. The scrubby growth had done its best to hide chopped-
out pits, but bushes and trees couldn't camouflage the damage.
If you wanted to be fanciful, the land looked alive—ravaged
and furious. I said something of the sort, and Mr. Van der
Westhuizen nodded soberly.

"A lot of work's gone into this country around here," he said.
"And a lot of wealth been taken out of it, too. Mr. Anthony, for
instance; he's spent a long time here at Gong Gong, and done
well at it, but it's all worked out now. I don't see much going
on, do you?" The car paused at the top of a steep incline down
to what must have been a river hidden in a gorge beyond; we
saw a steam shovel sticking up gauntly against the sky. It wasn't
working and the pit was empty.

A colored child sat drowsily on the veranda of a tin house

near the excavation. We drove over and jolted to a stop there. "I'll just ask this fellow," said Mr. Van der Westhuizen. A mongrel dog came out and yapped at us, and a tan-colored man followed. He knew Mr. Van der Westhuizen, and they conversed for a while in Afrikaans.

Mr. Van der Westhuizen came back and reported: "He says they've all gone; they went to the new diggings in that fissure Mr. Bishop was talking about. That's the way they are, you know; they chase around after the latest find." He climbed into the car, waved to the colored man, and backed out to the road. "Some of these fellows haven't got the money to outfit themselves, you know, but they have friends. Diggers stick together. If a man makes a good strike he often backs other diggers; he buys their outfits for them and pays his share of the boys and water, in return for half the takings out of the claim. A digger can get through a lot of money that way. In fact, that's what usually happens to it."

He talked some more about Lichtenburg. The diamond market was dangerously low in 1927 when that big discovery was made, and De Beers was not overjoyed, to put it mildly. But for the ordinary digger the name Lichtenburg still has a special luster that only the bigger strike at Alexander Bay, in South-West Africa, has ever dimmed. Of all the men Mr. Van der Westhuizen knew who made fortunes at Lichtenburg, he could think of only one still alive and in possession of a fair amount of his money.

"His family put it into a farm at the Cape," he said. "The rest—well, they kept on looking for diamonds, and every single one, if he's dead, died broke, and the rest are broke as well, you can bet, wherever they are."

We had come into sight of the river and were now following it as it meandered over a very wide, stony bed. Soon we came to the pretty town of Barkly West, identifiable for miles off because of its tall Dutch Reformed Church tower. It was a much more elaborate structure than most South African churches. They are usually made of stucco, but this was of rocks that had been carefully selected to give a variegated pudding-stone effect and equally carefully cut and fitted. Mr. Van der Westhuizen began talking about diamond dealers, who according to him were a different type of man altogether from diggers. Dealers knew how to hold on to their money, he said, and there was no denying they got more out of the business of digging in the first place. Diggers were notoriously easygoing and didn't know how to drive a bargain, but buyers were different. They had to be. As we rolled past the local hotel he suddenly stepped on the brake and called out in welcome to a big, pink-faced man in shirt sleeves who was walking by, carrying a leather box like a fat brief case or a small suitcase.

"Just the man I wanted you to meet," he said to me cheerfully as we got out of the car. "This is one of the biggest dealers in the district."

We all went into the hotel for a cool beer, and the dealer asked us where we'd been sight-seeing. We told him: Nooitgedacht and Gong Gong. He remarked that there was absolutely nothing going on at Gong Gong, and asked for the latest reports on Nooitgedacht. "I haven't been around there lately," he said.

"Well, we heard talk; somebody's supposed to have got hold of something," said Mr. Van der Westhuizen, rather to my interested surprise, for I had heard nothing of it. "You know how it is; you can't tell until they come in for the valuation, but these fellows could use a little encouragement. They haven't had anything big for months. How's it with you?"

The dealer said, "Oh, it's quiet here too. Still, I've found a few that aren't bad. Would you like to see them?"

He pulled a bunch of keys out of his pocket and unlocked his case. Inside it was like a giant jewel box with all the secondary prettiness left out; there was no white padded satin or anything like that, just diamonds, and they were hidden from first sight. The case was divided into a number of little metal boxes or compartments of different depth. Along one side paper money was tucked: all the rest was filled with paper packets.

These paper packets, as I soon learned in the diamond fields, are a special sign of the trade. Most diamond people carry their wares around with a splendid, airy carelessness. Everyone except the final middleman, who displays his rings and necklaces piously surrounded by black velvet and reinforced glass windows, seems to go out of his way to show who is master—his diamonds or himself. The people of Kimberley and Johannesburg and Orange Mouth carry gems in rusty tin pillboxes, old candy boxes, and especially in folded paper—simple pieces of paper, not particularly strong or tough, folded and opened and folded again around bits of stone worth thousands of dollars. This dealer was one of the paper-folders. He brought out packet after packet and unwrapped them to show me what he was buying and selling and keeping. Some were rough diamonds; some had been cut, and they blazed in the noonday light. He usually carried around his whole stock, he said; it was safer than leaving them at home or in the office.

"Ever seen a good collection of fancies?" he demanded. He

added to Mr. Van der Westhuizen, "I don't believe you've seen these." Diving into the case, he brought up a large packet of the most worn-out paper of all. There was a little hole at the corner where it had been wrapped once too often; a blue diamond nearly slipped out as he lifted it. But then, I've seen lots of diamonds fall to the floor and roll into the corner; somehow or other they are always found again without much trouble. They are easy to see.

The dealer unwrapped and displayed a splendid collection. They were all cut stones; several ambers, quite a few blues, two lovely pinks, and one that was nearly purple, as well as a few very clear greenish ones that I didn't like to say looked exactly like aquamarines. Their owner smiled at our enthusiasm: it was a pleased, proud smile. "I've been making this collection ever since I went into the business," he said, wrapping them up again, "and that's nearly forty years. It's my hobby, fancies. My wife thinks I'm crazy. Now, that's a funny thing; she doesn't like diamonds at all; never wears any, nor my daughter either. They want me to quit the business. My son's the same, he's never shown any interest in diamonds. After me all the time to give up, sell out, and settle down with him on the family farm."

"What about the breakwater? —Here's one of our leading breakwater men," said Mr. Van der Westhuizen to me in explanation. "He can tell you all about it. It's the way to make money fast."

The dealer said, "Oh, I don't know, you can lose money too. That last one of mine cost ten thousand pounds. But then, I expect I'll make it back again on the next one. . . . I don't know. Perhaps I ought to retire like the boy says."

He smiled and walked off down the road with his leather box. We climbed back into the car. "*He* won't ever go to the poorhouse, no matter how he talks," said Mr. Van der Westhuizen. Possibly realizing that he sounded a bit resentful, he added, "But he's a very good man, you know. He never smokes or drinks, he's very steady, he takes a lot of interest in this town. He was born and brought up here. The church there, you see how well built it is. Good Afrikaners are supposed to give a tenth of their income every year to the church; you people call it the tithe, don't you? Well, that man, he never misses out on his tithe. I expect he's paid for most of that new church out of his own pocket." He sighed and looked around at the red earth. "It's a funny thing to think this is all diamondiferous," he said. "You might find a diamond anywhere. Oh well, not everybody's lucky. I did right, quitting when I did. Yes, I did right."

Next day—Friday—I arrived a little later at Nooitgedacht. This time I went out with the valuer and purchaser, that same Mr. Cohen whose enamel sign I had seen on the company office door. We found Mr. Van der Westhuizen and his companion already there, and water for tea was boiling on the stove. Mr. Cohen had a pleasant manner and I recalled what I had been told about him; that he had a reputation for giving fair prices to the diggers and was a great relief after some of the people they had had to deal with in the past. It is important to diggers to have a good buyer on the grounds, for though they have the privilege of selling their stones elsewhere, most of them find it simpler in the end—and often necessary—to cash in then and there, on the spot.

"There are two ways he can make an offer," Mr. Van der Westhuizen explained over the teacups. "He sometimes gives a price they can take up right away or later on as they like. Or he makes a different kind of proposition, when he isn't so sure how he can dispose of the stone himself; they can turn it down and go out and hawk it around the other dealers, but if they do that and then come back, his price won't be as good as it was at first."

Mr. Cohen unlocked the door of his own cubicle and got it ready. I looked out the window at the diggers who had assembled before the shack. I wouldn't have guessed from my view the day before that there were so many people on the farm, vast as it was. Then I had seen only four or five houses all morning, but there were twenty or thirty people talking to each other in the shade of the big tree or leaning against the wall. Most of them were colored. All of them looked ready for hard work, some in ragged clothes; the general effect was a parched one, as if they would have been muddy if ever they could get wet, but that wasn't likely. There was one woman, a wide, low one in an old black felt hat and a skirt of indeterminate color and a brown sweater full of holes, buttoned to straining tightness over her big bust. Her skin was light brown, her hair was gray, and when she saw me looking at her, her smile was shy and sweet.

We went in to Mr. Cohen's room, which held nothing but a table, two chairs, and a pair of diamond scales. He unlocked his case and disclosed a lot of money—notes neatly stacked together with rubber bands around them, and rouleaux of coins in paper, like those at a bank. He sat down behind the table and put on a pair of jeweler's goggles. The diggers lined up at the door without any jostling. Everything was easy, slow-moving and familiar. I saw some of the diggers I had met the day before, but not Mr. Anthony; Mr. Van der Westhuizen said he had probably not found anything and so there was no sense in turning up.

First in the line was an old, old colored man in a hat full of holes; I suppose he wore it only to keep his hair out of his eyes. He pulled an inhaler tube out of his vest pocket and cackled as he shook out two or three lumps of brown bort. Mr. Cohen laughed too. They both sounded rather rueful. Mr. Cohen weighed the diamonds; he wrote something down on a pad of printed forms; he added it and looked up and said, "Eleven shillings. Can't do more."

The old man raised his eyebrows and hesitated. Mr. Cohen said, "I *can't* do more. That's all it's worth."

The old man shrugged, accepted a piece of paper as a voucher, and moved out of the office, giving way to another colored man, a younger one. Mr. Cohen greeted this one cheerfully. "Well, Van der Merwe, have you found another Jonker?"

Mr. Van der Merwe, a man with high cheekbones and blue eyes, didn't smile. He looked grave, like the bearer of important news, but he didn't speak either. With the hint of a swagger he pulled out a tiny box, rolled something into the palm of his hand, and put it down before Mr. Cohen. The two diggers behind him craned their necks to see and one whistled. It was undeniably a large diamond; from where I was, in the corner, it looked very good. Mr. Van der Westhuizen beamed and nodded at me. Mr. Cohen said, "Well!"

He picked it up and hefted it in his hand, up and down. "It must be about eight carats," he said. Everyone looked excited.

Mr. Cohen seemed to put off the moment of actual weighing on the scales to let all of us enjoy ourselves guessing. Mr. Van der Merwe still didn't smile. He looked proud and dignified, standing alone there, like the father of a new baby.

Finally Mr. Cohen pushed his goggles far back on his head, picked up his loupe, and studied the stone. We were all quiet while he did this, and a lot of the diggers outside looked in the window. At last he spoke. "Couple of specks there. Pity."

"*Little* specks," said Mr. Van der Merwe.

"Off-color too," said Mr. Cohen. "Pity. If only it weren't quite so yellow——"

Mr. Van der Merwe laughed at last, sternly and scornfully. "The color's *good*," he said.

"Frankly I'm not sure," said Mr. Cohen. "I can't be sure about the color until I get back to the lab in Kimberley. It's a nice stone anyway," he conceded. He put it into the scales and we all waited tensely. "Eight. Eight and a half—no, it runs more than that. Eight and five eighths. Well now, let's see." He picked up his pencil and got to work on his pad. At last he said, "Five hundred twenty pounds, even. That is, if you sell it now. That will leave you, without the royalty, four hundred and sixty-eight."

All our eyes turned toward the digger. He shook his head and said calmly, "That's the best stone I've ever found in all my life's digging."

"Listen, Van der Merwe. It's a good big stone, but it's just a little off-color. You won't get a better price anywhere, I'll tell you that," said Mr. Cohen.

Again Mr. Van der Merwe shook his head. Mr. Cohen picked up the diamond and the loupe and studied it some more, saying as if to himself, "If only I could be sure that big spot was near enough to the middle; it wouldn't lose so much in the cutting in that case." He immersed himself in thought. The office was dead quiet. Then he sighed and said, "Make it four seventy-five. That's just about top price for the color."

Mr. Van der Merwe in turn thought and counted and considered. After a dramatic pause he did something—he must have made some sign, though I didn't see it—that indicated acceptance. We all let out our breath, and he took his piece of paper and went through the door, grinning. Outside, a number of men crowded around to congratulate him.

After that everything seemed anticlimactic. Mr. Bishop brought in a little stone for which he got six pounds, and he said it was just about enough to pay for his water. He stood around and exchanged pleasantries with the next man, a European who was able to sell his take for ten pounds. "That's pretty good," said Mr. Bishop ironically.

The other man grunted. "I've got to pay ten boys, man," he said.

"And how are you, Mrs. Bartlett?" said Mr. Cohen, greeting the lady digger. She was too shy to be talkative. She dug into her sweater pocket and produced a wooden needlecase, made in the shape of an elongated acorn; from this she rolled out a stone that brought her twenty-five pounds. This was good from Nooitgedacht standards, and everyone looked at her admiringly, which made her more bashful than ever. She went out to the tree and stood there, curious to see if anyone else had any luck. Nobody had. The Van der Merwe diamond was the biggest that had been found for several weeks, and everyone had evidently decided that it was going to be a high spot for

some weeks to come. The last man in line was a toothless ancient who haggled gently but stubbornly until he brought Mr.
Cohen's offer up from thirty-two shillings to thirty-five.

"It's not worth thirty-five," said Mr. Cohen to me as he
packed up, "but you get to know these old boys, and it's hard
not to let go once in a while. I wonder if I made a mistake on
the big one?"

It was time for the pay-off; once again those diggers who had
decided to take their money lined up, papers in hand. Everyone fell silent again, respectfully, as Mr. Van der Merwe collected his. He asked for it in small notes, nothing more than five
pounds. Then in little groups or couples the diggers strolled
off and disappeared. The red, baked land looked bleached now
in the fierce sun. Mr. Cohen locked his case and we all had tea.

Mr. Van der Westhuizen said, "They're supposed to go back
to work now for the rest of the day. The weekend doesn't begin
officially until tonight. But not many people go on digging after
the pay-off. Well, Mr. Cohen, how do you feel about your big
diamond?"

"I may have made a mistake. I hope not," said Mr. Cohen.

"Much going on out at Nooitgedacht?" a diamond buyer in
Kimberley asked me, over a pot of tea, when I got back to town.
He spoke in the manner of an adult inquiring how nursery
school had been today.

"There was one pretty big diamond, weighing more than
eight carats," I told him. "There wasn't anything else. But I
noticed there's been quite an imposing record of big finds out
there over the years. They've had lots of luck in their day,
haven't they?"

"Some luck, maybe," he said, "but in my opinion their day is over. Those fellows at Nooitgedacht go out and sweat in the sun, and haul up boulders, and sort their wash, and what do they come up with? Three or four hundred carats a month, at most, for the batch of them. You know what the Premier Mine produces? A hundred thousand carats a month. I'm against digging on principle. It's wasteful, it's disorganized, and it's useless. And I say—though this isn't the official attitude, it's only my own—that it's time they gave it up."

"Oh, come now!" I protested. "After all, people have made fortunes out of digging. What about the Jonker?"

"The Jonker?" said the buyer. "Well, since you mention it, I've never gone along with the theory that the Jonker just happened to turn up where it did. It's my belief that it originally came out of a deep mine. The Premier, no doubt." And, as if he had not just pronounced a heresy, he took a deep draught of tea.

CHAPTER THREE

# The Giants

The long tables that formed a continuous counter around the room were heaped with diamonds, as neatly stacked as could be managed with such irregularly shaped things. Crystals have points, yet some diamonds are apt to roll. It was a businesslike room, and the heaps should have been businesslike, too, for they were as much merchandise as if they had been stacks of carbon paper. Through the door leading into a larger room I saw more tables in rows, where more diamonds were being sorted by aproned young girls using implements like eyebrow tweezers. All this should have been prosaic, but diamonds even in commercial bulk are never prosaic. They were in the rough, they weren't cut, but they flashed. Johannesburg's sun struck them, through the high windows and skylights, and they gleamed as if their light came not as an answer, but from some inside source.

"These in the lot here," said the man who was showing me around, indicating the nearest heap, "are what we call close goods, that is, of the best quality. They're pure; unspotted. As you can see they're graded according to size as well as color.

This one would be about four carats; this a little farther on would come to about two and a half. There are a hundred and forty-two carats to an ounce; it's a very ancient unit of weight." I imitated him and picked up a diamond here and there and put it down again, trying to look insouciant. Moving on, he continued talking: "Here are spotted ones, what we call piquéd; as you probably know, they've got to be cut carefully so the spots won't be included, and that lowers their value. These, less than a carat, are called melee; small, as you see, but fairly regular. Anything less than a carat that's broken, though, is considered a chip. It hasn't much value. Broken stones that weigh more than a carat are known as cleavages."

We stepped back and surveyed the length of the table, and he showed me how the different colors of the grades were plainly visible—blue, white, and various shades of yellow from pale to amber. Near the end of the room was a pile of brownish stones. They were marginal, he said. Anything of lighter color would be categorized as "fancy," worth whatever price it might fetch from a man whose taste was for fancies, but a stone of deeper color would be merely industrial, selling for much less than gem price.

"Diamond values are tricky things," he said. "A shade of color makes all the difference; it's what you might call dramatic. Fashions in colors come and go. There's a great demand at the moment for a rare greenish shade. We're doing some work on color in the research laboratories just now; it's never been discovered to a certainty what makes it. It's hard to generalize, but certain colors in stones do seem to occur in special parts of the mines, associated with certain other minerals. That doesn't apply, naturally, to the diamonds we find in alluvial deposits. . . . Here are the industrials."

We had got to the door and stood near a heap of dark stones. "We call these dressers in the trade. And here is what diamond looks like when it's been ground into powder for polishing. Here's diamond dust." He handed me a glass jar.

I had thought diamond dust would glitter like the stuff strewn on pictures of snow-topped roofs, on Christmas cards. It doesn't. It is gray powder like snuff, very heavy. He told me to dabble my fingers in it; I did, but gingerly, because I couldn't get over a silly idea that every grain counted. It felt as fine as face powder.

The guide said, "You've come at the right time of month to see the goods, because we're just making up our parcels for the sights. That's when all the diamond buyers come in to get their lots, either here or in London. The only way to allocate fairly is to make up each parcel with the same proportion of all the grades, and that's what we're doing now."

"Then there's no choice?" I asked.

"No choice outside of the value of the parcel. The buyer is given a look at his parcel, of course, to see if he wants it; sometimes he turns it down if it hasn't got enough of what he's after and too much of what he feels he can't use, but that doesn't happen very often. Each buyer is allowed to study his lot alone, in a room by himself, and make up his mind at his own speed. That's why it's called a 'sight.' Nobody's allowed to pick and choose from several packages, naturally."

I was about to ask where the other diamonds are kept—the ones rumor says are hidden away in a store to which more are added whenever the supply gets too plentiful for price support.

But we were interrupted by a second man who carried in a
metal box to show me. It held various specimens of freak diamonds that turn up from time to time in the mines. In some
the crystallization was incomplete and the diamonds were
partly hollow, for all the world like ice cubes not fully frozen.
In others the crystals were twinned in peculiar shapes. Finally
we got back to the subject I had on my mind.

"You've got a lot more diamonds put away, haven't you?" I
asked. "Where do you keep them?"

My question had a peculiar effect: the two men looked at
each other with weary expressions. My guide said, "We don't
keep any put away. The demand for gem diamonds is greater
than the supply, as I told you. That's why we have to be careful
allocating them."

I said, "Oh, come on. You know perfectly well it's all controlled. If all the diamonds you people had were thrown onto
the market at once, they wouldn't be worth anything. You keep
them back and dribble them out."

The second man said earnestly, "No, you've got it wrong.
Everybody thinks that, but it's not true. We do control production. It's true that not every one of our sources is working flat
out the whole time; for instance, since they started serious production in South Africa we're letting the Kimberley mines work
two out of each three at a time. But that's partly to conserve
gear, partly because it's a simple matter of working economy.
You'd apply the same principle to any kind of mining. You
don't want to work them all out at once."

"You can take my word for it that we've got no accumulated
stock, this year of all years," said my guide. "You probably
won't, though. We get this argument all the time. A few weeks

ago we had a lady journalist who came into the office, and she certainly did have a chip on her shoulder. She stood in front of my desk and accused me to my face of manipulating the market by the most devious methods. She said she knew for a fact we've got a vault full of priceless stones right here under this building, and when I wouldn't fall on my knees and confess she walked out swearing she was going to tear the whole racket apart."

The second man said gloomily, "And here we are without any backlog. I only wish she'd been right about that vault. Though mind you, I *have* seen this place practically choked with diamonds. That was a long time ago, in the thirties."

"Yes, the journalist girl should have seen us then," said the first man. "We had milk cans full of goods, literally milk cans, you know—those great big ones. It was in the depression of the early thirties when luxuries weren't selling. In times like that diamonds are always hit. But then the war came on and the slack was taken up. People buy during a war. A diamond's a good, compact way to invest your money, and you can smuggle it out of the country if you want to escape from some iron curtain or whatever."

I said, "You called it a good investment. That is to say, even if all the diamonds you've got were to be released——"

He moaned, interrupting me; he leaned forward and spoke slowly and carefully and loudly. "They—are—being—released. As fast as we can get them out. We can't keep up with the demand. As true as I'm here talking to you, we haven't any hoard hidden away. Just now we are selling every gem diamond we produce, and we could sell a lot more; we get requests for more every day. I admit it hasn't always been like that. This market has its ups and downs like any other. We probably have thin times ahead as well as behind us; that's what we have controls for. That's why from our point of view the monopoly is a good thing. The public doesn't like the word 'monopoly.' No more do I like it when it's applied to anything that's necessary, such as food, or clothing, or anything else utilitarian, but a diamond's not food or wool. A diamond—I'm discussing the gem, of course, not industrials—it's the essence of luxury. That's its appeal. If it became valueless, the dealers would be the first to complain—those same dealers who criticize us for controlling the market. Where would they be if the value fluctuated? I'll tell you. Right back where they were near the beginning, before the amalgamation, when in the price war between Rhodes and Barney Barnato the price of top-quality goods went down to ten shillings a carat, and every outgoing vehicle from Kimberley was full of people running away from the mines."

He was expressing a philosophy that applies to a lot of other commodities that are dug up from the ground, though diamonds are indeed, as he pointed out, a rather special thing even among minerals. The diamond mines of South Africa in their early days could hardly have been called typical of mines in general, though there were some points the industry had in common with other new mineral strikes. There was the familiar program: the discovery, the rush, the reign of the little man, and in the end, by the inexorable logic of technology and finance, the absorption of the little man by the big man, or, in this case, by the two big men—not that the little man didn't resist. Kimberley laws were passed to prevent monopoly, but they weren't applied for very long. No law could halt the march of natural disaster; neither could any action taken by individuals in their separate pits. It was this natural disaster that worked on the side of the monopolists.

When the Kimberley diggings were first staked out, the diggers stipulated that no one person could work more than two claims, of 31 feet by 31, at a time. Later the permission was enlarged to include ten claims under one management, and even that protective rule was shelved in 1876, when all restrictions on the size of claims were abolished. This was inevitable because of the conditions under which the diggers found themselves working when they abandoned surface washing and concentrated on digging in the "blue ground" where most diamonds were found. As they went deeper and deeper, hundreds of feet down, they dug themselves into trouble. Overhead the surrounding wall kept sloughing off and falling in, smothering men and pay dirt alike. Underfoot water became even more of a menace than this falling reef. During the surface-washing era, water had been a much desired commodity, rare and expensive in that arid climate, but even under diamond fields there is an underground water table, and the deep pits had tapped it. Hand pumping didn't afford fast enough action to deal with it. Sooner or later someone was bound to think of steam-engine pumping; it was typical of Cecil John Rhodes that he should have been the one, and also that he should have set about finding a steam pump before anybody else did.

He was twenty-one at the time, in 1874, and the rush was five years old. Three years before, he had come to South Africa from England for his health, gravitating to the Fields from a Natal farm in the wake of his elder brother who was also a restless, adventurous individual. Cecil did a certain amount of digging: the residents of Kimberley still point out the thorn tree

under which he is said to have sat when he sorted out the wash
from his first claim. When digging didn't pay, Rhodes turned
his hand to other ways of earning his living. He sold ice cream.
He peddled water when water was still desirable and not a menace. He was a man bound to turn his surroundings to advantage,
and as it happened he got his first real start over the encroaching water. By 1874 he had acquired a certain amount of money
that would have seemed very respectable for such a young man
to have earned at home in England, and when he went into
partnership with two other young Englishmen, Charles D.
Rudd and Wallace Alderson, they were able to put up the capital for the pump project out of their own pockets. It wasn't easy,
but finally Rhodes found a steam-engine pump for sale in
Africa, at Port Elizabeth. He wrote to Rudd:

"I had to give £900 and a bill at four months for £100. . . .
Wallace used to wake up fancying himself an engine. I wake
up fancying myself meeting various little bits of paper ranging
over 3, four and five months with my blessed signature at the
bottom."

It was a story with a happy ending, up to a point. The pump
paid off to such good effect that it might be called the foundation of Rhodes's famous fortune, and was thus indirectly responsible for his swift, fantastic career, which did so much to
expand the British Empire. The pump was hired out everywhere to diggers who still believed they could carry on as they
had done before, working their own claims and beholden to no
man. Rhodes and his partners formed a proper company around
it, and sent for better pumps and spare parts from England.
Soon they had enough capital to branch out pretty widely.

Even at that time, Rhodes had visions of a grandiose com-

bine that would take over all the mines in Kimberley, and of an
even more grandiose combine that would dominate and exploit
all there was to dominate and exploit in South Africa. The year
before he went into the pumping business, he had bought a
small claim in the De Beers Mine, and now, with his new
wealth, he began annexing other small holdings, by either buying the owners out or going into partnership with them. Bit by
bit, over the next few years, he enlarged his little domain in the
De Beers pit until by 1880 he was one of its largest claim owners. That year he took a great step. His combine coalesced with
two other large combines to form the De Beers Mining Company, Ltd. Like all other limited-liability companies in the
British colonies, this concern was issued a charter, or trust deed,
by the Colonial Office in London. At first, nobody except
Rhodes was much concerned about the terms of the charter,
but later they became celebrated. There was virtually no restric-
tion on the activities that De Beers could undertake; the company could go into practically any business it chose to and could
stake out claims of practically any sort in great stretches of un-
explored territory in Africa. For the moment, though, Rhodes
was kept busy with diamonds. There were still some obdurate
little companies with holdings in the De Beers Mine, and it
was to take him until 1887 to buy them all out.

As Rhodes made his way up in the world, step by step, another very bright young Englishman, Barney Barnato, was
climbing as swiftly, with just as much energy, toward his own
pinnacle in the diamond trade.

Considering everything, it was mildly exasperating to these
men who were making surprising fortunes in the Diamond
Fields that England should not admit the state of affairs. Ac-

cording to the people at home, there weren't any diamonds in South Africa—not indigenous diamonds, that is. Probably the majority of Hatton Garden merchants knew where the new supply of stones was coming from, but the general public remained skeptical for years. Most of them persisted in declaring that it was all a hoax. *The Times* and other papers, while carrying quotations of Cape diamond prices in their financial columns, sturdily refused to accept this information as evidence. The so-called South African diamond mines, they insisted, were salted with stones brought from Brazil. Everybody knew that tricky fellows abounded in the colonies. The whole thing, they said, was obviously a ramp designed to lure unwary investors into sinking capital in African real estate. "A land swindle," said *The Times*. Nobody remembered—well, after all, they could hardly be expected to remember—that at the beginning of the eighteenth century, when diamonds were first discovered in Brazil, exactly the same kind of story went the rounds among jewel merchants. It was said that the Brazilian stones could not possibly be genuine diamonds because, as everybody knew, diamonds came only from India. Then when tests proved that they were as hard as Indian stones, it was claimed that if they were indeed diamonds, they must be the sweepings, or refuse, of Indian mines, sent over to Brazil and sold to foolish traders as first-rate gems. For a long time the Brazilian miners had to smuggle their stones into Bengal by way of Goa and sell them as Indian produce. When this was done they were snapped up. It took years to overcome the rumors; years before Brazilian diamonds were bought for their proper worth in Brazil.

Here was the same thing happening again, only this time the South African diamond was the victim. In vain did an earnest

South African, during a visit to England in 1880, make the rounds of the newspapers in an attempt to convince the die-hards. Rhodes by this time was firmly established as a magnate and so was Barney Barnato, and Kimberley had become quite a town. But the self-appointed missionary of truth couldn't convince *The Times* of all this, nor the *Observer*, nor the *Telegraph*. *The Times's* city, or financial, editor did listen for a while and promised to publish a letter on the subject, but later on he changed his mind. He had made inquiries, he said, and discovered that the mines were in the hands of unprincipled men. Besides, he pointed out, such a letter might affect the share market.

In the meantime the picture was changing on the Fields: many of the original diggers had acknowledged defeat and pulled out, whereas others saw beyond the difficulties of individual mining to a solution of their troubles by combining. Rhodes wasn't the only one who realized that consolidation was inevitable. A lot of men were busy snapping up relinquished claims. For a while the Kimberley, the most important mine in the Fields, was split up and owned by a bewildering number of companies, but the best claims in the place belonged to Barney Barnato.

No novelist could have created a neater character than Barnato to set in contrast against the empire-builder Rhodes. Barnato was a melodramatic, mercurial figure: Rhodes was cool and well-bred in the English fashion. Barnato came from London's East End: Rhodes was a clergyman's son with a middle-class background. Rhodes had been educated and continued doggedly to acquire more education all through his early career in the Diamond Fields, returning to Oxford at intervals until he finally got his degree. Barnato left school at the age of fourteen, and it is not recorded that he ever expressed regret at having done so. Rhodes was tall and fair, Barnato short and dark—the differences could be catalogued for pages, but there were similarities, too, and the chief of these—unbounded ambition—resulted in a battle that still lives vividly in South African legend.

Barnato arrived at the Fields in 1873, having come out, like Rhodes, to join an elder brother; he was twenty-one years old and possessed something less than £60 to start out with. His real name was Barnett Isaacs, but with his brother Harry he had adopted the name Barnato as being more exotic and thus suitable for the stage. For both the Isaacs boys had appeared on the boards of London music halls.

In the year of Barnato's arrival a brief depression hit the world's luxury trades. In addition, there was an overproduction of big stones. There were too many diamonds on the market, and the price had sunk to below what the sellers considered a normal level. Like Rhodes, Barnato turned his hand to anything that would earn him a living. "There is nothing this country produces that I have not traded in," he said, after he had become a diamond king, "from diamonds and gold right away through wool, feathers, and mealies, to garden vegetables. I have always found that I was as good a hand at buying and selling as most people." That was blatant understatement. Barney was a wizard at buying and selling. He was quick-witted, and he had much more zest and vitality than the average man. Inevitably he settled on diamonds as his best bet —that is, until gold was discovered on the Rand—but he had many side lines in the early days before diamonds paid. He taught boxing, and tried his hand at running a cabaret. As the market improved, however, he became what was known as a "kopje-walloper," a man who traveled from one digger's house to another, buying stones. He earned a reputation for keen judgment and intelligence. At the time when the yellow ground, which was believed to be the best pay dirt, was exhausted and gave way to harder blue ground underneath, Barnato was one of the first to figure that this wasn't necessarily the end of the diamond mines. He listened to arguing geologists, and it seemed to him that Dr. Guybon Atherstone of Grahamstown made the most sense. You will recall it was Atherstone who argued that since the yellow soil was obviously not water-laid it must be of volcanic origin; the diamonds in it must therefore be the result of volcanic activity. Barnato told himself that there was then no reason why more diamonds shouldn't occur farther down, either actually in the blue ground or underneath it.

While the savants wrangled, he began buying claims as near as he could get them to the middle of the tube, or pipe, of ground that made up the Kimberley Mine. He had formed a private theory to add to Atherstone's which as it happened didn't work out quite so conclusively; since the stones found in the yellow ground were often bigger and better than those the diggers had scratched earlier out of water-laid deposits, it followed that this was because they were nearer the center of the world and so under greater pressure. Therefore, the deeper one dug, the bigger they were sure to be. (Here, for once, his shrewdness failed him.) By the time the blue ground was discovered to be productive, and when the individual diggers gave up because of the depth problems, Barney already had a lot of claims in strategic positions, and in 1880, the year Rhodes formed his company, he formed the Barnato Diamond Mining Company, which later was merged with the Kimberley Central Mining Company. There were other large syndicates in the Kimberley Mine, but Barnato's was easily the most aggressive. The last digger of all, a man named Stewart, held six claims in the very middle of the Kimberley pipe. He pulled out in 1881, at which period a number of companies were chasing whatever could be had, and Barney found himself bidding for the Stewart claims against a lot of rivals. He topped all bids and paid the record sum of thirty thousand pounds for each of the six. It seemed to the rest of his world a fantastic waste of money.

New problems were overtaking the trade—the capsizing reef, the collapsing inner walls, and the encroaching water which cost so much to pump out. The added plague of I.D.B., or illicit diamond buying, was at last under control to some extent; not conclusively, but at least better than it had hitherto been. After ten years' discussion, a suggestion which had long been urged by the diggers had been adopted, and native workers were now not only searched thoroughly when they left the mines; they seldom left the mines at all. They had to live in compounds on the premises, where they spent all their contracted time, forbidden to go outside. In spite of these precautions and the slowing up of stealing, business was bad. It wasn't so much a question now of I.D.B. or overproduction as of the expense, under such difficulties, of extracting the stones at all. The Mining Board, which was the miners' first attempt at concerted action, tried stopgap activity. For a while the reef was cut back from the edge of the pits: tunnels were dug in to blue ground at a gentle incline, or shafts were sunk well outside the pipes from which the workers made tunnels, or drifts, straight in to the blue ground. Some people tried drilling and blasting the blue ground as fast as possible in order to get it out before the reef fell. None of this was of any avail in the long run; it cost too much. By 1881 the landslides in the Kimberley Mine were becoming so catastrophic that a man who went down into the pit was taking his life into his hands, and it seemed, indeed, that all Barnato's money and drive had been wasted.

Then, in 1883, the Kimberley Mine made the most spectacular of its repeated comebacks. For years there had been talk in the diamond fields about underground mining, and now Kimberley Central had no choice but to try it. The company sank great shafts into the ground surrounding the pit, and it dug tunnels leading from the shafts into the heart of the blue ground under the mine. There was a good deal of trial and error, but by the end of 1884 Kimberley Central was running a scientific underground mining operation, resembling, in all its important particulars, the method used for mining diamonds today. In all this, Barnato, not Rhodes, led the way. Landslides did not become a crucial problem at the De Beers Mine until 1886, and it was in that year that Rhodes sank his shafts and dug his tunnels.

By 1887, Rhodes and Barnato were fully established as the two big men of Kimberley. Rhodes was thirty-four years old, and Barnato thirty-five. Rhodes, as chairman of the De Beers Mining Company, was in full control of the De Beers Mine. Barnato wasn't that firmly in the saddle, and his fingers were itching to take over the remaining companies in the Kimberley Mine. As for Rhodes, his fingers were now itching to take over all the mines in and around the town of Kimberley—primarily the Kimberley Mine, of course, but also the two smaller ones called Bultfontein and Dutoitspan. He felt that diamond prices must be kept up by the concerted action of the producers, and he could see no hope for such action unless a one-company monopoly ran all the mines. He had a point. During the middle eighties, the various owners of the Kimberley Mine had got into a short but intense price war, in which diamonds went down to ten shillings a carat, or five shillings less than it cost to produce them. Barnato naturally resented this as much as Rhodes did, but he saw things differently. He wanted to be the boss of the Kimberley and he felt that Rhodes should be content to be the boss at De Beers. The two of them, he thought, could work out the price problem together. However, both men figured that with control there was no way the business could go wrong for very long at a time, because there would always be a demand for diamonds. As Rhodes put it, the relationship between men and women was the foundation of the diamond's worth, and as long as men fell for women, diamonds would be in demand. Not that he would ever have handed diamonds around to girl friends himself. Rhodes was a cold fish as far as pretty ladies were concerned, but he was observant of the frailties of others. Whenever a man and a girl got engaged, he pointed out, a diamond was bought. (He called it, with true nineteenth-century delicacy, the "licit relationship" between the sexes.) So many people engaged every year meant so many diamonds sold that year. Barney's nephew Solly Joel was to say the same thing years later, during World War I: "Women are born every day, and while women are born, diamonds will be worn."

If you produced just enough, argued Rhodes, that was all

right. If you didn't produce enough, somebody went without diamonds and you lost money. But if you produced too many, people would be able to buy them cheap and you lost money again. The trick was to be able to hand out just the right amount to the customers, and you couldn't do that unless you had control of the entire output. Rhodes's theory didn't tell the whole story. Not all diamond-swapping relationships between men and women are licit, and, as today's De Beers directors would be able to testify, it is not easy to keep the demand neatly geared to the number of engagements that take place during a year. Irregularity has a way of creeping in. On the whole, however, Rhodes guessed right. Though some men do hand out diamonds to blondes they don't marry, and a lot of women get more than their ration of one diamond per engagement, the great bulk of the trade still relies on the supplying of gems for engagement rings. The only other important thing Rhodes didn't foresee, though it would not have upset him, was that there would be so many more people nowadays buying his rings.

Kimberley Mine, then, with Barney Barnato holding many of its best claims through the Kimberley Central Mining Company, was a threat to Rhodes's ideal monopoly because it meant he couldn't be boss of the whole setup. (At that point he knew of only the big four mines and the outlying smaller pipes that had been discovered during the rush: as far as anyone could tell, this one patch of the African map covered the entire important production of the world, for India's and Brazil's mines were nearly worked out.) Among the various owners at Kimberley, there was only one other company besides Barnato's that was important, a French group, the Compagnie Française des

Mines de Diamant du Cap de Bon Espérance, which everyone, not unnaturally, called simply the French Company. Barnato was piqued when he heard that Rhodes, right under his nose, had tried to buy out the French Company with money borrowed from the Rothschilds in London.

The story of the maneuvering that followed brings in names that were later to be famous in England as well as South Africa, when the English at last got around to admitting that there *were* diamonds down there. Alfred Beit was Rhodes's good friend, and he lent money for Rhodes's schemes. Rhodes himself didn't yet have much money to throw around. Beit came from Hamburg; he had been sent out originally to represent Lippert's, a diamond-buying firm, that had been in Africa since the beginning of the rush. Then there was Julius Wernher, a German who helped to organize the French Company: later Wernher and Beit were to combine. There were Max Michaelis and a number of others, who were destined to build palaces in London's West End as befitted millionaires, and make costly collections of paintings or ivory carvings or jewels or race horses, or in some cases all these things together. Beit was already rich, but he didn't have enough money for Rhodes's enormous plans, and that is why Rhodes had gone to Rothschilds in London. Until then Rothschilds weren't very much interested in South Africa. They had been influenced by pronouncements such as those of *The Times*, and distrusted far-off colonies. However, Rhodes had great powers of persuasion, and without much argument they agreed to lend him a million pounds with which to buy the French Company's holdings. The French owners accepted an offer of £1,400,000, half of this to be in De Beers shares. Rhodes and Beit would be able to manage this, and

everything seemed to be going nicely, with De Beers shares rising right along, when Barney Barnato showed his resentment
in a very practical manner by making a new offer to the French
Company of £1,750,000.

Negotiations between the French Company and De Beers
slowed down abruptly. The French Company, as it happened,
was jammed with pro-De Beers people, but a difference like
that was considerable and most French Company shareholders
naturally wanted to accept the better offer. Everyone waited
expectantly, heads turning toward Rhodes, as they do in tennis
matches, to see what force he would put behind his answering
ball. Rhodes put plenty of force behind it. He went to Barnato
and said, "You can go and offer the French Company three
hundred thousand pounds more than we have done, but then
we will go three hundred thousands better, and you can go on
bidding *ad infinitum* for the benefit of the French shareholders
(but) we shall have it in the end." Rhodes did have the French
Company in the end, but not just then. After delivering his
ultimatum, he thought up a compromise: Barnato would with-
draw his offer to the French Company, Rhodes would go ahead
and buy it out at the original price of £1,400,000, and then he
would sell it to Barnato. The price he asked was a fifth interest
in Kimberley Central, plus three hundred thousand pounds.
Barnato readily agreed. He now had what he wanted—the
French Company—and, even after sacrificing a fifth interest in
Kimberley Central, he and his friends still had seemingly im-
pregnable control of that company. Rhodes now had part of
what he wanted—a foothold in the Kimberley Mine. That was
when the real fight started.

Rhodes wanted to combine the De Beers and Kimberley

Central companies, so that they could be controlled from one center. As Chilvers, the historian of De Beers, put it: "Rhodes always wanted diamond production equated with demand. New producers make this difficult." Barnato, too, wanted production equated with demand, but as he saw it, it was Rhodes who made this difficult. His own was the better mine, he said, and was on its way to being even better, since it was undergoing reorganization and would soon be worked by new, underground methods. He needed no outside control. Production would soar, he said happily. This was so true that it scared Rhodes to death. Both mines would be producing hand over fist, and before they knew it the world would be flooded with diamonds and they would be ruined.

"We had to choose between the ruin of the diamond industry and the control of the Kimberley Mine," said Rhodes in a later recapitulation of events, with the beautiful simplicity that always characterized his reasoning. "We saw this, that you could never deal with obstinate people until you got the whip hand of them, and that the only thing we had to do to secure the success of our industry was to get the control of the Kimberley Mine."

With Beit and Rothschild money to back him up he began buying Kimberley Central shares. Barney was sure of his own holdings and those of his friends: added up, he thought, they would retain control, no matter how many shares De Beers might acquire outside. He took a long time to get worried, but after a while he discovered that even his trusted friends, tempted beyond fidelity by the prices that were being offered, were selling out. Barnato's reaction was born of desperation: he bought Kimberley Central shares from his former friends, in competition with Rhodes. The price of shares went up and up, and soon the price of diamonds went down and down, for Rhodes and Barnato began trying to undersell each other. It was a lovely, unreal time for diamond buyers and a harrowing one for the two great antagonists. Finally, early in 1888, Barnato had had enough; he was ready to capitulate. Rhodes laid down the terms, and Barnato accepted them; he turned over all his Kimberley Central shares to Rhodes, in return for a substantial but not decisive block of shares in the big new company Rhodes now created—De Beers Consolidated Mines, Ltd.

A small group of Kimberley Central shareholders protested the amalgamation, and this was when Rhodes's charter became famous. Kimberley Central's charter, the dissidents pointed out, provided that it could merge only with similar mining companies, and they maintained that De Beers wasn't a similar mining company at all but a potential empire. The shareholders took the matter to court, and during the proceedings, as the two charters were discussed, Rhodes's grand design was exposed for everybody concerned to see. It was plain he visualized a company that would not stop with the mere mining and selling of diamonds but would use its resources to branch out into all sorts of interests as it expanded northward until it dominated the whole of Africa, and after that, perhaps, the world. He dreamed of a huge corporation, or a collection of huge corporations, in which a few supermen would run everything. The disgruntled Kimberley Central shareholders, for their part, thought that digging out and selling diamonds were functions enough for any diamond mining company. Barnato had always felt the same, but now they feared that, by merging their interests with De Beers', he was steering them right into those uncharted seas that he himself had long been leery of. The potentially almost limitless scope of De Beers' operations, as set forth in its charter, prompted one of the judges before whom the dissident shareholders brought their case to remark that it would take less time to say what the company could not do than to say what it could do. "They can do anything and everything, my lord," the shareholders' counsel replied. "I suppose since the time of the East India Company, no company has had such power as this. They are not confined to Africa, and they are even authorized to take steps for the good government of any territory, so that . . . they would be empowered to annex a portion of territory in Central Africa, raise and maintain a standing army, and undertake warlike operations."

"The powers of the company are as extensive as those of any company that has ever existed," the court said in its judgment.

Ultimately, the court decided in favor of the dissident share-holders, but this didn't for a moment faze Rhodes and Barnato. If they couldn't merge Kimberley Central with De Beers, they could liquidate it and have De Beers buy its assets. That was what they did, and De Beers gave the authorities responsible for the liquidation the staggering sum of £5,338,650 for distri-bution among the shareholders. The payment was made by a single check, and this check—believed to be the largest ever written and honored up to that time—was framed and now hangs prominently on a wall of the directors' room at the De Beers Consolidated office in Kimberley.

Though beaten, Barney Barnato was not a pathetic figure. As the largest individual shareholder in the new company he was treated with respect. Reluctantly he gave in to Rhodes's arguments and consented to the larger program outline for De

Beers Consolidated Mining Company after an all-night sitting, during which he and his nephew Woolf Joel talked it over with Rhodes and Beit. Surrendering, he said, "Some people have a fancy for one thing, some another. You want the means to go north, if possible, and I suppose we must give it to you." That was how the push northward began; it was the beginning of the Jameson Raid, too, though Barney had no way of knowing that. He consented, but at his insistence Rhodes and Beit in their turn consented to the creation of new posts in the company: four life governorships, these governors to keep an eye on company policy and restrain the others, if they thought necessary, from too much enthusiastic use of their powers. Barney was one.

The suddenly friendly relationship between Cecil Rhodes and Barney Barnato was a spectacle that fascinated Kimberley. Of it were born two anecdotes that have carried down through the years. One has to do with the Kimberley Club, an institution which is still the center of the town's socio-business life. Of course, wherever Englishman meets Englishman they start a club, and this one, unlovely shack on the veld that it then was, followed the usual tradition of its kind; it represented social success and exclusion. Rhodes belonged to it in the natural course, and in the same natural course of events Barnato did not. Barnato was exactly what most horrified Rhodes's clubfellows, or at least what they professed horrified them—noisy, volatile, and talkative. His father was a shopkeeper, and the glorified diggers, however lately, had learned to look down on shopkeepers. "You couldn't help loving him," an elderly Kimberley lady once told me, but the members of the Kimberley Club seem to have resisted his charm. It was a fact that annoyed him. He knew the club members said unkind things about him. "I thought that was the trouble," he said simply, when Rhodes reported that one man in particular was holding out against him. He told Rhodes that he had never lunched at the Kimberley Club and that he would like to. Rhodes promptly took him, more than once. Other members complained. Rhodes's reaction was quick: he forced Barnato on the club as a member, and that settled that.

The strange alliance led next to the affair of the bucket of diamonds. Rhodes remarked to Barney that he had never seen such a collection, and that he had a fancy to do so. Barnato thereupon produced a bucketful and allowed the great man to dabble in it and play with the pretty things. That's all there is to the story, or all there would be if it weren't well known that Rhodes had a special way of looking at diamonds and reckoning up what he called "the power" contained in them. Without that knowledge the anecdote is meaningless; yet there is usually a reason when stories persist. Rhodes hasn't been dead such a long time that every scrap of his history is precious. Plenty of people who are still living remember him, and though hero worship plays a large part in the legend (I was rebuked in Kimberley because I had neglected to go and look at the stone he used for a mounting block) such hero worship could hardly be the explanation for the story of the bucketful of diamonds. I think it is remembered chiefly not because of Rhodes or Barnato, but because of the mental picture itself: the thought of that fabulous lot of diamonds. It was a symbol. It was treasure. It was South Africa. I caught myself gawking at the things in the top-story office in Johannesburg, and for the first time felt I could sympathize with Cecil Rhodes.

The familiar diamond names—Barnato, Beit, Joel, Dunkels, Robinson, Wernher—have come to mean to the public things that were very far from their owners' thoughts, back in the eighties. Their great London houses are coming up for auction nowadays, sacrificed to the welfare state. Their collections are bequeathed to cities, their jewels dispersed among heirs who, like as not, auction them off as they do the houses. Libraries have been founded on some of their fortunes, museums on others. The secondary uses of this money they made would have bored its original amassers to tears, for their tastes were earthier if not simpler. Life didn't get really gay and extravagant in South Africa until late in the decade of the eighties when gold had been found on the Rand and the erstwhile diamond financiers hastened to found Johannesburg. Before this second rush, however, Barney Barnato and his companions did what they could in Kimberley to amuse themselves. They raced horses, they played poker, and they laid bets.

"They never trusted each other even when they were playing," said a diamond man in reminiscent mood. "There was one poker game I used to hear about. Barney Barnato was playing against a fellow named Sager. Sager made a high bid on his hand, I don't recall how much—it could have been a hundred pounds, it could have been more; they played for high stakes, you understand. Barney said he'd better that one, and Sager said, 'I don't believe you've got that much. Let's see your money.' Well, naturally, Barney wasn't carrying that much around on him. He was good for it, of course, everybody knew that, but Sager wouldn't take his word for it. One thing led to another, and it ended with both fellows putting their hands, sight unseen, into envelopes and sealing the envelopes and

handing them over to a third party. They met next day each
with the money in his hand and opened up the envelopes in
the presence of witnesses. As it happened, Barney lost. . . .
No, they never trusted each other in that town."

The diamond millionaires were keen on any form of betting.
They bet on prize fights, on races between native children or
themselves, and they exchanged astronomical sums over the
horses. But more than any of these pursuits Barney loved amateur theatricals. He was an acting fool. His friends insisted that
his interpretation of Mathias in *The Bells* outdid that of Irving,
or if it didn't quite outshine Irving's it was every bit the same,
gesture for gesture, rant for rant. Given this taste and the
added stature he acquired in De Beers, it was natural that
Barney should enter politics. Rhodes was already there, a long
way ahead of him; in 1881 he had been elected to the Cape
Colony Parliament as the member for Klip Drift, and in 1890
he was to become Prime Minister. Barnato plunged in in 1888
and ran for Parliament from Kimberley, and for the campaign
he bought the famous barouche, a photograph of which deco-
rates practically every old-timer's wall in Kimberley. It was a
splendid turnout, designed, one would have said, for a circus
rather than an election campaign. There was a huge monogram
on the door, and it was drawn by four matched grays, each with
red-clad postilion. There were two cockaded footmen in green
livery, gold-braided, and Barnato when he rode in it wore fancy
clothes and a gray, curly-brimmed topper. His campaign was
eventful. There was fierce opposition to him among the towns-
people, some of whom were beginning to hate and fear De
Beers, assuming that as the company had already taken over the
municipal water works it would soon absorb all private business

as well and crowd them out. But Barnato won the election and became M.P. for Kimberley at the Cape. He said it was "the Dutch"—the Boers—who elected him; that he had been doing business with them ever since he arrived in the Fields, and that though they were keen, cunning traders Barney Barnato was a match for them, and they respected his quality.

What with fancy-dress electioneering, dramatics, and his success altogether, he must have continued to be an irritation to the more pernickety of his clubfellows. But in spite of his ebullient nature and all his resistance, respectability crept up on Barnato. He became the father of a family and a power in London's financial circles. These things sober a man. He never went so far as to collect oil paintings, but he did build a house in Park Lane, a pretentious gesture he had always sworn he would avoid. The porch of the mansion was supported by two stone figures, commonly known in the City as the Petrified Shareholders. Barnato also set up a racing stable in England and, given the time, might even have endowed a library. Instead, he went mad.

No one knows exactly what caused Barnato's madness, but two of the contributing factors were undoubtedly the Kaffir Circus and the Jameson Raid. In 1886, gold had been discovered on the Rand, near Johannesburg, in the Transvaal. Within a few years, both Rhodes and Barnato had made heavy investments in the gold mines; Rhodes at one time was receiving four hundred thousand pounds a year from his gold holdings, and although Barnato's income from the Rand is not known, his holdings eventually employed twenty thousand whites and a hundred thousand natives. In September 1895, there were spectacular goings on in the gold markets of London and Paris—an imbroglio popularly known as the Kaffir Circus. First there was a sudden boom, then a sudden bust. Barnato, who was in London at the time, singlehandedly and feverishly set out to restore order by buying, and he succeeded—at a cost of several million pounds and, some of his friends believed, his sanity. Three months later came the Jameson Raid. Many Britons, including Rhodes and Solly Joel, who was Barnato's nephew and protégé, had been casting a covetous eye at the Transvaal, and, in December 1895, a somewhat quixotic force of six hundred men, led by Dr. Leander Starr Jameson, a close friend of Rhodes, headed for Johannesburg with the idea of taking over the city. Jameson's raiders were captured by a Boer force forty miles west of Johannesburg, and four of their leaders were sentenced to death. Among these was Solly Joel. Barnato, who was still in London, was deeply disturbed, and he made a tremendous and ultimately successful effort to get Joel and his colleagues pardoned. What may have convinced the Boers was Barnato's threat to close his gold mines and thereby throw more than a hundred thousand people out of work. Soon afterward, Barnato's mind, which had always worked at an extraordinary pace, began to run away with him altogether. He had lucid intervals, during which he carried on his business in England and Africa, and it was during what Joel thought was one of these intervals that, one day in 1897, Barnato managed to evade his family's watchfulness aboard ship on the way to London. He jumped overboard and was drowned. He was only forty-four years old.

During his lifetime as well as after it there were plenty of scandalous stories about Barnato's methods of making a fortune. But South Africa is a fertile forcing ground for this sort of thing, especially when a man goes into politics, and there is small doubt that he was often unfairly traduced. It was during the famous election campaign that an orator, speaking for one of Barnato's opponents, started considerable excitement by say-ing, "Men are being put forward who, if returned, would be a disgrace to any society; and it is quite possible that we may see the spectacle of the dupe on the Breakwater and his employer in Parliament." This quite clearly referred to Barnato and an alleged connection with I.D.B., as a term on the Table Bay Breakwater was the customary penalty for such infractions of the law. When asked to be more explicit the orator was canny, saying, "I am not such a fool as to render myself amenable to the law of libel." But what made Barnato particularly indignant was another allegation that he had salted his claims in the Kim-berley pit. He confessed, shortly before he died, that he had been so bitterly hurt by the talk he had nearly pulled out of South Africa altogether. "I never showed that I felt it"; he told his biographer, Harry Raymond; "and I determined never to give in, but to face it out. I knew that if I only stayed long enough I should get justice. So I stayed and faced it out, and fought that Kimberley election as no election has ever been fought in South Africa before, and came in at the head of the poll. And then no dog barked."

Rhodes outlived Barnato by only five years. Once he had cleared up the situation in Kimberley (after the merger, it had taken him practically no time to buy out the lesser Kimberley mines), he went north, as he had always wanted to. First, he bought up gold fields in the Rand. Then, in 1889, largely with

De Beers money, he set up the British South Africa Company, and this firm received a charter that was even more fantastic than the De Beers charter. It permitted the company not only to strike north into the vast territories now known as the Rhodesias but "to make treaties, promulgate laws, preserve peace, and maintain a police force." In 1890, while Rhodes's men were moving north and founding cities, he became Prime Minister of the Cape Colony, and he was still holding that office when the Jameson Raid took place. He had known in advance that there would be a raid, had appeared to approve of it, and then, at the last moment, had sent a telegram to Jameson telling him to call it off. The telegram never arrived. There was a great deal of indignant clamor about the raid all over the world, and Rhodes quickly resigned as Prime Minister. In 1899, the year the Boer War broke out, he was in high favor again, both in Africa and England, and he said, "My career is only just beginning." During the war, he set up a small munitions factory in Kimberley. Every shell it turned out was inscribed "Compliments from C.R." For a long time he had had serious heart trouble, and in 1902, just before the war ended, he died, at the age of forty-nine.

The careers of Rhodes and Barnato were closely intertwined with those of a number of other South African millionaires whose names became famous in England around the turn of the century. Suddenly arriving in England as they did with their fabulous fortunes to buy horses and houses and paintings and cases of champagne, they were more noticeable in the London of that day than Texas millionaires are now in New York. Things have changed since. The diamond industry has grown

up. The gold industry has grown up. And the diamond and
gold millionaires have grown up, too. Today's leaders of the
diamond industry—notably Sir Ernest Oppenheimer, the present chairman of De Beers, and his son Harry—are quiet, self-
effacing, public-spirited men. In the old days, the South African
millionaires, as a class, were anything but self-effacing; in 1902,
they were lampooned in *The Girl From Kay's*, a popular musi-
cal that was staged in London. The leading male character
was billed as "Max Hoggenheimer, a South African millionaire," but he was more generally referred to by the shopgirls,
bathing girls, and hot-spot girls to whom he was partial as
"Piggy." "Piggy will pay, pay, pay!" the ladies of the chorus
caroled blithely as they went through their dance routines. And
in the finale the heroine sang:

> *It's very nice to be*
> *A dame of high degree*
> *With blood and reputation beautifully blue;*
> *But folks with cash can get*
> *Into the smartest set,*
> *And that's what I shall proceed to do!*
> *When driving through the Park,*
> *Perhaps you may remark*
> *A silver-mounted perfumed petrol motor trap;*
> *You'll see me on the box*
> *In furs of silver fox,*
> *With just a few big diamonds in my cap.*
> *I'll marry Hoggenheimer of Park Lane,*
> *The money he is winning*
> *I'll set it gaily spinning;*

*And ev'ry one that sees me will explain*
*That I'm Mrs. Hoggenheimer of Park Lane.*

Songwriters were generous with their lyrics in those days.
This number ambles on through several verses, describing how
Piggy rises in the world, and it ends triumphantly:

*He may be made a peer,*
*A baron, viscount, or a belted earl!*
*He'll be Lord Hoggenheimer of Park Lane,*
*And prove he is descended*
*From Norman barons splendid!*
*And she'll have royal blood in every vein*
*When she is Countess Hoggenheimer of Park Lane!*

South Africans can, and do, argue with each other for long,
comfortable hours about the old scandals. Which of the millionaires, they ask each other, was the most dishonest? Who
among them were pleasant fellows, who unpleasant? There are
always plenty of opinions to the effect that Barnato among
others indulged in I.D.B., but the attitude of a lot of South
Africans toward that crime is rather like that of Americans toward bootlegging during Prohibition. I got the impression that
they thought I.D.B. reprehensible, of course, if you come right
down to it, but just the same everyone in the old days must have
done it. (Even now there isn't as much sincere indignation on
the subject as perhaps there ought to be; a young man was
caught during my visit and sentenced to three years in prison,
and his acquaintances took what I considered a rather philosophical view of the matter, merely saying that he'd been unlucky and a bit of an ass.) Only one old man, more than seventy

years old, showed any genuine warmth in condemning the
I.D.B. that he said was carried on by Barnato, and he had
clearly inherited these sentiments from his father.

"Barney lived next door to us when I was a child," he said,
"and my father didn't like the goings on at his house. It was
queer altogether—funny sorts of people came knocking at his
door all hours of the night. Father finally went and told him
what he thought of him. He said, 'Barney, you'd better watch
out. You'll get into trouble one day.' It didn't make any difference; Barney wouldn't listen or change his ways. After a while
Father moved out. We went across town. We didn't want any
trouble."

I heard stories about some of the other diamond millionaires
that were even less admiring. There was Mr. J. B. Robinson,
for instance, later Sir Joseph; he drove a very hard bargain and
was famous for it. One tale about him deals with the gold rush
at the Rand. It had been common knowledge for years that
there was gold in South Africa, but no one was sure if the ore
was there in paying quantity. As things turned out, it was, to
put it mildly, and the diamond kings hastened to invest in the
new project. Though such a new project, it posed some old
problems, among which was how to persuade stubborn farmers
to sell their farms. Some were actually the same people who had
first lived in Griqualand West on diamondiferous land and had
been persuaded with great difficulty to sell their farms and move
away, only to be disturbed again by these persistent treasure
seekers from the outside world. More than one Boer was stubborn about selling. It was the same story as before, but Robinson was good at bargaining with Boers and he usually got his
way in the end. An acquaintance of his told of one occasion

when he bought a farm, Langlaagte, from a widow and paid her
fifteen hundred pounds for all rights, mineral as well as surface.
(This was necessary, as otherwise he would have been able to
claim ownership only of the produce grown and the animals
grazing on the land.) Like most of these farms it was a huge expanse of not very fertile land and the widow had not bothered
to have it surveyed, since she had an old survey chart that dated
back to her family's purchase. She said she thought the chart
was more or less correct, and the contract was drawn up with
the acreage as represented on it. Later, when Robinson had the
farm surveyed, he discovered that there was less land than
the widow had said, and though it was already known that the
place was full of gold he deducted a certain sum from his purchase price. Robinson's farm is estimated to have produced gold
worth from one hundred to two hundred million pounds
sterling.

Robinson himself used to tell with amusement and pride of
another deal he made with an old couple. He had had to work
on the man for a long time, arguing, persuading, and tempting,
until the Boer at last agreed to sell the farm complete with
surface and mineral rights or, as he himself put it, "everything
on and in it." Robinson was in the act of writing out the contract when the old woman burst into tears. They discovered
after some questioning that what was really breaking her heart
about leaving the farm was the thought that she must give up
a favorite pot plant of which she was very fond. Robinson
didn't reassure her by saying he had no desire for the plant. On
the contrary, he only gave it up after long argument and a re-
duction in his purchase price.

After the First World War, Robinson, who by then had been

made a baronet and was evidently generous enough in the right quarter when there was something to be got out of it, was scheduled to receive a peerage. It was to be bestowed "in recognition of his services": the usual formula. Lloyd George who was Prime Minister at the time, had never been to South Africa, and evidently had no idea of Robinson's reputation there. However, the London *Morning Post*, a paper which was later to merge with the *Telegraph*, was edited by a man who had. This editor started a campaign of indignation against the award and succeeded in raising such an outcry that the promised peerage was actually revoked, an act of Indian giving that has never, before or since in all Great Britain's history, been equaled. Definitely, Robinson wasn't popular.

He may have taken comfort in the fact that, anyway, he was rich. When he died, in 1929, he left a collection of paintings worth three million dollars. Yet other South Africans outdid even that. Sir Julius Wernher was one, with his collection, and Sir Alfred Beit was another. Incidentally there is a story about Sir Alfred that in my opinion surpasses any Robinson anecdote. It is in the private records of Walter Stanley Whitworth, who came out to South Africa in 1893 and went to work in the Koffeyfontein (or Coffeyfontein, or Kaffyfonteyn) diamond mine near Jagersfontein, a place that was to become one of the most important of the Fields. Koffeyfontein was not yet a De Beers mine, for though Rhodes's idea of amalgamation continued to march, the company was slow and deliberate in its swallowing. The men who owned Koffeyfontein were nearly broke and for some time had been asking De Beers either to buy them out or extend a helping hand with a loan in it. Whitworth wrote, "On one occasion Mr. Hirschhorn wrote to say he was

bringing Mr. Beit, a Life Governor of De Beers, over to have a
look at Jagersfontein and Koffeyfontein. They would spend the
night with us. Fradgley and I were rather alarmed at the prospect and gave a great deal of thought to the preparation of a
good dinner for our guests. We also went to find out what wine
the bars had and were delighted when Fred Edwards produced
a bottle of champagne which had been lying on the top shelf of
the bar for many years. We agreed to pay him 35/ for the champagne, if it was not flat on opening; if it was flat, he must take it
back. After some argument he agreed to this, and as it proved
to be exceptionally good Mr. Edwards received his 35/. Mr.
Beit appeared to enjoy the champagne very much, and he
dropped off to sleep after dinner. Mr. Hirschhorn whispered
that he was very tired, but after he had had his nap he would
talk to him about Koffeyfontein. When later Mr. Hirschhorn
tried to persuade Mr. Beit to support us with a loan of £20,-
ooo, which we were needing badly at the time, he replied,
'When the plum is ripe it will drop into our mouth.' The following morning they went on to Kimberley and I never saw
Mr. Beit again."

Shortly before his death, Sir Alfred Beit went to look at a
new mine near Pretoria, the Premier, which was to become the
proud show place of all the Diamond Fields. It was here that
the Cullinan was found. When Sir Alfred visited it, it hadn't
yet become a part of the De Beers combine. The sight of its
size so shocked him that he had a stroke, and died five months
later.

# CHAPTER FOUR

# The Premier

Early on Christmas Day, 1954, a BOAC Stratocruiser flying from London to New York in a heavy rain crashed and burst into flames while attempting to make a routine landing at Prestwick Airport, in Scotland. Of the thirty-six people on board, only ten survived. Twenty-one of the twenty-five passengers had been intending to disembark at Prestwick, most of them to spend their holidays in Scotland. Even if the tragedy had not been peculiarly poignant because of the date, the size and scope of it would have horrified the public. For a few days the human angle of the accident pushed all other considerations pertaining to it out of mind. But most people who use air mails sooner or later ask themselves, whenever they hear of a crash, if by any chance they have lost letters thereby. In New York, about twenty diamond merchants had more to worry about than mere letters. They began to wonder, after a few days, if they weren't more closely concerned with this disaster than they had at first supposed. They had bought a considerable stock of diamonds from the Diamond Trading Company, the name under which the selling department of De Beers now operates. These stones should in the ordinary way have arrived at their destination, and they had not arrived. In the reports of the salvage operations at Prestwick there was no word of any diamonds, but, after all, the investigators who were working on the problem hadn't been alerted to look for diamonds. The waiting merchants were uneasily aware that their gems, if they had been caught in the plane's fierce combustion, might very possibly be so damaged and blackened that they would be unrecognizable to any but a trained eye. They were not unduly perturbed, however; in accordance with a long-established practice, they had all insured their shipments against loss or damage—most of them at Lloyd's of London—for 10 per cent more than the actual purchase price.

It was not strange that they shouldn't have known for certain on what plane their costly cargo had been sent. Air mail doesn't operate in the cut-and-dried manifest manner of deep-sea transport; nevertheless a lot of jewels are sent by plane, and successfully, across the Atlantic. After all, they don't weigh much. American dealers buy their diamonds abroad in the rough because there is no duty to pay on uncut stones, whereas cut and polished diamonds are dutiable to the amount of 10 per cent. Buying at the Christmas season is generally pretty heavy; in 1954 it was exceptionally so. When the perturbed authorities began looking into the records of registered packages and insurance, it appeared that the dealers had reason to feel misgivings. Nine hundred thousand pounds worth of diamonds might very well have been aboard the wrecked Stratocruiser: at any rate that amount had been sent by the company, by air mail, in forty separate registered packages. The company usually splits up its large shipments in this manner so that the stones will be distributed among various carriers and the risk of loss through accident lessened. This time of all times, it seemed, the precaution had not worked. It was so unusual that all the stones should have been put on one plane that the British Post Office itself was surprised, as well as appalled. The officials postponed admitting the truth until no more doubt was possible; on December 30 they made a statement: "About 250 bags of letters and parcel mails . . . were on board the aircraft. It is not unlikely that a number of packets declared to contain diamonds were in the letter mails, but it is not yet possible to confirm this. The post office has received no claims from the senders of registered mail posted at about the time concerned, although inquiries have been made by insurance assessors."

In other words, the Diamond Trading Company had not been bombarding the post office with anguished demands for reassurance. But there was no reason for the company to be unduly alarmed. The lost property wasn't theirs any more; it belonged to the purchasers. Lloyd's the insurers, however, being heavily involved, lost no time getting in touch with their insurance adjusters, and on December 30, five days after the crash, one of their investigators with several associates went to Prestwick. All this time the salvaged mails were being dried out and shipped to post office headquarters in London for identification and sending again. (As it happens, one of these letters was mine. It arrived two weeks late at its destination in New York, water-stained and muddy, stamped "Salvaged Mail, Aircraft Crash, Prestwick 25-12-54.") Research had finally turned up the fact that it was more than likely the whole diamond consignment had indeed been aboard that plane, owing to an unusual circumstance: another plane which had been carrying some portion of the shipment had at the last minute been with-drawn, and its cargo, including the registered diamond pack-ages, was transferred to the unlucky Stratocruiser.

The Lloyd's investigator and his helpers made their way through the debris-strewn muck, searching. Plenty of other people were busy on the spot, loading everything large and ob-vious that came to hand, but these men were looking only for particular things, the wrappings of diamond parcels. They didn't have to wait long. Almost immediately one of their num-ber, picking up a handful of mud near the outskirts of the area, found three diamonds in it. A few minutes later they discovered nearly a whole packageful in the center section of what re-mained of the fuselage, near the nose of the plane. The ground under their feet was studded with the things—large, once val-uable diamonds, scorched and blackened or trodden out of sight. The whole area was hastily cordoned off, and thereafter only authorized persons were allowed inside the rope. For a while the men merely went on looking as well as their eyes permitted, now and then finding more stones, but the early winter dark soon came down on their labors. Prestwick was un-dergoing a cold spell with night frost. The searchers gave up for the day and covered the ground with tarpaulins so that it wouldn't be too stiff for more searching in the morning.

"Experts Take Over at Prestwick," said a London *Times* headline on January 1. All day long for the next few days the telephone rang at the offices of the Anglo American Corpora-tion of South Africa, of which the company is a part. Inter-ested parties, newspaper reporters, and just plain curious people wanted to know whether diamonds could be destroyed by fire—which they can, if the fire is hot enough—or, if they weren't destroyed, what the effect of a burning airplane's heat would be. The official in charge could only reply cautiously, "Well, it wouldn't do them any good." The fact was, nobody knew the answers right off the bat. Such a quantity of valuable material is seldom available for experimentation. Even De Beers has never tried it out in just the conditions obtained at Prestwick Airport. As it turned out, few of the diamonds, if any, had been completely consumed, as far as the experts know. (Some are still missing, but that doesn't mean they were burned up.) A lot of them, however, were covered with charred black material. Ultimately they were cured with a fair amount of success, though with loss in weight. Lloyd's had to pay off, and the salvaged diamonds became its property; eventually, with the help of the Diamond Trading Company, it sold them—at some loss, of course—to other diamond dealers who had them cut and polished and offered them for sale.

As far as the dealers in America were concerned, the story ended pretty well; any loss they suffered was more than made up by the insurance. One firm's directors felt so squeamish at making a profit out of calamity that they sent the extra 10 per cent back to England for distribution among families that had been bereaved by the accident.

The fact that nearly 90 per cent of the lost stones were recovered is a triumph in the history of diamond mining. For it was definitely by a mining process that they were finally extracted from Scottish mud. In Britain, engineers set up a miniature washing plant modeled on the big plant of the Premier Mine in South Africa. Next to the Prestwick runway the mud was four inches thick. All this top covering, two hundred square yards in extent, was scraped up and washed. The chief difference between that material and the stuff that usually goes into the bin at the Premier Mine was that the miners were certain it would produce: you might almost say that for a week or two Prestwick Airport was a legitimate salted prospect.

The knowledge that was applied to the emergency of the Prestwick diamonds had been gained slowly and painfully from the beginning, more than half a century ago, in the Diamond Fields of South Africa. At that time the fabled millionaires of Kimberley stood on the heights and knew they were successful and could safely branch out. They had consolidated the companies; a recent world depression had been weathered; they held the necessary monopoly and could get ahead with production, secure in the knowledge that they had power to hold back their produce if and when necessary. They were in the transition stage between old-fashioned, happy-go-lucky digging methods and new, sober, businesslike underground mining. Another important step had to be introduced. Control of the workers must be tightened so that they might no longer smuggle out any diamonds they filched during working hours. This precaution was necessary not only because the owners were facing a steady loss in diamonds themselves, but because such sales inevitably lowered the market price everywhere through extensive underselling of illicitly acquired stones. Already the people who clamored for stricter surveillance of the native workers, or "boys," had met with considerable success. The boys were no longer permitted to go home after hours and move about as they liked, selling stolen diamonds to dealers. They were shut up in compounds where what they had stolen couldn't profit them until the end of the period they were contracted for, and even then when the boy had done his term and was ready to go he was not

only carefully searched, but held in a special detention room for
several days so that he might digest whatever he had eaten—including diamonds—before taking his leave. For it was the sad
fact that as mine guards grew more adept at searching topknots,
beards, between toes, earholes, and all the other natural orifices
of the body, natives grew equally adept at thinking up new ways
to hide diamonds. Swallowing was a favorite method until the
mine owners figured out how to beat it. During the period of
incarceration the boy had to wear big, clumsy gloves to prevent his recovering stones on his own and swallowing them
again, or hiding them after he had been subjected to thorough
search. Today, of course, the invention of X-ray searching has
rendered unnecessary this process, which was one of the most
picturesque aspects of old-time diamond mining, but in the interests of history the De Beers board room at Kimberley displays a remarkable photograph. It is of an elderly native
presenting toward the camera a plate, or tray, on which lie ten
of the biggest of the twenty-one diamonds he swallowed all at
one time, which later he was forced to relinquish. Their total
weight was 348 carats. It is a very graphic picture. You wouldn't
believe the feat possible for anything but an ostrich, but it happened. The native's expression, perhaps naturally, is perturbed.

It was hoped that when machinery was introduced to mining,
with its resultant lessening of intimate contact between worker
and diamondiferous earth, all this I.D.B. would be avoided. It
did slow down to some extent, but the earliest underground
machinery wasn't very efficient and didn't obviate manual labor
to that extent. As mining history goes it was still early days,
and the workers found plenty of chances to pilfer. Working out
of tunnels that were driven over from the hard, nonproductive

reef, the miners hacked out the blue ground, dynamiting it when necessary, and hauled it out to the surface and carted it some distance to the "floors." These were vast level spaces of veld where the lumps of blue ground were spread out and exposed to the weather. In time, under sun and rain, blue ground deteriorates until it becomes soft, crumbly yellow dirt. Some of this blue stuff is more resistant to erosion than the rest, but on a general average the miners reckoned it took nine months to weather. Waiting seemed a slow business and entailed a lot of expense in security measures; the floors had to be fenced in firmly and checked every so often. Even inside they had to be patrolled against depredations of dishonest workers, white and black. It was as widespread a business as riding range on a western ranch, and much more money was involved, but at the time no other method seemed satisfactory. In principle, mining was still nearly as primitive as it was in the seventeenth century when Jean Baptiste Tavernier, a French jewel merchant with a wandering foot, visited the diamond mines of Kollur in India. He watched sixty thousand people toiling away there. "After the miners have selected the place where they desire to work," he wrote, "they smooth down another spot close by, of equal or rather greater extent, round which they erect an enclosing wall of two feet in height. At the base of this little wall they make openings, at every two feet, for the escape of the water, which they close till it is time for the water to be drawn off. This place being thus prepared, all who are about to engage in the search assemble, men, women, and children, together with their employer and a party of his relatives and friends. . . . When dinner is finished, each starts work, the men to excavate the earth, and the women and children to carry it to the place which has been prepared as I have said above. They excavate to 10, 12, or 14 feet in depth, but when they reach water there is nothing more to hope for. All the earth is carried to this place, men, women and children draw water with pitchers from the hole which they have excavated, and throw it upon the earth which they have placed there, in order to soften it, leaving it in this state for one or two days, according to the tenacity of the clay, until it becomes like soup. This done, they open the holes which they made in the wall to let off the water, then they throw on more, so that all the slime may be removed, and nothing remain but sand. It is a kind of clay which requires to be washed two or three times. They then leave it to be dried by the sun, which is quickly effected by the great heat. They have a particular kind of basket made something like a winnowing fan, in which they place the earth, which they agitate as we do when winnowing grain. The fine part is blown away, and the coarse stuff which remains is subsequently replaced on the ground.

"All the earth having been thus winnowed, they spread it with a rake and make it as level as possible. Then they all stand together on the earth, each with a large baton of wood like a huge pestle, half a foot wide at the base, and pound the earth, going from one end to the other, always pounding each part two or three times; they then place it again in the baskets and winnow it, as they did on the first occasion, after which they spread it out again and range themselves on one side to handle the earth and search for the diamonds. . . . Formerly, instead of using wooden pestles for pounding the earth, they pounded it with stones, and it was that method which produced so many flaws in the diamonds."

The mines Tavernier saw were probably in alluvially laid deposits, or the matrix couldn't have been pounded up after two days' soaking, not even by sixty thousand workers. In South Africa, nobody was able to crush by hand, and so reckoning of a mine's resources in business circles always gave first place to the tonnage of blue ground waiting on the floors. Nowadays, no mine works on this basis. The blue ground is crushed and processed as soon as it is brought out, and the extensive floors have become a memory. When the change-over came to Kimberley it was a great relief, because a lot of acreage was set free for building, and Kimberley is a rather squashed town between its gaping pits. Today at Koffeyfontein, however, about sixty miles away, where another great pit yawns and there is no town waiting for space, the floors still exist, complete with fences and guardrooms at the entrances, simply because nobody wants to use them for anything else. During World War II, however, they came in very handy as a ready-made concentration camp for enemy aliens.

The mechanization of underground mines went slowly, and while it was going on a lot of mine managers found themselves in great difficulty with the compound system. Mines that had not yet come into the prosperous combine of De Beers Consolidated encountered particularly tough going. The records of Mr. Walter Stanley Whitworth, who joined that same Koffeyfontein in '93, give as good a picture as can be had of what it was like to manage labor in these conditions. For his times, Whitworth was an enlightened liberal. (Today his daughter is a social worker in South Africa.) Nevertheless he found himself forced to participate in practices that enlightened men do not approve. Koffeyfontein couldn't depend on a steady supply of volunteer labor, because there weren't enough workers to go round and the boys who could manage it went to mines where conditions were more inviting. These natives were a tough lot for the most part. They had come into the Diamond Fields from the north; before the rush there had been very few natives of any sort living on that part of the veld. Away from their homes, mixing up with roughs, the newcomers soon became wild and unmanageable, and "faction fights" were a constant hazard, when boys of one tribe engaged in battle with those of another. There were other complications in their mass behavior too.

"Strike for more pay being organized in Compound," Whitworth's notes read for May 1895. He wanted to start a new system of feeding the boys communally, deducting something from their earnings to pay for it; for when left to themselves they often did not eat enough, preferring to gamble or drink with the money. "We now have such a number in a half-starved condition that they have not the strength to work. . . . Saunders is against the idea of feeding them and advocates pay being increased. . . . I think we should take advantage of the experience gained by other companies." Like other managers, Koffeyfontein's sometimes contracted for groups of workers through their village chiefs, for varying periods. Noting that they had got a number in this way, Whitworth added, "West thinks we should get all boys from this source and turn out the location boys in the compound. They are always a nuisance and Armstrong's people have now practically thrown open their compound so we should not be able to keep them if we did not allow them out frequently." A few days later he wrote, "A great many boys have left us and gone to Armstrong Company's claims during the last few weeks—not because their compound is open but because we hear there is any amount of liquor to be had there and a large number of boys will have their liquor at any price—it is the only thing they live for. For this reason we are increasing the supply of liquor to the boys for a couple of weeks to see if this has the effect of making the boys less anxious to get special passes out to the location, as if they go out simply to obtain liquor, which in the greater number of cases is the reason for getting out, it will be better for us to let them have more in the compound if it will keep them in." He added a few days later, in an uneasy note, "From a moral point of view of course brandy is all wrong, but we are a Diamond Mining Company, not a Temperance Society."

Whitworth continued to have trouble with his labor. He tried out various methods of distributing the brandy that was to keep the boys contented, but some of the leaders outwitted him and cornered the supply. He went on fighting for a new system of feeding them, and at last won out. Then sickness struck the mine and traveled with horrible speed through the compound, so that Whitworth listed a number of deaths every day. A government doctor came to inspect the sanitary arrangements and said the authorities were doing as well as could be expected—which, though probably true, was qualified praise: not much was expected of mine authorities in those days. Yet boys still presented themselves in ragged little bands or in solitude, asking for the work they had become used to, and native chiefs still sold indenture rights in the bodies of other less sophisticated boys, and various independent companies continued to poach labor from each other until the Boer War suspended all activities. Whitworth lived to see a transforma-

tion in the industry; he died only three years ago. At the home
of his widow in Koffeyfontein, I saw an old group photograph
of some of his mine boys. A more tatterdemalion crew could
scarcely be imagined.

"Yes," said Mrs. Whitworth, "those were some of the earliest lot we had to deal with. They look the most terrible rascals,
don't they? Poor dears, I'm afraid that's just about what they
were."

The Premier Mine near Pretoria, which didn't even exist
when Whitworth first came to the Fields, affords the most dramatic contrast that can be offered to his portrayal of early
Koffeyfontein. It has been developed carefully and expensively,
with all the foresight De Beers could afford. The Premier is a
company pet. For this reason some of Kimberley's residents
patriotically resent it, since the working of the original Kimberley mines, the great pits that were once little hummocks on
the open veld, has been slowed down. They are not being neglected merely because of the competition from fields which,
like the Premier, have been discovered since their day of glory;
there is another reason. These Kimberley mines have had their
day, and within the foreseeable future they might even be
worked out. This is an ominous fact for Kimberley, patriotism
apart, unless the De Beers people continue nursing the town's
chief resource, the diamond industry there, but there is no
doubt they will. De Beers is a huge company, and along with
the vast powers it acquired with its original trust deed it took
on vast responsibilities as well. Kimberley is one of these. Fortunately for her (I suppose towns, like ships, are feminine) the
company's policy is opposed to that of many lesser organiza-

tions that develop mines in a remorseless manner, working them out and moving on. Towns that depend on such mines, growing up around them, die out as quickly as they have grown. Without De Beers' careful management this might easily have happened already to Kimberley.

In a civic history report drawn up just before World War II, the fact was pointed out somewhat ruefully: "The development of the City of Kimberley has been influenced, perhaps more than other cities, by external historical and economic factors, whose primary effect has been elsewhere, but whose effect on the city itself has been considerable. The transition from mining camp to city has never been entirely effected, since until now, the city has been entirely dependent upon the diamond industry, and has never succeeded in relating itself closely to the surrounding region and its mineral and agricultural potentialities."

Although a ghost town is a sight to fill the observer with gloomy musings, most mining towns don't represent big tragedies, even when they're dead. For South Africa, however, Kimberley is a big city, and her demise would be disastrous for a lot of people. Therefore, the authorities feel, until her secondary interests have been built up to an extent that will support the people, the mines must go on. They aren't worked all together, and some outlying pipes have not yet been developed at all. For example, for many years after it was closed because of the great world depression, Jagersfontein, where the prettiest diamonds are supposed to come from, remained inactive; only lately has it started up again, whereas its neighbor Koffeyfontein is still left undisturbed. Someday no doubt work will start at Koffeyfontein again, but for the moment it is completely quiet, a great hole alone on the veld, with only one old native watchman moving around the wastes of the floors.

The Premier is its opposite in every respect. It was the Premier that gave Sir Alfred Beit, Cecil Rhodes's associate, that stroke when he saw it for the first time and realized what competition it would mean to the De Beers domain in the Kimberley district. Not being able to foresee that De Beers would in time acquire this treasure house, too, Beit literally almost died of fright. It had been discovered by Thomas Cullinan, who had been a bricklayer in Johannesburg and made a lot of money as a builder before he turned to prospecting. Cullinan guessed he was onto something special, though he was a long way from the Diamond Fields, nearly at Pretoria east of Johannesburg, when he met a man who proved that he had found a handsome three-carat diamond thereabouts, alongside the fence of a farm. This happened in 1898, by which time people in South Africa had a pretty good idea of what diamondiferous land looked like. Cullinan was familiar with the history of the De Beers and Kimberley mines, and he studied this untried region with an expert eye. His acquaintance's diamond had been found in alluvial soil. This might have meant that it had been washed out of some nearby eminence, and when he looked around for such an eminence he saw one—a little hill or kopje not unlike Colesberg Kopje, at which the De Beers New Rush had begun. Might not this bump conceal a similar blue-ground pipe? Cullinan resolved to take a long chance and buy the farm just in case, though it was far away from proved diamond ground, but at this point he ran into a snag. The farm, it seemed, belonged to an elderly Boer named Joachim Prinsloo, who was already well known to prospectors—for two very good reasons.

Prinsloo had been living and farming at Madderfontein in the Transvaal when the gold strike was first made, in 1886, and his farm was right in the middle of all the excitement. It had proved a difficult matter for the gold speculators to persuade him to sell out. He was a man of habit: he didn't like moving. But he listened, finally, to the voice of temptation and sold Madderfontein, which was soon developed into a prosperous gold mine. Prinsloo put the large purchase price in his pocket and moved off glumly, and bought another farm at a place called Kaalfontein. Hardly had he begun to feel settled, however, when those pesky prospectors were at his heels again. This time, it seemed, he was sitting on diamonds instead of gold, but the net result was the same. Bewailing his bad luck, he accepted another large sum and wearily moved on to a third location in the vicinity of Pretoria, and that was where he was when Cullinan decided to buy his farm—sitting on his *stoep* with a loaded rifle by his chair, determined to stay put this time, come what might.

Cullinan sent an agent to negotiate, riding as everyone did in a two-wheeled Cape cart. When the agent asked that all too familiar question as to what the farmer wanted for his land, Prinsloo flatly refused even to discuss the matter. The agent persevered; that is, he came back a second time, whereupon the old man yelled at him, "You had better not get off that cart or I will shoot." One sees his point. At any rate the agent did: he stayed on his cart and drove away, and reported to his employer that there was nothing doing. Cullinan gave up for the time being, but he remembered the *kopje* and the big diamond, and as soon as he heard of Prinsloo's death not long afterward he returned to the attack. The old man's daughter, who inherited the farm, was much more reasonable. Cullinan finally got it for fifty-two thousand pounds.

It is worth noting, however, that Prinsloo's spirit is far from dead among his fellow Afrikaners; their process of reasoning still shows signs of similarity to his. One of the De Beers geologists told me a story he heard just before the last World War: it still haunts him. There was a farmer who set out to drill a well. Much to his disgust—for well drilling is very costly—he didn't strike water. All he got was oil. He swore, and capped the borehole, and went away to look for water elsewhere.

Two years after the Premier was opened, in 1905, it was being worked as an open pit, seventy-five acres in area and thirty feet deep. Late one afternoon in June the manager, Mr. Frederick Wells, happened to notice something glittering in the sun's slanting rays, high up in the side wall of the crater, nearly at the surface. He climbed up and dug the thing out of the earth with his penknife, growing more incredulous with every jab of the blade. Even for South Africa, where stupendous finds are not uncommon, Wells's was enough to make anybody question its possibility—a great heavy chunk of blue-white diamond so big that he couldn't close his hand over it. He made double-quick time to the office to test and weigh it. It was a stone of 3024¾ carats, much the biggest diamond that had ever been seen. Mr. Wells received two thousand pounds as a bonus, and the diamond was named the "Cullinan." As everybody in the diamond world knows, the giant was bought in 1907 by the government of the Transvaal for a hundred and fifty thousand pounds and presented to King Edward VII. The King had it cut into nine main stones. The biggest of these is set in the royal scepter of Britain's crown jewels, where it holds first place.

Uncut, the Cullinan—four inches long, two and a half high, and two broad—was not by any means the ideal diamond-shaped or octahedral crystal of textbook specifications, which looks like two pyramids joined at the base. (Tavernier called any good example of this ideal crystal shape a *"pointe naïve."*) The Cullinan was a mere portion of this form; it had three natural faces of the right outline and one large face that might or might not have been a "cleavage," i.e. the plane left by splitting off from a larger stone. Many diamond people among miners and buyers and admirers insist that the huge stone was indeed a fragment, that what it broke off from must still exist, and that the rest of the Cullinan still waits somewhere to be discovered, buried in alluvial sands perhaps, or possibly in an African witch doctor's regalia. Others, less romantic, point out that except for its size the Cullinan was a quite ordinary crystal, imperfect, but of a shape often found, for diamonds do not by any means always present ideal octahedra. The joy killers, however, are heavily outnumbered, and the glittering dream of finding the other half of that outsize brilliant has spurred on many a prospector. If they are right it is hard to imagine what the two pieces put together would look like—in real life, that is to say. I have handled a life-size model of the Cullinan, and it made me wonder how even the most experienced mine manager could have dared to believe he had found what he had found.

Like the Kimberley mines, the Premier went through a number of depressions and was closed down more than once, when diamond mining didn't pay. Between 1931 and 1944 it wasn't worked at all. Until that closing, because of its great size, it had been worked only by opencast methods, and by then the pit was more than six hundred feet deep. Meanwhile, it had passed into the hands of De Beers. After Sir Alfred Beit's visit, De Beers patiently and relentlessly bought up Premier shares, and by 1922 it had won control of the mine. At the end of 1944, though the war was not yet over, the diamond trade was showing signs of recovery, and it was decided that the Premier should be outfitted with underground gear and set in motion as the latest thing in diamond mines. It was a lengthy, expensive process. Five years were spent on it; for ten months of this the engineers merely pumped out water—nine hundred million gallons of water. Then, while four shafts were being sunk and development was under way, a model separation plant was set up and tried out. Not until 1950 did the mine go into production with a full scale plant.

Sir Thomas Cullinan's hopeful daring in going so far afield was impressed on me at the beginning of my visit to the Premier. I had been long enough in the Union of South Africa, though that wasn't very long, to have learned the simple rule that Kimberley is for diamonds, Johannesburg for gold, and it seemed unnatural that I should be going to look at diamonds straight from Johannesburg. It didn't make the adjustment any easier to remind myself that the head offices of the Anglo American are themselves in Johannesburg. The travel bureaus, however, are not confused on this point. They are quite content that the Premier should be so easy of access, and a visit to this genuine diamond mine is one of their routine recommendations for a one-day trip; it is something that tourists can easily do even when they haven't the time for safaris to the game reserve or plane trips over the Victoria Falls. It was not strange that my visit should coincide with the presence of a large party of American tourists who had been floating around the neighborhood for some days. They were taking a week ashore, having left their ship in Table Bay at Cape Town, and I bumped into portions of the party wherever I went in Johannesburg. In fact, I was crowded out of my hotel by them, for it was a well-organized party that had booked rooms months in advance. I moved into another hotel farther out of town but nearer Pretoria, on my way to the mine, and though it was a very bad hotel even by South African standards, which are not exacting, the tourists were there too. We shared our misfortunes. Early on the Premier day I got up, in my sixth-floor room, and attempted to order breakfast by telephone. There was no reply, nor did anybody come in, and that in itself was odd, because room boys are always coming into your room in South African hotels, especially when you haven't invited them. A Johannesburg hotel boy is one of the most persistent creatures on earth. If your door is locked he scratches at it until you open up, when with a sweet smile he pads past you and either puts down a diminutive cake of soap, or picks up one that is already there and carries it out. The fact that nobody had disturbed my sleep at five-thirty in the morning with a cup of tea I hadn't ordered was also worrying because it was abnormal. I began to feel lonely as well as hungry. After waiting on the phone, and clicking it, and waiting again for some minutes, I decided to go downstairs and investigate. The elevator didn't work either. Was this, perhaps, the beginning of an uprising like that of the Mau Mau in Kenya?

A hush of death pervaded the floor; I couldn't even hear the bell buzz. Finally I found a staircase and walked down the six flights. On the last floor but one I began to hear a noise, like a swarm of angry bees, and when I reached the lounge I had to push my way through the crowd. They were all agitated American tourists who had been unable to get anybody on the telephone. They were telling each other about it while they waited their turn to besiege the desk and complain that they were going to miss buses, and ships, and all sorts of important appointments. Behind the desks were two pretty white ladies, quite calm, slowly and without fluster permitting the tourists to pay their bills and listening without emotion to their complaints. Behind them was the switchboard, which they ignored, and sitting at the switchboard was the cause of all the trouble; a raw native, barefoot and very lightly clad. He looked as if he had stepped from the forest for the first time that morning. Great round white bone circles filled his stretched ear lobes. He was dreamily and idly plugging wires into the board and pulling them out again, not caring what he did nor asking himself why.

A furious old man just ahead of me waved his cane in the air and demanded loudly, "What's the matter here?"

One lady behind the desk said, "The proper switchboard boy isn't here today. That will be four pounds ten, please. Thank you."

Emulating her admirable example, I remained calm. I went down to the corner store and bought an apple for my breakfast: I don't know what all the other guests did. By the time I had eaten it, the mine official who was to show me over the Premier had arrived; he said we should be there rather early and at a fixed time in order to get ahead of a tourist party. Pretoria, through which we drove on our way, is a rather strange capital city in that for the important part of the political year no

Union government officials are there at all. Annually they must
pack up and move eight hundred miles south, to Cape Town for
the House of Assembly sessions, accompanied by foreign ministers and other ambassadorial dignitaries. This was one of the
times Pretoria had been deserted for Cape Town, and all the
official residences and buildings were therefore closed and
empty. We peered through noble iron gates at the Prime Minister's estate and wandered as we liked through the archways
of the Union Building. This is a lovely and impressive sight
high on a hill, built rather in the style of the top tier of an especially elaborate Colosseum. A great stretch of park land rolls
down from its gardens to the town level. There are rare trees
and shrubs; there are statues in the heroic tradition in Pretoria,
with prancing horses and wreath-bearing Muses: there are,
above all, lovely wooded slopes and spaces continually remind-
ing one of how little room we have left, over on our side of the
equator.

Outside town we stopped by for a look at the Voortrekkers'
monument. This is well worth seeing if you like monuments,
which I don't very much. It is like a great kiln or truncated
gas tank, surrounded by a circular wall built in lifelike imitation of covered wagons. The entrance is decorated with
bas-relief designs of a pioneer woman and children wearing sun-
bonnets. At this entrance there is no covered-wagon wall; instead, a great flight of steps leads up to the doorway with its
bas-relief. An iron fence is cunningly fashioned to resemble
assagais. I think there are big guns, too, somewhere in the design, but in this I may be mistaken. It is all very handsome
and clean and fierce and a little bit meaningless, for to be
significant, monuments should be erected by the people who

actually remember and live through the events they are com-
memorating. This building has only lately been erected. These
treks and battles seem to have happened a very long time ago,
and it is hard to work up much feeling over Voortrekkers'
grievances.

South African mines can be seen far off on that flat land because of their headgear, the tall, skeletal shape rather like a
smaller Eiffel Tower that stands astride the main shaft and
holds the hoisting apparatus. Closer at hand one sees the
broad expanse of roofs and its long, slanting conveyer belts and
the dark smokestacks characteristic of mines all over the world.
It is not until you drive through the town and approach the
gardens that surround the managerial offices that you come into
the De Beers atmosphere. This is hard to describe but very easy
to recognize, once you have visited a few of their establish-
ments. There never seems to be anything unnecessarily grimy
about a De Beers mine. There is always paint wherever paint
should be; the gravel paths are squared and trim; wherever it is
possible to grow flowers, flowers are. The De Beers influence
can be best summed up, perhaps, by saying that the company's
mines always look as if they were ready for a visit from the
board of directors.

Underground, though I knew better than to expect a lot of
ragged boys hacking away at the walls with pickaxes, I was
surprised nevertheless by the immensity and the neatness of
the layout. The passages were spacious and whitewashed, and,
except in the blue-ground pipe itself or where blasting had only
recently been carried out, they gave a strange impression of
permanence. These white walls and the electric lights, the great
pumps, the safety gadgets and special doors to be used in case

of flooding, the railways; they were all the paraphernalia of a mine de luxe, as long as we walked along the tunnel walled in by reef. Where the blue ground began and blasting was being carried on, the impression was different. Here it was dark except for the lanterns carried by the workers. Here, in spite of air-conditioning, was a smell of explosives and wet ground. Here it was possible, looking down at the grizzly through which the hunks of rock were dropped, to believe at last that we were hundreds of feet down in the earth.

Because the Premier is the pet mine of the De Beers group it has a final touch of elegance the others cannot claim: a crusher inside the mine instead of out in the open. Grounded in the bedrock a thousand feet below the surface, foundations rein-forced by concrete, it does its mighty work without producing any vibration, and considering the noise it makes, this seems very unnatural. It is possible by standing on a platform close to the machine to see part of the crushing process. Great jagged lumps fall into the hopper and gradually disappear; there is an incredibly loud crunching, and the gravel that results is carried off on an endless belt in immense containers, or skips, and hoisted through the main shaft to the plant outside. It is hard to realize that this dark green-blue stuff is diamond-bearing, or even if one grants that, it is still hard to suppose that the crystals can be extracted. The statistics, too, are discouraging; nearly four tons of blue ground must be crushed and washed and screened and all the rest of it to produce one carat of diamond. Nevertheless, even at this rate, diamond mining pays. Once that idea is firmly fixed in the mind one begins to mistrust the efficiency of this admirably efficient method at the Premier. In vain the officials assured me that recovery was quite adequately accomplished: I didn't trust the system. As the waste was carried off my eyes followed it. I was worried. How could they be so sure, day after day, that no diamonds had slipped past in the tailings? And another thing; what would happen nowadays to a big diamond, I asked, as for instance the other half of the Cullinan, if by chance it turned up in the blue ground and fell into that crusher?

It was evident that I had asked a rather awkward question. I learned that it is on record that one or two big stones *have* as a matter of fact been destroyed in this manner. It is true that the blue ground is carefully inspected throughout the process, from crusher to crusher, down to the working size of ⅜ of an inch or less. Men are stationed to inspect the conveyer belts that carry the gravel along, and anyone who catches a big diamond in this manner is paid a good bonus. Nevertheless a stone does slip past now and then and is ruined. The tactful visitors learn not to lament this fact too strenuously, for mining engineers in the diamond industry are rather touchy on the subject of big stones. They resent the publicity received by the giants. They take the side of the littler, unsung diamonds, the gallant small things that are extracted in bulk and put into ordinary engagement rings or factory tools, for on these the whole trade depends today. It is unfair, say the engineers, to act as if diamond mining were simply a matter of digging up a Cullinan once a week.

"You wouldn't keep a mine going steadily on the proceeds of the big fellows," one of the men said to me indignantly. "You couldn't run this industry on fancy stones. Where would we all be if we tried?"

I couldn't answer. All I knew was that it seemed a shame to risk missing the big ones, but then I am an amateur.

Above ground, the gravel goes to the jig, which is a sloping rectangular screen. As the water washes the gravel along, the table jumps and jiggles and shakes. The small pieces sift through; the big ones dance down, hopping, skipping, and bouncing on the screen, to fall into a trough at the bottom. From this they are swept into another conveyer and carried back for a further go in a smaller crusher. What has passed through the screen is carried in the opposite direction and dumped into heavy-media separation vats. These are industrial-ized versions of the drums in which the old-time diggers swirl and separate their washes; they are full of a specially prepared solution, and they whirl around constantly, sorting out the material by a combination of gravity action and centrifugal force. Diamond is heavy: its density is 3.5. Therefore the diamonds, if there are any, sink to the bottom outside edge of the tanks, along with any bits of gravel that may be equally heavy, and from there the whole lot is carried, as concentrate, to the last stage of separation on the grease tables. It is at this point in the concentrate that the gravel becomes pretty; a mass of multi-colored stones like those found in water-laid diamondiferous areas. Jasper, chalcedony, agate, garnet, ironstone: the original dull blue ground has been separated and sorted out into these. It all flashes decoratively as it passes on the belt, and a stray handful scooped up from the procession feels surprisingly weighty.

The whole building thudded. I leaned over and watched, fascinated, as the stones marched past. I sniffed the air, which smelled of wet earth. "There was a diamond!" I said.

"Saw one, did you?" asked the official. He sounded uninterested. "If you did, you're the first who's spotted a diamond on the belt in all the years I've been working. Come on over to the other place and look at the grease tables if you really want to see a few."

Deep-mine diamonds are hydrophobic. This doesn't mean, as for a startled moment I thought it did, that they bite, but only that they don't like water. They have a rather greasy surface on which water behaves like mercury, or as if it were on a duck's back. It collects in droplets, it rolls off, it does anything except spread down over the diamond and wet it. This is true, however, only of mine diamonds taken from blue-ground matrix. Water-laid diamonds, after their long sojourn in the river or sea, are more friendly to water; they have collected an invisible film over their oily surfaces on which water readily sticks. Hydrophobic diamonds, while refusing to stay wet, are hospitable to oil and grease, and when given a chance will stick to greasy stuff or allow it to stick to them. Going on this principle, mining engineers have evolved the grease table, which is constructed in a series of three descending, sloping steps, or little cliffs. The surface is of aluminum, coated all over with grease about half an inch thick or even more. Along the top of the table is the lip of the chute, down which pours the concentrate. At the last stage before it emerges it is spread out and distributed evenly, so that it comes out in a regular flow all along the edge of the table, rattling down on the grease and urged on its way by the jiggling, dancing movement of the table. Over the edge of the step or cliff, the gravel-filled water rushes like a miniature cataract, and every pebble as it slides over comes into contact with the grease. Wherever a diamond comes down and rubs along the grease it is caught and held. Each blow from passing gravel only shoves it deeper into its bed. Most diamonds are caught and held as soon as they fall from the hopper, and if you have a rich concentrate it is not long before there is a whole ridge of crystals, big and little, burrowing down into the grease and showing as glassy specks in the yellow. A few of the bigger ones go down to the second step before they get stuck. The third and last step is the widest and is only there to make quite sure; very few diamonds get as far as that. Every so often the flow is stopped so that a worker can scrape off the grease, diamonds and all, and put it into a fine-wire basket. This is placed in another bigger container and put over a hot fire, where it is all boiled in water until the grease can be skimmed off and the diamonds alone are left—a small handful out of a great mass of rock. Four tons to a carat.

Throughout the entire process, from mine to boiling pot, the diamonds have been accompanied on their journey by natives. Natives cart supplies to the mine lifts; the tools and sticks of dynamite and the spare parts for machinery. Natives stand by respectfully while whites adjust the explosives, and they hurry forward to help break up recalcitrant blocks after the blast. They swarm over the grizzly, relieving jams and coaxing the lumps through into trucks, and then they drive the trucks through the long, dimly lit corridors. Two thousand natives man the mines, and when their shift is over they are brought out by special passages into their own shower rooms, and thence back to the compounds. By special arrangement, very ingeniously, they have not gone out of doors once. This is an important improvement, for in the days of Mr. Whitworth's self-questionings and up until a good deal later, boys easily caught pneumonia from coming out of the heated underground into cooler air.

We saw the compounds where they live when they are not underground—blocks of cubicles and iron-framed double-decker beds; playing grounds; an all-purpose church. While I can't say the quarters were enticing, they appear to be a far cry from the compounds of half a century ago. There are classes in tailoring and woodwork, in reading and writing. There are great kitchens and eating rooms, and special arrangements for making the mild native beer that is today's safe equivalent of Mr. Whitworth's mischief-making brandy. The bloody faction fights don't happen any more. The boys lead lives of what must be intense boredom in their isolation, but they are kept clean and are well fed and, by South African standards, well paid—the minimum wage is four pounds a month, excellent pay for a native in South Africa. (Food, schooling, and medical care are free.) They can bank this money if they want to, or send it home to their families; a good deal of it, however, is spent in the mine shop on clothes. South African natives generally are well dressed to a degree that astonishes tourists. This is due partly to a widely spread prejudice among natives in favor of clothes: clothes stand for wealth almost as currency does; but there is another reason. When food is paid for there is really very little else a native in South Africa can use money for.

Whether or not a mine worker's life is dull, the De Beers Mine managers never find it necessary to go out "recruiting" labor, as the process of indenturing is called. They have more applicants for work than they can use. It is one manager's cynical belief that some of his most persistent repeaters are men who don't like too much of their wives' company and come to find refuge behind the fences. In any case, after a man has signed on two or three times running, and spent his period of nine months or whatever has been nominated in the bond that many times, the labor manager rather discourages another term.

"I tell him to go home and visit his wife for a few months, and come back later if he wants to," he said. "I think they like the security of the life here. You get to know them pretty well after a while."

Finally we reached the house where the end produce of all this activity could be seen, in trays of diamonds undergoing sorting according to size and color. There were little *pointes naïves*, big ones, in-between ones, yellow, amber, white, and blue—and, of course, a life-size model of the Cullinan, and again I thought sadly of what might happen to a stone that size, or anywhere near it, in the works of the Premier today. The fact is, though they consist of the hardest substance in the universe, diamonds are brittle and easily breakable if you hit them at just the right angle. This casts a lurid light on some of the stories of the early days of Kimberley, when one of the supposedly scientific tests of a doubtful stone was to give it a good swipe with a hammer. The diggers honestly believed that though quartz crystal would smash under this treatment, genuine diamond would not. Louis Cohen, who was Barney Barnato's first partner when they were both green boys, recounted in his memoirs how on his first attempt at diamond buying he invested three of his very few pounds in a small crystal which he hastily took to a buyer. The buyer looked at it closely, sneered, put it on one of his metal weights, and brought down another weight on it with a great blow. The fact that the crystal splintered was proof to both of them that it hadn't been a diamond. In view of what is known today about diamonds, Mr. Cohen may have been grievously wronged.

There *was* a narrow squeak at the Premier in June 1954, I learned; a diamond weighing four hundred and twenty-six and a half carats appeared on the grease table, nipped and gnawed slightly at one end by the machinery but miraculously whole. It was strange that such a whopping stone should have come through intact; anything of that size really has no business escaping the jaws of efficiency in the journey from mine to grease table. The officials at the Premier showed me the diamond. It is gloriously clear and a pure blue-white, but, like its distinguished predecessor the Cullinan, it is not a perfect octahedron. It is a good deal longer than it is thick, and one end is smaller than the other, which may be one reason it survived the machine. Luckily, only the small end was caught in the crusher.

A few years ago, the Premier people had a less fortunate experience; some fragments that appeared pretty much all at once on the grease table brought the men in charge to the melancholy conclusion that a very large diamond of superior quality had been crushed, and they were able to reconstruct enough of it to get a fairly good idea of the tragic loss they had incurred. It fell to the lot of the engineer who told me about the incident to break the news to Sir Ernest Oppenheimer. Sir Ernest loves diamonds with a passionate fervor, and he took it hard.

"He said, 'Do you realize your machines have destroyed one of the noblest things in nature?'" the engineer recalled. "So I said to him, 'Sir Ernest, I'm awfully sorry. You must know how sorry we all are. But if you'll permit me to be frank, I admit I can only look at it from my special point of view.' He said, 'What's that?' and I said, 'Well, sir, all I can say is that I'm glad, speaking purely as an engineer, that my machines are so efficient. I would have known there was something wrong if that stone had got through whole.'"

# CHAPTER FIVE

# . . . And Son

It was raining hard in Johannesburg one morning a few years ago when a very young man saw that he was going to be late to his new job with the Anglo American Corporation of South Africa. He hurried. He ran up the soaking steps of the corporation's impressive building in Main Street that with its subsidiaries occupies a large hunk of Johannesburg's financial district; and he ran into one of the elevators and stood impatiently, his raincoat dripping, while it carried him to the correct floor. Then, dashing down the corridor at least ten minutes past the proper time for starting work, he was briefly gratified when somebody ahead of him, seeing him approach like a cannon ball, paused and held open a door for him.

"It was a little old fellow in a raincoat something like mine but not so new," he said later in horrified tones. "Such a quiet little man, so polite, that I must have had a vague idea, if I thought about it at all, that he was somebody who worked around the place like a kind of older office boy. Mind you, I wasn't much more than an office boy myself. I just said, 'Thanks!' and nodded in a lordly way as I swept past, and it

was a week before I saw the little old man again and one of
the other fellows told me who he was. My God, it was Sir Ernest Oppenheimer!"

Head of one of the most complicated empires of industry in
the world, Oppenheimer is a very rich and powerful man, but
a shy one. Rich and powerful men are sure to be referred to in
the press, sooner or later, as "mystery men," though the description may not apply at all. As far as Britain and the United
States are concerned, however, Sir Ernest really is a mystery
man. He's almost unknown personally in those parts. It is true
that he endows colleges and scholarships, and contributes to
libraries and all the rest of it. His name pops up copiously on
the financial page, but the general public doesn't pay much attention to endowments or financial pages. The general public
reads society columns instead, and Oppenheimer isn't a soci-
ety-column type. He is not seen at Cannes; he doesn't give
parties at racecourses. He doesn't wander about in a yacht.
He likes books and paintings and staying at home: he is a man
much preoccupied with family affairs. His general interest is
chiefly in South Africa, which is a long way from England and
the States. Though he was born in Germany and spent a good
part of his youth in England, he has been in South Africa most
of his long life and is a South African by nationality. London
and New York are the main distribution centers for diamonds,
and diamonds have been the foundation of his fortune, though
his financial interests are widespread through other commodities now, but Sir Ernest doesn't visit London often and he goes
even more seldom to New York, leaving such voyages to
younger people such as his son Harry. Sir Ernest likes Johannesburg, a city he watched grow up. He enjoys his house there,

with its pretty grounds; he likes the space and the air. When he is at leisure he walks and reads biography. It is the gentle simplicity of his life that makes him a mystery.

Of course there are other factors: for example, when the public does become aware of Oppenheimer, as sometimes even the non-financial-page type of public does, it usually asks that great question of comparatives; just how rich is he? People are fond of knowing how many times a millionaire a millionaire may be, especially in our income-taxed world. People are especially partial to succulent bits of information that apply to diamonds and gold. The normal mind dwells naturally on Aladdin's cave and Golconda, on treasure chests and towering palaces with jeweled roofs. Unfortunately the mind as far as Oppenheimer is concerned is bound to be frustrated. Nobody in his list of companies would risk making a guess, far less a statement, as to just how much money he owns. It is not at all certain that even Sir Ernest could tell, though he has a fabulous head for figures. The difficulty that faces the average man in such a matter is that Oppenheimer's activities are so many and so complicated. At the moment of writing he is a director of forty-one companies and chairman of twenty-eight of these. Four of them are in the United Kingdom: namely the British South African Company, the Commonwealth Development Finance Company Limited, Hambros Bank Limited, and Tanganyika Concessions Limited. Twenty-four more are in South Africa, and they are *all* limited companies.

In Northern Rhodesia he is chairman of all six of his limited companies—Bancroft Mines, Nchanga Consolidated Copper Mines, Rhodesia Copper Refineries, the Rhodesia Broken Hill Development Company, Rhodesian Anglo America, and

Rhokana Corporation. He is also chairman of the Anglo American Rhodesian Development Corporation Limited of Southern Rhodesia, and a director in the Belgian Congo of the Société Minière du Beceka, and in Portuguese West Africa of the Companhia de Diamantes de Angola.

Sir Ernest doesn't subscribe as Cecil Rhodes did to the theory of empire: on the contrary, he's not at all nationalistically minded. But, as the presiding judge said of the De Beers charter at the time of the Kimberley Central law suit, it would be easier to say what in the world of finance he isn't than what he is. It was an association of such ideas, no doubt, that produced an uncharacteristic burst of literary allusion to him in the financial columns of the British weekly, *The Economist*, in June 1954. "In the diamond trade," said *The Economist*, under the heading "King of Diamonds," "the De Beers group 'doth bestride the narrow world like a Colossus.'" The derivation is clear: Rhodes-Colossus, Rhodes-Oppenheimer, therefore Oppenheimer-Colossus. It is an oversimplification. In most respects the two men could hardly be less alike, though there is no doubt that Oppenheimer firmly believes in one of Rhodes's basic tenets, that amalgamation is a good thing. It is his application of the tenet that differs. He supports the fundamental theory of control in diamond trading, but he doesn't carry his passion for tidiness to the extent of using diamond profits to grab land for colonial glory. The control itself, whatever the occasional disgruntled trader may say in attacking it, is a measure that has won general approbation among diamond men, in Rhodes's time and in Oppenheimer's. But Sir Ernest *has* gone further, in his own way, just as Rhodes went in his: he uses diamond profits to develop a large number of other interests in Africa, predominantly mining interests but not necessarily so—copper, gold, coal, the secondary industries arising from these interests, and whatever else seems to him promising. And whatever seems promising to Sir Ernest usually fulfills its promise.

"It is argued," said *The Economist*, referring to the latest Oppenheimer venture in gold, "that shareholders might have been allowed to decide for themselves whether to invest their money in the speculative ventures of the Orange Free State, but Sir Ernest would have none of it." He had his way and invested their money in West Reef, and the shareholders profited, and people talked more than ever of Sir Ernest's similarity to Rhodes, who also made money for his shareholders without asking their blessing. Most British newspapers mention the matter from time to time.

Considering all this comparison with the empire builder, it is not surprising that the few members of the British public who saw Oppenheimer at last when he came to England in 1954 should have thought at first that they were looking at the wrong man. It was unusual that he should have come, and it was even less usual that he should have granted an interview, as he did, to the press; in fact he has never before done such a thing in Britain. The reporters, who were all fairly well up on the contemporary affairs of finance, had been thinking of him as a biggish type—a captain of industry, or better still a generalissimo. Rhodes was a big man. Rhodes looked rather like Nietzsche's superman, and Hitler would certainly have used him as a model. He was tall, broad, and blond. The only way he failed to maintain the Nordic ideal was in his voice, which was squeaky and apt to rise to falsetto pitch. Rhodes

was a boisterous man when he relaxed: he loved camping out
on the veld, and always moved about with a number of male
friends in his train. He was what is called a man's man, and
the shrines to his memory that dot South Africa always feature
photographs of him posed among cronies, in big hats and boots
and carrying guns. While he wasn't exactly flashy and never
forgot he was a clergyman's son, there was no modesty about
him.

Sir Ernest is a very different type, and the newspapermen
found the difference piquant. It is true that at the time
of the interview he was approaching his seventy-fifth birthday,
whereas Rhodes was only forty-nine when he died. But Oppenheimer at forty-nine, or even at twenty-nine, was never in
the heroic mold beloved of Nietzsche. He is small and slender,
with gentle manners; though his voice is resonant it too is gentle. He has shining brown eyes and an alert expression. When
he talks to someone he looks at that person with a gaze so
direct and unflinching that, regardless of what he is saying,
the impression he gives is of great intensity, and also of
great simplicity. This bright brown gaze and his soft voice usually arouse in people an emotion that can best be called protective. Why a man of Sir Ernest's resources and record should
need protection is a question that doesn't cry out for answer at
the time.

Possibly the close attention he pays to strangers' speech is
his form of escape from embarrassment. Sir Ernest is shy
—which is one reason he avoids press interviews—but he tries
not to let his shyness carry him to extremes. When his advisers
said he ought to meet the British gentlemen of the press he
did meet the gentlemen of the press, and when he fluttered

nervously just before the hour arranged, and said he hadn't the slightest idea what he was going to talk about, the advisers, who knew him well, were not at all perturbed. They had heard him go on like that many times before. Sure enough he had a statement prepared in his head, which he delivered admirably. He showed no signs of nervousness. He answered questions promptly, with an amazing flow of statistics for which he carried no notes, and by the time it all came to a close he was completely at ease and thoroughly efficient. The reporters were just putting away their pencils when Sir Ernest quietly fainted.

"Though what else he could have expected after behaving as he did I don't know," said Lady Oppenheimer to an acquaintance, when the crisis was over and her husband was safe back in Johannesburg. "All that excitement and the bad air. He's not used to the tension of London in any case, and there he stood in a crowded, smoke-filled room for more than half an hour, and he was talking the whole time. Of course it was the smoke. After all, he's an old man, but he's very strong."

It is necessary for his family to mention this truth about his strength from time to time, for another deceptive impression he somehow imparts, without in the least wishing to deceive, is of constitutional delicacy. (Though when he's been ill he likes to get credit for it. "You must never tell Ernest he's looking well," said a close friend. "Just tell him he's looking much better.") He is small and quiet, and people want to take care of him and cosset him, but he has a reputation among his cronies for extraordinary bodily toughness.

These cronies can fairly be described as few and faithful. Oppenheimer has led a sheltered life, in spite of its excitements. He has always dwelt in the stability of one overpowering in-

terest, which, though in the ordinary sense it would not be considered stable and though it has subjected him to a dramatic
series of ups and downs, nevertheless adds up to continuity of
a sort. Except for these ups and downs of finance, Sir Ernest
has not had a checkered career. The variety of his life was not
geographical or vocational: not for him the pattern of cow-
punching, or bartending, or elevator operating, or windjammer
sailing that we usually think of when we hear of men who have
made their fortunes out of mining in the colonies. Sir Ernest
went into the diamond trade when he was sixteen, and he's
been in diamonds ever since, though admittedly he has been
in a lot of other things as well. His circle is largely made up
of people he has known for many years, who have known each
other, too, all that time. One of these men was in a reminiscent
mood the other day, rendered thoughtful, as septuagenarians
are, by his old friend's birthday.

"I recall the day I first saw Ernest," he said. "It was in the
sorting room where he was working in Kimberley. He had just
got to town and I noticed him immediately; it was a little place
and you always did look twice at strangers in those days. It
was 1902, a warm summer day. His sleeves were rolled up, and
I noticed his arms immediately. I thought I'd never seen such
muscular arms on any man. Ernest's still immensely strong,
though you mightn't think it because he seems to be lightly
built. Harry Oppenheimer's the same; they're short and slight
but sinewy. Well, I asked the man in charge of the office,
'Who's that fellow with the big arms?' and he said it was a
new man, Ernest Oppenheimer, who'd just been sent out from
London. He said, 'I don't think very much of him from what
I've seen so far. He's terribly shy, and he doesn't seem to be

very bright.' I never saw that fellow in later years that I didn't
rub it in, what he'd said about Ernest Oppenheimer. I never
let him forget it."

There is a much wider circle of people who know Oppenheimer and see him often, though they aren't his intimate
friends. Outside of his business employees and apart from the
men who help distribute the money he gives away is a marginal group of his neighbors, in Johannesburg and other centers
of European South Africa. All these people hear constantly of
Sir Ernest and often see him going about his affairs: entering
his office, lending the light of his presence to important public
gatherings, meeting relatives at the airport—that sort of thing.
Like other small communities of Europeans surrounded and
outnumbered by another race, white Johannesburg is ingrown
and tends to be gossipy about local celebrities. Its malice, like
that of university faculties or literary groups or any other sort
of isolated crowd, is practiced and sharp. Added to this, one
would expect a natural envy of Oppenheimer wealth to mount
up to a quantity of unkind comment about the family from the
rest of Johannesburg. Somehow, though, it doesn't happen:
Oppenheimer is usually spared. This is not because the gossips
are afraid. There are lots of other rich men in South Africa,
and they get the works without mercy. Even Sir Ernest's political opponents, or rather Harry's—for Sir Ernest gave up his seat
in the House of Assembly some years ago—leave him personally alone, though they attack Oppenheimer business concerns
with a bitterness that shocks travelers from more inhibited
lands. There are several reasons for this forbearance. The chief
one, probably, is Sir Ernest's own personality. Even a determined reputation wrecker could hardly hope to convince any-

one who knows him, however slightly, that here is an evil or haughty character. Besides, he lives quietly. Envy is not exacerbated by the spectacle of wild Oppenheimer extravagance. Moreover, he is generous, and he is quiet about that too. He makes many of his donations through the Anglo American Corporation, and these are on record: what he gives away privately is a matter of speculation. The money admittedly given away by him as separate from the De Beers donations as a company comes to more than one hundred and fifteen thousand pounds to charitable and other institutions and more than seventy thousand to educational and other institutions, not counting a recent gift, in partnership with his son, of one hundred thousand pounds to Oxford University to found the new Queen Elizabeth House, devoted to the study of Commonwealth relations. There is good reason to suspect, however, that this is only part of the story, but, if so, Sir Ernest isn't telling the rest of it.

Ernest Oppenheimer was born in 1880 in Friedberg near Frankfurt, Hesse Province. The revolution of 1848 had affected his family, as it did many other middle-class people of the period, with a dissatisfaction that showed itself in a strong urge to get out of the country while the getting was good, before the reactionary Prussian influence crushed all liberalism. Ernest's parents remained in Friedberg to rear their large family, but several of his uncles found their way to England and settled down there. Ernest was fifth of the six sons of his parents: there were four girls besides. The state of Germany did not improve as these children grew up, and most of them followed their relatives across the Channel and found jobs in London. When Ernest was sixteen years old his elder brother Bernard

suggested that he come to London and join him in the firm of
Anton Dunkelsbuhler & Co., diamond dealers, as an apprentice.
Dunkelsbuhler was a name familiar on the Diamond Fields of
South Africa. Anton Dunkelsbuhler had been on the spot since
the early days of Rhodes and Barnato. His firm had been one of
those that pledged themselves after the amalgamation of Kimberley mines to buy De Beers Consolidated's output according
to fixed percentages: finally, in 1890, they evolved the Diamond
Syndicate. In 1893, just three years before Ernest emigrated to
England, the Syndicate achieved its aim and controlled the
world sale of diamonds. The group became known to gem dealers all over the world simply as "the Syndicate," and this name
fluctuated in popularity just about as general prosperity fluctuated. When demand outstripped supply, dealers liked the
Syndicate well enough and admitted that in times of stress it
was a good thing. But whenever depressions set in or somebody
found himself in possession of a lot more diamonds than the
rest of the suppliers, the Syndicate stood in the way of individ-
ualists who would otherwise have undercut the selling price or
flooded the market in an attempt to make a fortune quickly
and then get out. Then there were curses on the heads of the
Syndicate that so cruelly restrained the merchants. The Syndicate itself is no longer with the trade, but the system remains
in essence under another name and the connotations of the
word itself still hang round Hatton Garden. It will take Sunday
newspapers a long time to forget it.

In London, Ernest acquired a room in Camden Town, a
quiet section of the city that was to become famous some years
later because Dr. Crippen lived there and buried his dismem-
bered wife in the cellar. Every day the boy went to Hatton

Garden, where diamond merchants congregate, and set to work learning his business. Things don't change much in that world, and the training he underwent was just about what an apprentice in the diamond trade would undergo today. At Dunkelsbuhler's in London rough stones came in from South Africa, where they had been bought by the firm's representatives, and were sorted and graded and sold. He enjoyed the work. He soon became so proficient in judging diamonds that he gained a reputation for it, even in that society of experts.

There are dozens of stories current in Johannesburg and Kimberley about his knowledge of stones. One is told in several versions, but the main point of the tale is that during a recent meeting of De Beers directors someone played a practical joke and slipped a phony in among a handful of good stones that were being passed around from hand to hand, a piece of bottle glass that closely resembled a rough diamond. It is said that Oppenheimer spotted it even before it reached him. Certainly his Hatton Garden training was intensive and arduous. During the six years he was in London he found only one opportunity to pay a visit to his parents in Germany, and it wasn't that he didn't want to go.

"Only the other day when I was playing with my grandson, who is soon going away to school, I thought what it must have meant to my parents to send their children away from them into the world," he recently told a colleague. In 1902, Dunkelsbuhler's sent him to Kimberley, where they needed experts of his caliber even more than they did in London.

Kimberley wasn't quite the rough mining camp it had been twenty years earlier, but it wasn't exactly a suave metropolis either. The tents and shacks had mostly given way to solid

dwelling places and shops and office buildings, but the sense
of get-rich-quick urgency that had earlier animated it had now
moved on to Johannesburg, where many of the old-time Kimberley magnates were settled in happily making second or third
or fourth fortunes in gold. Yet Kimberley was far from dead.
The mines were working and diamonds flowed up to the surface, but the town was already becoming what it is today, a
residential place where citizens lived quietly and talked a good
deal about old times. They had a stirring lot of old times to
talk about, with the Boer War so recently over and Cecil
Rhodes only just dead. (He had died six weeks before Ernest
arrived in South Africa, gasping for breath in his little cottage
at Muizenberg at the Cape.) The memory of Jameson's Raid,
when a band of British volunteers tried to wrest Johannesburg
from the Boers, was still vivid, and the rights and wrongs of its
famous debacle were hotly debated: for that matter they still
are, in Kimberley.

Ernest was twenty-two years old when he arrived in South
Africa. He was keenly ambitious: he knew exactly what he
wanted to do, but it sounded so startling that he hesitated to
confide the scope of his vision to any of his contemporaries.
His aim was simple but gloriously out of reach: he intended
to make a huge, specific fortune—fifty thousand pounds, no less
—and retire on it. He figured that if he could save up that much
and invest it wisely at 5 per cent, he would have enough of an
income—twenty-five hundred pounds a year, or twelve thousand
five hundred dollars at the current exchange rate—to live on.
He would then settle down to reading and studying for the
rest of his life. But an achievement of this ambition was wildly
improbable, he knew, and in the meantime he went to the

Dunkelsbuhler office every day, and carried out his various duties and sorted diamonds, sitting at the table with his sleeves rolled up. The social life of the community was not remarkable for variety or stimulation, but people did get to know each other very well. One of Ernest's earliest friendships was that with Jameson. Belligerent little Leander Starr Jameson, or Sir Starr, or "Dr. Jim," had survived his early vicissitudes and lived down the raid to such an extent that he was elected M.P. and for a time attended the House of Assembly in Cape Town. Now he lived quietly, spending the last years of his life sometimes in South Africa, sometimes in Britain.

"He used to stay in the same house I did in Kimberley," said Sir Ernest. "I remember him sitting on the *stoep*, his right leg crossed over his left, reading about swashbucklers."

Jameson never set himself up as a business expert, but after all he had made money out of his long association with Rhodes, and he must have picked up a certain amount of practical philosophy as well from him. It was from this special fund of knowledge that he was able one day to give Ernest Oppenheimer valuable advice. The young man was complaining that his youth put him at a disadvantage at the office.

"Everyday I go there, and I work as hard as anybody in the firm, if not harder. I sit down and sort diamonds with them," he said. "Yet they don't respect me."

Dr. Jim said, "That's the trouble. Of course they don't respect you for working hard. Don't sort diamonds: let them do the sorting."

Taking the older man's words to heart, Oppenheimer stayed home more, and when he went to the office it was to buy and sell diamonds that had been sorted by lesser mortals. For the

rest, he busied himself increasingly with the loftier aspects of
the diamond business and soon, as a rising young executive, he
had a hand in the operations of the Syndicate. "But I was bored
without the diamond sorting, and I was forced by this boredom
to read," he said. "That may also be why I went in for municipal affairs so hard: having nothing else to do."

When he thinks back to his first few years in South Africa,
Sir Ernest is puzzled to account for that rather unusual taste.
Why should he have been so keen on the mechanics of government, especially in a frontier town like Kimberley? It wasn't a
customary yearning among his colleagues: most of them were
completely absorbed in business. The town was full of men
who concentrated on the making and investment of money,
and in these sentiments, it must be understood, he heartily con-
curred. He was very keen, himself, on making and investing
money. He had no prejudice against the stuff at all. Yet for
some reason he wanted to take a hand in the management of
human affairs as well. It was not the usual desire for power, as
he remembers it now; it was just that he wanted to see things
going smoothly, and when they didn't he wanted to help readjust them.

"I was always interested in people," he said. "Only four
years after I arrived in Kimberley I joined the Town Council.
It was a small thing, but you must realize that no one in the
sphere of life in which I was had done anything like that before."

Actually it wasn't such a small thing as all that to have
joined the Council, because in communities such as Kimberley these organizations are tremendously important. Oppenheimer remained an active member of the Council and became

more and more of a figure in it. This suited him thoroughly: he had already identified himself with the place and its future, and entertained no idea of going back to England or Germany to live. Within a year of his arrival he had adopted South African nationality. He did go back to England on a visit, however, in 1906. It was in the nature of an old-home tour, for by this time a large proportion of the Oppenheimer family had left Friedberg for good and settled down in England; Ernest's brothers, Bernard, Gustav, Louis, and Otto were all there. Louis, who was ten years older than Ernest, had married a London girl named Charlotte Pollak. She had a younger sister named Mary Lina. By the end of the year Ernest was on his way back to Kimberley with Mary Lina as his wife. Mary Oppenheimer was an unusual woman, with a true understanding of the mysteries of finance. Old friends of the Oppenheimers all agree in saying that she had a man's mind. A mind like a razor, they sometimes add when they feel that the first description is perhaps inadequate as praise. One extremist even said, "Sometimes I used to think she was even better than Ernest at business."

They had two children, Harry Frederick, who was born in 1908, and Frank Leslie, born in 1910. Frank was drowned at the age of twenty-five, swimming off the coast of Madeira.

Ernest's career in the government of Kimberley kept pace with his rise in the diamond industry. He was elected a city councilor in 1908, while still in his twenties: that was remarkable enough, but it was more remarkable that he should have become mayor when he was only thirty-four. In spite of what happened later it still pleases him to think he achieved the post so young. The drawback wasn't obvious at the time, but it be-

came so later—it was the date of his election: 1914. The misgivings of his forebears were about to be justified, but early in
the year the European residents of Kimberley weren't watching
the home countries very closely. Instead, they were absorbed
in a troublesome situation that grew more of a nuisance day
by day: the rivalry between Kimberley and its very close neighbor, the town of Beaconsfield. Beaconsfield was what would
have been a suburb of Kimberley, if the latter town had
been big enough to lay claim to a satellite. There were inter-
municipal quarrels and squabbles over utility services, police
protection, and the like, and it was all very silly because the
communities were separated by a mere few miles of road which
even then was rapidly filling up with houses. The situation had
long annoyed Ernest Oppenheimer's orderly soul, and his fellow townsmen's lackadaisical acceptance of it annoyed him still
more. As town councilor he had tackled the problem but
found himself alone on his side in the battle. As mayor, of
course, he had much more power. The minute he got a chance
he rode blandly over the patriotic protests of his fellow Kimber-
lites and put through a combination of the towns under the
name of Kimberley. He did it by sheer insistence and quick,
flowing conversation, and anybody who has ever encountered
civic pride will realize what a feat of persuasion it was. In spite
of his gentle ways, Oppenheimer roused is a Juggernaut talker.
Once he gets under way there is no holding out against him.

The job of combining Beaconsfield and Kimberley appealed
to him not only because it was practical, but because it was
in the true Rhodes tradition of amalgamation. He figures
that the more you combine factors, the easier it is to handle
them. Today Beaconsfield harbors no grudge; it plays West-

chester to Kimberley's New York as a smart residential quarter.

The diamond trade had undergone a bad depression since Ernest's arrival in South Africa; in 1907 the mines actually closed down for a space. About the same time something else happened that was calculated to put wrinkles into De Beers' brows. Troubles always seemed to grow in clusters in South Africa. This time it was the discovery of diamonds at Lüderitz-bucht on the coast of German South-West Africa. The diamond trade shuddered in any case, at every new discovery, but this was worse than most because it wasn't in territory that the Syndicate could control. Although for the moment the production at Lüderitz, as the settlement on the bay is called, was irregular, depending as it did on diggers, and the diamonds were very small, it was probably only a matter of time before the Germans would organize it and start mining in earnest, and what might happen then didn't look too rosy for the South African diamond-mining people. At least that is how the situation appeared to Ernest Oppenheimer, and though other diamond men didn't seem to worry as much as he did once the first shock had passed, De Beers asked him to go and have a look at the German fields. In 1914, early in that significant year, he did go to Lüderitz with Alpheus Williams, a geologist, the son of Gardner Williams. In their report they assessed the possibilities of the fields and the probable productive life of each section. Oppenheimer's calculations based on these observations have since turned out to be remarkably accurate. Through the offices of the keenly interested government of South Africa the leading diamond producers, including the Germans, held a conference and agreed to go in all together in the matter of control. This gratified the South Africans, as until then the German Régie, which controlled output and sales in South-West Africa, hadn't co-operated very enthusiastically with the Syndicate. The war naturally canceled all these arrangements, however, and later the German dealers had to fall in with the others, willy-nilly.

But by 1914 diamonds weren't Oppenheimer's only interest, though they were still, as they are now, his favorite. He had begun to branch out, and his investments were varied. Those which were to prove most important were in the gold mines of the Witwatersrand, usually called the Rand for short. They were being developed by a firm called the Consolidated Mines Selection Company, with headquarters in Johannesburg. Oppenheimer was named resident director of Consolidated, and, although he was not actually a resident of Johannesburg, he began spending a good deal of time there. He also had a stake in the new coal mines, and he was interested in base-metal mining as well, and the secondary industries that sprang up everywhere in the wake of prospectors. He was watching a nation grow up.

Then the war broke out. Nobody was busier than the young mayor of Kimberley. He helped raise and finance the 2nd Battalion of the Kimberley Regiment, and launched a charitable relief fund, and was altogether concentrated on winning the war efficiently. Those were the days when enlistment was voluntary, and in South Africa there were many ticklish situations, for a lot of South Africans weren't of British descent: they, or their parents, had come from all over the world. Anyone who decided that the colony was a place of mixed loyalties would have been correct. There should never have been any doubt about Ernest Oppenheimer's loyalties, however, and he was bit-

terly offended when it came to his attention that people were
whispering against him.

It was 1915. "General Botha had already taken South-West
Africa from the Germans, and General Smuts was driving the
enemy out of East Africa. And then they suddenly remembered
I had a German name," he said.

Of course he wasn't the only one who suffered from this
sort of thing. In England even Earl Battenberg had hearkened
to the voice of hysteria and changed his name to Mountbat-
ten. The Dunkelsbuhlers, who also suffered unpopularity,
truncated their name and became the Dunkels family. Oppenheimer, however, didn't take that way out because it was different in South Africa, and such action wouldn't have done
him any good. Britain was a much bigger place socially; nobody can answer for millions of people, and you can blame the
unknowns for whatever idiocy might crop up among the public, but Kimberley wasn't in England and Ernest knew practically everybody there, and they knew him. He felt they
should have known him better by that time. He was hurt. It
became more than a mere matter of whispering: one evening a
mob gathered outside his house and threw stones at it. The
authorities decided he had better have a guard, and a man from
the local police force was put on duty. Late that night Oppenheimer invited him in for a sit-down and a glass of something.
They had an amiable visit, and after a little while Oppenheimer
asked the man his name.

"Schumann," said the bodyguard.

Somehow this incident helped the mayor to make up his
mind. Hitherto he had hesitated to follow his inclinations, to

resign his post and renounce Kimberley, but now he did this. With his family he moved away, down to the Cape.

Along the coast east of Cape Town, serving as a summer resort and suburb, is a magnificent stretch of beach at the foot of the mountains known as Sea Point. Oppenheimer went to stay there at a hotel for a bit. For days he walked along the sand or climbed the rocks and sat high up, looking out to sea, struggling with disappointment and resentment, and thinking things out. He had to plan the future. He was only thirty-six, but he had amassed capital and reputation: he had a wide choice of alternatives. Certainly he would not return to Kimberley, but he didn't want to leave South Africa altogether. He decided at last to go to Johannesburg, and he has lived there ever since.

The gold-mining company had on its staff an American consulting engineer named W. L. Honnold. Honnold and Oppenheimer became friendly, and the American told Oppenheimer about his theory that there were other undiscovered gold deposits at certain points relative to the Reef that was then being worked. Honnold proposed to investigate by means of boring, and of course a program of judicious land buying was indicated, too. But this was all by way of being a major operation in the future: the project called for more funds than the two men could supply for themselves. It was a situation like that of Rhodes with the diamond mines when he wanted to amalgamate. The two friends in 1917 organized a company called the Anglo American Corporation of South Africa, a name they hoped might strike a responsive chord in the only group of investors who were likely to have ready cash at that time; that is to say, Americans. Among Honnold's friends was Herbert Hoover, then in London as head of the commission for Belgian relief. Honnold arranged a meeting with Hoover, and went on ahead to prepare the way. Oppenheimer soon joined him there, and the three men held a conference in the Savoy Hotel to discuss the project. It may be presumed that Honnold presented the technical and scientific arguments in its favor, and that Oppenheimer showed a persuasive grasp of the financial intricacies involved; in any event, Hoover appears to have been favorably impressed. He told the partners that he was pretty sure he could find American money for the project: he mentioned J. P. Morgan as a likely bet. Later things developed as he thought they might.

His business thus satisfactorily launched, Oppenheimer sailed from Southampton for South Africa in the *Galway Castle*. Early in the morning, the third day out, two hundred miles southwest of Land's End, the ship was torpedoed by a U-boat and all hands took to the lifeboats. It was a stormy sea. Many boats capsized: one of them was Oppenheimer's. More than a hundred passengers were lost in that incident, but Oppenheimer's tough constitution saw him through. He gave up his place in the lifeboat, swam around in the icy water for an hour, and was then picked up by a rescuing destroyer. Wrapped in a blanket and very much the worse for wear, he was carried back to England with the other survivors. Just before Germany surrendered he managed to get another passage home, this time making it without incident.

In 1921, in recognition of his services to the Empire during the early years of the war, Oppenheimer was knighted. Honors were descending thick and fast on the family. His brother Bernard, for having given employment to disabled soldiers in his diamond-polishing works, and aiding and employing Belgian refugees, and generally encouraging rehabilitation measures, was made a baronet, and Sir Ernest must have felt, with all this British recognition, that the mob scene in Kimberley not so long before had been adequately wiped off the record. Certainly he bore no malice. A few years later he was elected Member of Parliament for Kimberley, and he continued to represent the town at the House of Assembly for eleven years.

Anglo American was a great success from the first. J. P. Morgan and other American bankers invested something over five million dollars in the corporation. The gold fields were so productive that Oppenheimer, who had become chairman of Anglo American, began casting his eye about for further opportunities. He didn't have far to look. One of the consequences of the war was that Germany's holdings in South-West Africa were thrown open to development by British capital; the German mining firms there were, in fact, going broke. So Oppenheimer stepped in and bought out the German firms, merging them into a single company called Consolidated Diamond Mines of South-West Africa, Ltd., in which Anglo American held a controlling interest. This act made him an important figure in the diamond-producing world—within a year Consolidated Diamond Mines was accounting for a fifth of all the diamonds mined in Africa—and he determined to use his newly acquired power to influence the other large producers, notably De Beers, in the direction of a more rigid marketing arrangement than the old Diamond Syndicate and stricter control of production. He had a poor opinion of the De Beers directors' breadth of vision. His breadth of vision, on the other hand, scared them to death.

Meanwhile, the diamond business had its ups and downs.

Following the usual postwar boom, a depression overtook the industry and stayed with it from 1920 to 1922. Then the market rallied; Anglo American installed a new plant in South-West Africa, diamond mines all over South Africa were making a good recovery, and everything seemed ready to hum, when, in 1926, the industry received one of the most severe shocks in its history—the discovery of alluvial diamond fields around Lichtenburg. Nobody who specializes in diamonds will admit that in the last analysis you can have too many of the things, but in the Syndicate it was widely felt that the timing of this find was tactless, to say the least. And far worse was to follow. The Lichtenburg mines were rich, and the prospectors who were digging up the stones were not governed by the existing rules of marketing, for these were alluvial diamonds and the control laws had been formulated only for diamonds of the crater mines, extracted from blue-ground matrix. The Lichtenburg diggers happily returned to the old rough-and-ready methods of the eighties, selling their finds wherever they could for whatever they could get. Because of the new plenty this was not as much as the Syndicate had been getting for their controlled-price stones. To keep themselves from being swamped in the flood, the Syndicate members bought up as much of this output as they could, which as the flow continued proved a dangerously expensive proceeding. The industry was still reeling from the shock when a geologist, Dr. Hans Merensky, prospecting the Crown lands of Namaqualand south of the old German territory border, made his historically lucky strike and disclosed the fabulous coastal terrace deposits of Alexander Bay.

For some time Oppenheimer had been urging De Beers to

take alluvial deposits seriously enough to include them in their
controlled areas: the old-timers, however, worried though they
were by developments, refused to budge. Alluvials had never
bothered them much in the early days; alluvials were just alluvials; no doubt this emergency would pass and all would be
as it had been before, without any action on their part. While
they sat quiet and shook their heads over the expense of buying
up the new stones, and possessed themselves in patience, and
waited for the flood to subside, that flood rose higher and
higher. Oppenheimer was in London during the worst of it.
He cabled a strong warning to De Beers, and got a reply that
he still recollects in scorn, "stating that Rhodes had said in
1893 that alluvial diamonds did not interest him. . . . Can
you imagine such an attitude? At the time when alluvial production was increasing and the market was flooded with alluvial diamonds, De Beers refused to recognize the danger from
this source to the whole industry. I suggested that De Beers
immediately incorporate all the alluvial mines, but my proposal
was turned down."

Sir Ernest decided to act without the lethargic directors, and
bypass them. He roused friends who were able and willing to
help, and in combination they hurried to buy for themselves
as much land as possible in the Lichtenburg and Namaqualand
areas.

Gradually the old guard at De Beers began to listen to Oppenheimer. In 1926, yielding to pressure from a powerful group
of shareholders, it had appointed him to the company's board
of directors, and from then on he was able to wage his battle
from the inside. Then, in 1929, just before the stock-market
crash in New York, a fresh crisis overtook the diamond trade.

At the time, De Beers had no chairman—only an acting chairman. The company's need of a strong leader was obvious. The De Beers board had a special meeting in Cape Town, and in the course of it Sir Ernest referred pointedly to the large interests that he had in the industry—in South-West Africa, Namaqualand, and Lichtenburg—and the other directors reluctantly realized that here at least was a man who seemed to know what to do. They elected him chairman—almost, as it were, on his own proposal. "You see, I had clear ideas," he said recently, recollecting.

Oppenheimer needed clear ideas during the months and years that followed this remarkable maneuver, for the diamond industry had a rough time of it during the depression. Immediately after his appointment as chairman of De Beers, he took action on a variety of fronts, and the result was the massive monopolistic structure that is De Beers today. He had De Beers buy out Anglo American's interest in Consolidated Diamond Mines and in the alluvial field, thereby welding the producers into a firmer unit than any envisaged since the days of Rhodes. Then, he set up a firm called the Diamond Corporation, capitalized by producers and dealers alike, to buy up alluvial stones and control their prices. Before long, this replaced the Syndicate, taking over the latter's business in crater-mine diamonds, which was rapidly becoming little more than a matter of sitting on surplus stones that nobody wanted except at ruinously low prices. As the market bogged down, operations in the mines again faltered, slowed to a crawl, then ceased altogether. Well aware that when times are hard miners and dealers alike, no matter how thoroughly organized, are sorely tempted to cut prices, Oppenheimer made personal appeals to scores of dia-

mond men in South Africa, extolling the advantages of solidar-
ity, pointing out the dangers of a go-it-alone policy, and beg-
ging them to hold the price line; he made a tour of England,
Holland, Belgium, and France, carrying the same message to
diamond traders wherever he went. As time passed and the
mines remained closed, it began to look as if the whole industry
might collapse, but in the dead hush of the shutdown Oppenheimer persevered with such success that when things began
to pick up again he had not only all the former members of the
Syndicate and the alluvial-mine owners lined up behind him
but also producers in the Belgian Congo, West Africa, and the
Portuguese colony of Angola, three regions in which alluvial
deposits had only recently been discovered.

In 1933, Oppenheimer set up a subsidiary firm called the
Diamond Trading Company to serve as the sole channel
through which the diamond producers sold their wares. Inevitably, such an out-and-out and large-scale monopoly brought
cries of indignation from certain quarters, prompting the South
African Government to appoint a commission to look into the
matter, but the commission accomplished little and was finally
disbanded. Oppenheimer was convinced that if the diamond
industry was to survive, it had to be a monopoly. As he saw it,
competition in diamond trading is of necessity unhealthy because of the limited number of diamond deposits in the world
and the hard fact that there are just so many stones still to be
mined; these would soon all be taken out of the ground if mine
operators were given a free hand, and this, of course, would
mean the end of the industry. But it would not die in a blaze
of glory, because while the mining companies were breathlessly
digging away, in furious competition with one another, and

dealers were dumping their output on the market, the price of diamonds would fall disastrously. The thousands of employees in the industry—miners, assayers, cutters and so on—would suffer as much as the financiers, if not more, from such a sudden dislocation, Oppenheimer pointed out, and in the end no one would profit. The death of the industry had to come someday, but he felt that everything possible should be done to forestall it. And monopoly was the only answer.

Oppenheimer lives in Parktown, a residential section on the outskirts of Johannesburg. His house, Brenthurst, sits well back in a forty-acre plot of ground. It is a white house with the big-roomed and high-ceilinged architecture that people living in warm climates usually develop. Sir Ernest's first wife, Mary, died about twenty years ago: he is now married to the widow of his nephew, who was the son of his brother Bernard. The nephew was named Sir Michael Oppenheimer, so Sir Ernest's wife, who was Miss Caroline Harvey, has been Lady Oppenheimer twice. The fact that her son by her first husband is in his turn Sir Michael Oppenheimer, and that *his* wife is thus also Lady Oppenheimer, doesn't make matters any easier for a newcomer to the Oppenheimer family circle.

Sir Ernest's days in Johannesburg follow a set routine. He goes to his office at nine and deals with business, spending much of the time in conference with his son Harry. He has never been one of those great minds for little things. He likes the theory of affairs, but the executive details don't fascinate him and he delegates them to a number of helpers. They say he is a good man to work for: he doesn't interfere. A little past twelve he knocks off and has a whisky and soda, and then he goes home. He is always at home for lunch and usually he doesn't return to his office. For several years, under the mistaken impression that he had diabetes, he followed a strict diet, but now he has a doctor who recently decided he hasn't got diabetes at all, so life at Brenthurst has relaxed accordingly.

One evening not so long ago there was a small dinner party at Brenthurst. Lady Oppenheimer's sister Lady Balfour was there, and a few people from Anglo American with their wives.

Sir Ernest was asked by one of the Anglo American men about one of his recent donations to a library somewhere in the States. Lady Oppenheimer was surprised, and in the amused tone of a woman who never knows what is coming next, she asked, "But Ernest, *are* you a librarian? What is this library?"

"No . . . no, I'm not a librarian," he said, looking confused by the table's attention. "Only, if you give money to one organization the others all expect it too. This Queen Elizabeth House has brought a lot of requests."

He had been pleasantly engaged that afternoon with some of his pictures that had just arrived from England, where the Oppenheimers used to keep a flat they have now given up. He took the guests after dinner to look at them where they stood on the floor, propped against chairs and tables in a ring as they had been all day while their owner made up his mind where to hang them.

"Here is a Sisley, and this I'm very fond of, this Renoir," he said. "But have you seen my Goya? Come and look. She's in here."

The Goya, a portrait of a woman in court dress, hung in a library. "Who is it?" asked one of the women.

"A duchess," Sir Ernest replied absently.

The party talked, inevitably, about diamonds, especially about a big stone that was recently found on the grease tables of the Premier Mine. It is one of the most beautiful specimens ever found, and the guests had heard a rumor that Sir Ernest wanted to buy it himself. He is not like a lot of diamond men who are bored by their own stock in trade and whose wives never wear such things. Lady Oppenheimer's diamonds are famous, and she enjoys wearing them, though not in profusion. Someone once asked her if it is true that she has a diamond of every color in the spectrum, and she seemed surprised.

"Oh no," she said. "I have a few colored stones, it's true, but not as many as all that. I have a blue, of course. And a pink. And——" She paused, looking thoughtful. "Come to think of it," she said, "I'm not exactly *underfed* with diamonds."

Now Sir Ernest talked eagerly about the new stone. "It is beautiful," he said. "It is lovely. I wish I owned it."

A guest asked, "Why don't you buy it, then?"

"It would cost a lot of money," said Sir Ernest.


"Politics were different then," said Harry Oppenheimer one day when he was talking of his father's experiences as a Member of Parliament. Like most political careers in South Africa, Harry's is stormy. "The House wasn't the same then; it was quieter, because it represented a much more restricted group. Men in his position had things more their own way."

Sir Ernest as a Member did have an occasional fight on his hands, especially when he first took his seat in 1924. To go to the House of Assembly was part of the tradition of South Africa, inherited from Britain, though it was very much to his taste in any case. If you were one of the privileged classes— and thanks to diamonds and gold a lot of whites were privileged —you sought election as a matter of course. Rhodes went beyond that; he was Prime Minister until the Jameson Raid forced him to resign. Jameson himself was Premier later. Many De Beers directors, notably Barney Barnato, had sat in Parliament, and Sir Ernest like Barney—and Harry like Sir Ernest— faced the accusation that he was nothing but a tool of the big business interests. But it was indeed different, as Harry said, in the twenties. South Africa's interests were then almost indistinguishable from that same big business, and the taunt was rhetorical rather than sensible. Bitter Boer nationalist spirit hadn't yet pushed the Afrikaner party into power. Afrikaners were still overwhelmed by British superiority in education and knowledge of world affairs. In that atmosphere, Sir Ernest's liberal sentiments did not afford the contrast they do today.

As his son and heir, Harry finds himself when he is in the House of Assembly the representative of a body of concerns that occupies a peculiar position. In almost any other country in the world, modern fashion would point at a great firm like Anglo American with accusatory forefinger as the epitome of reaction. A monopoly based on exploitation of the lesser breeds. A crowd of money-grabbing, power-grabbing millionaires. Haughty wealth in the saddle, riding down the lower classes. The trouble with this picture is that in South Africa wealth isn't in the saddle. The Oppenheimers are strong supporters of the United party, which is in opposition to the Nationalists who control the country. The United party has been out of office for seven years, and there are certainly no signs at the moment of its getting back in. As things are counted in South Africa, the Oppenheimers are dangerous radicals. They believe in the advancement of what politicians there always refer to as the "native." They treat the native too well, for according to the Nationalists their rate of pay boosts the wage scale of everybody else who uses native labor, and their welfare policy is equally difficult to compete with. They've got to be watched, moreover, lest they import dangerous ideas from Rhodesia, where the native (who suffers a land change at the border and in Rhodesia suddenly becomes, politically speaking, the African instead) is as a matter of policy due for advancement. There is the Copper Belt of Northern Rhodesia, where the Anglo American Corporation of Rhodesia is developing a group of mines. Sir Ernest has done something on a grand scale there in building whole townships of comfortable houses for the African workers, where they live with their families and send their children to school. He proposed doing the same thing in the gold fields of the Orange Free State. He thought, and he still thinks, that workers who are contented will do better work, and they are more likely to be contented if they live with their families near their jobs than if they are pent up in barracklike compounds as they are at Johannesburg. But the South African Government didn't like the idea at all. This would never do, the Ministers concerned explained, because such action would create new, permanent "black spots" in the middle of white country. Sir Ernest wasn't permitted to put up his buildings, and the Nationalists were more than ever convinced that you must be very, very careful with Anglo American. There is also the suspicious fact that Sir Ernest is interested in the University

of Witwatersrand and has from time to time endowed it in one
way or another. As everybody knows, universities are hotbeds
of radicalism—Wits University especially, because it accepts
native as well as white students. Indeed it seems probable that
if the Oppenheimers weren't so important to the country's
economy they wouldn't be suffered at all. It is not long since a
Minister, enraged by a criticism from Harry in the House,
shouted across to the Opposition benches, "Perhaps we'd better
raise taxation on the mines. How would you like that?"

"They talk," said Sir Ernest. "They talk, but they don't carry
out half what they threaten against us."

Harry is not quite so confident, quite possibly because he is
very much in the thick of things and gets around a great deal
more than his father. It is one thing to observe the parliamentary battle from your own home, and quite another to be taking
part in it. As for getting around, in a very literal sense Harry
is constantly on the go. He is deputy chairman of Anglo
American as well as director of De Beers and an imposing list
of other companies. Quite apart from the talent required for
these various tasks, it isn't easy to manage them all from a
geographical point of view. Harry's main business office is, of
course, in the Anglo American building in Johannesburg, and
he is domiciled in that city, but the House of Assembly is in
Cape Town, eight hundred miles off. Therefore when the
House is sitting he spends the week in Cape Town, where he
and his wife have found and refurbished an old house in the
middle of the Malay quarter, near the parliamentary buildings.
His wife Bridget doesn't mind commuting on this rather
breath-taking scale, but it all takes time. Harry flies back to
Johannesburg for long weekends and attends to his business

affairs on these occasions; in moments of urgency he comes back in the middle of the week when necessary. But his constituency is Kimberley, and he has a stud farm nearby at Mauritzfontein. He is very fond of the farm, so he manages to stop off now and then, Kimberley being roughly halfway between Johannesburg and Cape Town. When the House isn't in session there are a lot of places Harry must visit from time to time—his farm in Southern Rhodesia, and the Copper Belt, and Tanganyika, and the Congo, and, now that his son Nicholas is going there to boarding school, England at least twice a year.

In South Africa they don't subscribe any more to the old axiom about remarkable fathers having unremarkable children. They haven't had time to think about it since Harry Oppenheimer grew up. Instead, a lot of the old-timers are apt to declare aggressively that, given time, Harry might well outstrip his father in business acumen. You can't generalize from the particular, but his case is an argument in favor of the theory of heredity, instead of environment, shaping our ends, because Harry's youth and training have been completely unlike his father's. Sir Ernest had the ordinary schooling of a boy in a small German town, and he went to work at the age of sixteen. Circumstances forced him to specialize immediately: he learned all the rest of it from experience, though he learned unusually fast. Harry attended one of the best schools in Johannesburg— and Johannesburg has very good schools—until he was old enough to be sent to public school in England. He went to Charterhouse and then Christ Church, Oxford, where he took an honors degree in Modern Greats. (Modern Greats is sometimes known instead as P.P.E., that is, politics, philosophy, and economics.)

He is a little taller than his father, with dark hair and eyes. Like Sir Ernest he wears a mustache, but they don't really resemble each other very much: Harry is supposed to be more like his mother, Mary. He is compactly built: in the British tradition he keeps very fit with squash and riding. He moves quickly; somehow he gets out of or into a room with great dispatch but no fuss at all. He talks rather quickly. "He is an excellent listener," to quote the "Portrait Gallery" feature of the London *Sunday Times* in 1955, just a year after that paper's profile of his father appeared, "but the sensitive can recognize in a faraway look his slight impatience with a slower thinker who elaborates a point that he has grasped several minutes before." Harry was unaware of that trick until he read the article: he tries now to control it. Like Sir Ernest, he is really shy: this, too, he tries to control, because shyness isn't very useful in parliamentary debate.

The younger Oppenheimers' Johannesburg house is called Little Brenthurst, more in deference to the head of the family than in consideration of the relative size of the two structures. At any rate it is big enough to house the collection, made originally by Sir Ernest, of Africana: all the books that he could find dealing with South Africa's history and development. The first flush of literature on this subject (as distinguished from the second one which is going on right now) occurred in the days when books were really books. Publishers ran to big, heavy, two-volume works illustrated with plates on thick paper, bound in heavy gilt-tooled leather. These, with a number of smaller but equally elaborate volumes from the same

period, look very well in Harry's big drawing room. They are
keeping company with some unusual, very fine pieces of Chinese porcelain. On the high mantelpiece are a few late seventeenth-century plates bearing the insignia of the Dutch East
India Company. This company, of course, founded Cape
Town. There aren't a lot of the plates around any more.

"But I don't collect from a historical point of view," said
Harry one evening before dinner when his guests commented
on the Chinese pieces. "I don't really collect at all in the true
sense of the word. Collectors fix on one sort of thing at a time,
don't they? I just buy a thing now and then if it has beauty."

It was shortly before nine-year-old Nicholas was to leave for
England and his first term at boarding school, and Harry's wife
had gone upstairs to try to persuade the youngster, and the Oppenheimers' other child, twelve-year-old Mary, that the time
had come to go to bed. Sounds of giggling and scuffling at the
head of the staircase indicated that her efforts were not proving
altogether successful. Gradually, however, things became quiet
overhead, and then Mrs. Oppenheimer returned to the drawing
room. "Those children!" she said to her husband. "They simply
won't settle down. They were having a pillow fight and one of
the pillows came down the stairs."

An important debate was pending in the House of Assembly,
following on the annual presentation of "the budget" by the
Minister of Finance and a formal request to the government to
vote funds for the coming year's administration. For some years
now, Harry Oppenheimer's speech for the Opposition in reply
to the budget has been acknowledged as the high point of the
political year; it is a social event.

It was the third week in March. South Africa's winter was approaching, but in Cape Town the sun was still so hot at noonday that the beaches were deserted: the white children didn't come out with their colored nurses until after tea. Cape Town is a very old city and it retains a stately, provincial flavor. Friends of the young Oppenheimers exclaim at their ill-advised originality in having bought the house they have, protesting that it is in a noisy, unrestful part of the city. Other Cape people, who can afford to, live well outside, at the beach or in the woods, indulging in gardens and other bucolic luxuries. Sir Ernest keeps a house at Muizenburg, some miles from the city center. But the visitor from our industrialized Northern Hemisphere doesn't find the young Oppenheimers' neighborhood all that citified. It is a lovely little house, with a plain front in pink stucco, facing a street that slopes steeply; and in the back there is a courtyard shaded by tall trees and cooled by a small ornamental pool. Over the high courtyard wall the top of a mosque, gathering place of Cape Malays, is just visible. The muezzin had appeared on his gallery and called the faithful to prayers and gone in again: night was imminent but had not yet fallen. A small party was gathered in the courtyard for a drink before dinner. Oppenheimer was looking moody.

"How ridiculous politics is!" he said suddenly. "Take this budget. There's nothing in it this year, absolutely nothing, yet I have got to find something to discuss, merely because it's the custom."

The next day Mrs. Oppenheimer presided at the lunch table without her husband, explaining to her guests—a touring Englishman and a man from the office in Johannesburg—that he was already at the House, as his turn to speak would come early in the afternoon. The party must arrive in plenty of time as there was apt to be a crowd in the visitors' gallery for the occasion. The talk at table was political. There are always points of discussion between the Nationalist and the United parties that are good for conversation. Finally Mrs. Oppenheimer interrupted with the news that it was time to go. As she drove the short distance to the House of Assembly she explained further to the newly arrived Englishman that the first answer to the budget was being made at that very moment, probably, by Mr. Waterson, the Member for Constantia. He was to move various changes in the Minister of Finance's program, on behalf of the United party. Of course the changes wouldn't stand a chance of being voted in, but it was a necessary gesture for the Opposition to make: it was part of the game. Oppenheimer was to follow up by seconding the motion, and would take off from there.

The solid, handsome building, fronting a tree-bordered street, looked unusually animated, with a crowd moving slowly in at the entrance. There were many women dressed to the nines in pretty summery costumes: white hats, white shoes, linen or silk dresses; they all went indoors and climbed the stairs to the gallery. Mrs. Oppenheimer settled her party into one of the small compartments like shallow theatrical boxes that were built directly over the Nationalist side of the House, so that they looked down at the United party members across the way. Before departing to the special gallery reserved for family connections, she gave the Englishman one last explanation of an unusual and fascinating feature of South African parliamentary custom: the proceedings are bilingual. As a matter of policy, Nationalist Members make their speeches in Afrikaans.

The United party reply to them in English. This, too, is more or less a matter of policy, but it is also because some of them can't speak Afrikaans anyway. When today's adults in South Africa were school children, they spoke English at school, no matter what they learned at home, so that children of English extraction often grew up knowing only the few words of Afrikaans that they had picked up from servants and the occasional Afrikaner playmate. Today's children will presumably be better fitted to cope with difficulties in the House of Assembly because Afrikaans is now compulsorily taught in the state schools. But that is all in the future, and in the meantime conscientious M.P.s of British descent, of whom there are quite a few in the United party, must either brush up on the language this late in the day or wait until they can read the Nationalist speeches in translation. One of the ways in which Harry Oppenheimer annoys his opponents is by being fluent in Afrikaans.

The room is modeled on the Chamber of Commons in the British Houses of Parliament, but it is slightly smaller and the ceilings are not so high that members look like midgets, as they do in London. Nor are the benches benches: they are seats with desks in front of them, like school desks, placed in pairs. One of the Nationalists was on his feet speaking as the Oppenheimer party came in. Nobody seemed to listen. Members drifted through the door, bowed to the head of the room where the Speaker was sitting, and took their seats and talked to each other and generally behaved as carelessly and informally as the audience in a Chinese theater. In the crowded gallery, visitors found seats or went away disappointed. Mr. Waterson had not yet begun: now he took the floor.

In spite of Oppenheimer's complaint that there was nothing either to praise or attack in the budget, his party had managed to think of a few criticisms after all. Mr. Waterson listed them and made the motion that had been agreed upon. He expounded the United party's objections to certain proposed methods of taxation. He urged the government to "take active steps to relieve the acute shortage of manpower." He proposed that they "produce concrete plans for reducing the cost of living." There were routine attacks, but the fourth and last item touched on a very sore point: "to restrain the Minister of Native Affairs whose policies and activities threaten the progress and prosperity of the Union." At this the House and visitors all pricked up their ears. For some weeks the Minister of Native Affairs, Dr. Verwoerd, had been hitting the headlines with suggested implementations of *apartheid*. Though his ideas were startlingly comprehensive and embraced the possibility of complete segregation of the races in all walks of life, it was his statements dealing with domestic labor that was eliciting most comment among the people who can afford to pay for such labor. (Many poor Afrikaners cannot, and they love Dr. Verwoerd.) He said that the native should not serve in white people's houses in such propinquity, and that white housewives can perfectly well do their own work. For that matter it would do them good, he said; look at the pioneer women of the Voortrekkers! His other statements may not have been quite as attention-getting among white women, but they were pretty newsworthy at that, and Mr. Waterson now recalled them to mind.

"The Minister of Native Affairs talks—my goodness how he talks!—about 'trends' and 'directions' and he explains this and

he hedges on that, but he makes it perfectly clear that his ulti-
mate aim is a white South Africa side by side with a black South
Africa. A white South Africa in which, according to the Minister of Labor, the white woman will scrub her own floors and
the farmer will not, as at present, confine himself to riding in
his car to the co-operative society to collect his check whilst
coloreds and Natives sit on the tractor and plough and plant
and reap, and side by side with that a black South Africa self-
sufficient in its own territories. On the one hand industry and
agriculture is being worried and harassed with continual lec-
tures by the Minister of Native Affairs on the necessity of employing the minimum amount of non-European labor, because
gradually, according to his policy, it will disappear. On the
other hand there is not the slightest indication on the financial
side that the Government has even begun to think about the
implications of it all and of the necessity of making the Native
reserves capable of supporting this Native population which
must ultimately, under the direction of the Minister of Native
Affairs and the Minister of Labor, make its home there. . . .
Let the honorable Minister, and let everybody in this House,
remember that no manpower means no capital, no development, and no revenue. . . . Yet the Minister of the Interior
goes to Worcester, and if he is correctly reported, he begged
the industrialists whom he addressed there to use the minimum possible of Native labor. . . . These gentlemen are not
talking about a drop in the ocean, but they are talking about
80 per cent of the total amount of labor to be employed in our
economy."

It was all very reasonable, well arranged and nicely said, but
there was no fire in it: it was cool and gentlemanly and that

was all. When Waterson sat down, however, the House began to stir, and in the gallery people leaned forward. This was what they had come for. Harry Oppenheimer stood up.

He started on a calm note, easygoing and personal, like a man who hasn't thought out beforehand what he is going to say—unlike Waterson, he didn't use notes—yet it became obvious as he went along that he knew precisely what he was up to. He criticized a proposed gift tax and a proposed tax on dividends from outside South Africa. As he got into the theme his manner grew even more easy: he talked rapidly and clearly, swaying a little with the rhythm of the words.

". . . Now the Minister here is concerned with tackling an evil, a distinct evil, but a specific evil. He is trying to tackle the position which arises when a man, in order to avoid tax, transfers dividends which are earned in the Union to a company outside the Union, say in Rhodesia or South-West Africa, and gets back these profits as dividends from the company outside the Union and thus evades paying tax," Oppenheimer declared. "The Minister is quite right to stop that, but I must say that I think that on the face of it, it must be wrong to tackle a specific evil of that sort by throwing overboard what is a fundamental concept and has always been a fundamental concept in our taxation system. Because as long as I can remember (and no doubt longer) it has been a principle of taxation in South Africa that taxation should not be paid on income arising outside the country. Now the measure which the honorable Minister is proposing in the first place is going to have the effect to give the people a strong inducement—the people whom the Minister is trying to attack—to keep their profits outside the country, and to re-invest those profits outside the country, and so the honorable Minister in that way will not only lose the tax, but the country will lose the benefit of the profits also."

After attacking the Nationalists' restrictive immigration laws in a voice that became suddenly angry, Oppenheimer turned to the subject of Verwoerd's policy toward the Native. Verwoerd had announced, in one of his speeches, that there were to be no new industrial townships created in the Witwatersrand, and therefore no more "black spots" to worry segregationists. Henceforth, he had thus implied, mines must be found that were tactfully located near the borderline between white and black communities, but nobody was to worry about any consequent slowing down of industry since there is "already enough industrial ground open on the Witwatersrand to be sufficient for all possible requirements for ten years or more." Oppenheimer had some angry fun with that, making the House laugh several times, and he made a few hits at the chronic trouble faced by all employers in South Africa, where Native workers are kept out of all but the lowest-paid, least-skilled jobs.

It was an extraordinarily interesting performance—one that has perhaps not been necessary for a politician in any other country to put on since the days when Hitler was just coming into power in Germany. Oppenheimer was speaking against a party of determined, dangerously ignorant people, on behalf of a far more sophisticated, liberal group. He was addressing both these groups, and he had to hit a balance between their standards so that the message not only attacked on the Nationalist plane, but attracted and held the attention of the United party. In apparently succeeding he sounded like what he is, a man well trained in Britain. But a man born and reared in Britain could not have pulled off the trick in Cape Town.

No sooner had Oppenheimer sat down than the visitors in the gallery, as one man, stood up and started out. The business of the day was not over in the House, but for the spectators it was. A Nationalist Member took the floor and started to talk in Afrikaans, while upstairs the ladies in their white hats, the gentlemen in their dark coats, were moving in a great flood through the passageways, greeting each other with smiles and gushing little comments, drifting, in a mass, down and out to their shiny motor cars under the trees on the boulevard.

# CHAPTER SIX

# The Cutters

In 1887 most British thought that their country was getting along pretty well. Not so, said Mr. Lewis Atkinson, writing to *The Times*. Because of the stupid intolerance of their ancestors under Edward I, six centuries before, the British had sacrificed a thriving trade, that of diamond cutting, and British gem owners were having to ship uncut stones over to Holland and Belgium, "at great risk and expense," to be cut and set; and it was all due to the long-ago expulsion of the Jews. As director of the newly established Diamond Cutting Company, Mr. Atkinson wanted the state of affairs remedied as soon as possible. He was telling the truth when he said that there were very few men in the kingdom capable of cutting jewels, and his words attracted attention, but if he had brought up the matter only a few years earlier he would have found it very hard to work up any English interest, however accurate his report. It was the recent discovery of diamond mines in South Africa that had started Mr. Atkinson and his friends thinking about what they had lost, and growing belatedly indignant about religious intolerance.

As he pointed out, the diamond-cutting industry has always wandered about, following the peregrinations of world Jewry. Jewish domination of the industry dates back to the Middle Ages, when anti-Semitic guild laws rendered it impossible for Jews to take part in more than a few clearly stipulated trades. It was not so much that other people weren't permitted to cut diamonds as that Jews weren't permitted to do very many other jobs. They concentrated on jewel dealing and jewel cutting and polishing, until they had a large part of the trade and the majority of the cutting industry in their control. Jewel fanciers were apt to discover too late that anti-Semitism had great disadvantages: that when you expelled Jews you expelled their special talents as well. During the Inquisition, Portugal lost a splendid and famous group of cutters, who fled to the Low Countries, France, and England. Thereafter any fidalgo with a rough stone he wanted to have cut and set had to send it all the way to Amsterdam, Antwerp, Paris, or London, and, as Mr. Atkinson sorrowfully pointed out, London lost the trade a little later when her Jews were pushed out to the Continent. During the years preceding the South African discoveries, this fact didn't wreak any ostensible hardship on the British public: people had got used to sending jewels for polishing, when they had any, to Holland or Belgium. There weren't a lot of diamonds floating around, in any case. The early days of glory in India had stimulated the jewel trade about a hundred years before, as witness some of the East India Company's inventories, or the dazzling customs list of Mrs. Warren Hastings' possessions when she came back to live in England, but this excitement was dying down: India's mines were nearly worked out, and even Brazil's were an old story. After 1871 and the beginning of Kimberley, however, things changed. New, beautiful, big stones were coming on the market in London; jewels that needed expert handling. And where were those experts? Alas, they were still across the Channel, and the stones had to be shipped over to them "at great risk and expense," as Mr. Atkinson so truly pointed out. However, he added in happier vein, the efforts of his group to establish a new center in London were meeting with success. His associates were encouraging Dutch and Belgian cutters to let bygones be bygones and emigrate once more to England.

In thus handing the palm to the cutters of the Low Countries, Mr. Atkinson was possibly activated by a guilty conscience; the conscience of all knowledgeable gem men who had recently seen the Koh-i-nur. It wasn't a thing to admit openly, but they knew it nevertheless to be true that the Koh-i-nur, star of the crown jewels, that famous giant that had recently come into Queen Victoria's possession after nobody knew how many centuries' experience of blood and rapine, had been practically ruined in the cutting. In London at that, under the very eyes of royalty itself. It was a tricky business meddling with the reputations of famous stones, and it was trickier yet to insinuate that the royal family would have done better to trust such a treasure to people who understood their business. However, there it was; the thing was done.

Europeans have long been more particular than Indians about diamond cutting. This is odd, because until lately the East has been the traditional source of the world's jewels, but it is true. Perhaps it is just that Indians are satisfied to let well enough alone. Of course the more westernized of the rich men of India now have their treasures cut and set as carefully as

anybody else, but you often see Indian ladies wearing necklaces
and rings of uncut rubies, sapphires, or diamonds. It isn't that
Indian jewelers didn't try. In the early days when European
merchants brought back pretty stones for sale it was noted that
an occasional attempt had already been made to polish these
rough jewels. The men at the mines must have got the idea
from looking at natural crystals, especially those of diamonds,
which with their regular facets and sharp points often do look
remarkably fashioned, as if they had already been cut by man.
(Pliny described diamond crystals very accurately as colorless
and transparent, with polished facets and two points like two
whipping tops joined together at their bases.) With these as
models the dealers probably attempted to improve other diamonds that were not regularly shaped, grinding facets where
no facets were. It was a formidable task. Nothing cuts diamond
but diamond, so that one stone had to be ground against another by hand, a process that might easily run into months of
work. There is a short cut for making some of the facets, however, which the jewelers must have discovered by accident, possibly disastrously. Diamonds will split comparatively easily in
certain directions. Conversely, grinding them against this grain
is extremely difficult. Nobody tries to do this even today, on a
motor-run polishing disk, because a diamond ground the wrong
way simply gouges out the disk. There are other methods.

While the philosophical Indians were content to sell uncut
or half-cut stones, the restless Europeans got busy at improving
them. About the end of the thirteenth century a guild of gem
polishers and cutters was founded in Paris. The members probably worked more on sapphires and rubies than diamonds,
though diamonds were by no means unknown. The inventory

of the jewels of Louis d'Anjou in 1368 listed some cut diamonds, but they weren't big ones: the Indian rulers who owned
the mines always kept for themselves any finds bigger than
about ten carats, so only the little stuff was exported. Later another guild was formed in Nuremberg, not exclusively of jewel
cutters. There were some stone engravers there too, of whom
Gutenberg was one. (He could cut and polish gems with the
best of them.) The traveler Sir John Mandeville, who at this
time was making his famous journey in the East, knew what
diamonds looked like, but some of his ideas as to their source
were picturesque. They were found, he said, in the north of
India, "so cold a country that for the great cold and continual
frost the water congeals into crystal (i.e. quartz). And upon
the rock of crystal grow good diamonds that are of the color
of crystal, but they are more dim colored than the crystal and
brown as oil. And they are so hard that there may be no metal
polish them ne break them. . . . And they are four cornered
of their own growing and four square. And they grow together,
male and female; and they are nourished with dew of heaven.
And they engender and conceive, as it were, in their kind and
bring forth small childer, and so they multiply and grow al-
way. I have many times assayed and seen that if a man take
them with a little of the rock that they grow on, so that they
be taken up by the roots and oft sythes wet with the dew of
May, they grow ilk a year visibly, so that the small wax great."

Until a few years ago some Indian diggers held similar be-
liefs; perhaps they still do, though the fact that the Russians
are developing the ancient mine at Panna may have brought
them more sophistication. The great gem authority Edwin
W. Streeter wrote, "There is an erroneous impression among

the poor miners that the Diamonds grow in and about the huge fragments of the crust of the earth which has been heaved and broken up. Among the natives of the Madras Presidency, there exists a curious belief that the rock crystal, which occurs in the diamantiferous ground, will become Diamond when impregnated with electricity by the action of lightning."

The craftsmen of Nuremberg improved their technique; so did the cutters in Paris. The Duke of Burgundy in 1407 gave a banquet in the Louvre to the King and his court, and presented to his guests as party favors eleven diamonds set in gold. They were cut, probably, by a man named Hermann who had quite a name for dexterity. From the description, modern cutters think that these eleven stones, though by no means perfect, must have shown some rudiments of the true art of cutting, which consists in making the best possible use of the play of light. About fifty years after this banquet a Paris-trained cutter named Louis de Berquem moved to Antwerp and set up in an atelier there. He carried the art of faceting stones to such a degree that in the end he revised the whole system of cutting and evolved the pattern as it is known today. He cut three big stones for the Duke of Burgundy that immediately became famous among diamond fanciers all over Europe. The biggest, the Beau Sancy, had already been cut once, Indian fashion, in a random lot of facets all over its surface. Louis de Berquem made a complete new job of it and much enhanced the diamond's beauty. His pupils carried the light far and wide, and diamonds grew more and more sparkly. For two hundred years thereafter, Mr. Atkinson said in his letter to *The Times*, cutting went on in England just as it did in France and

the Low Countries, and the "old English cutters" were regarded
as the best workmen of all. This is not necessarily true: Mr.
Atkinson was grinding an ax rather than diamonds; but it is at
least possible that British workmen did, as he claimed, bear a
good name for their treatment of colored stones. Paris outdid
them, though, in fashionable reputation. Cardinal Mazarin
loved diamonds and that meant that everybody else in the *haut
monde* did, too: as long as he lived the French cutters flour-
ished. After his death in 1661, however, the French cutters fell
off nearly as badly as the English did, and so it went until the
discoveries of the mines of South Africa. There were very few
men who knew how to cut in France, and only one could be
found in all of London in 1869, whereas in Amsterdam there
were at least ten thousand. Nevertheless the Koh-i-nur had to
be cut in London. To understand the situation it would be as
well to go back again from Victorian England, but only two
hundred years this time, to Tavernier.

Jean Baptiste Tavernier was born in France at the beginning
of the seventeenth century, of a Protestant Belgian family that
had fled their country for the same reason so many cutters did,
to escape religious persecution. He was a jewel merchant who
traveled extensively, mostly in the Far East. It is apparent that
though he could reasonably claim his work forced him to make
the long, arduous voyages for which he became noted, he really
simply loved to travel. In the course of his life Tavernier completed six long voyages. As an old man he settled down to enjoy a prosperous existence, but when he was eighty-four he set
out again on a seventh journey. He said he had to do it because
his son had made reckless speculations, but I think he didn't
really mind. In any case he died on the way, of a fever, and

was buried near Moscow. One of the many people who have written up the histories of famous jewels tries to make out that he was a victim of the notorious curse said to follow the Hope diamond, for the Hope is a piece of a much bigger blue diamond, called the Blue Tavernier, which the traveler brought back from India and sold to the King of France. But surely it is stretching things rather far to say that it would take a powerful curse to kill a man of eighty-four, even a tough egg like Tavernier. Take it all in all, he could hardly be described as the accursed type. He looks very hearty in the portrait that serves as frontispiece to my copy of his works, a well-known edition by Professor Valentine Ball. In this he wears a splendid robe encrusted with gold embroidery under a fur cape, with a big turban, a costume given him by a royal Indian client.

The Koh-i-nur is one of those diamonds that have acquired personalities of their own and are spoken of by people in the trade almost as if they were flesh-and-blood personages in history. Rolling stones do gather moss. The Sancy, the Koh-i-nur, the Regent, and the rest of them have gathered a lot of it, sagas too long to be repeated here. Even longer than the sagas are the footnotes. Historians lead strenuous lives in their bookish way, and one of the hottest arguments that stirred their scholarly desks in the past century was that of the Great Mogul and its relation to the Koh-i-nur. Were they or were they not the same stone? Streeter didn't think so. Professor Ball, who edited Tavernier, was convinced that they were and that Streeter was wrong. With careful arguments based on weights and possibilities he convinced a number of people, including me. Even if Professor Ball and I are wrong, one thing at least cannot be disputed: that the Great Mogul disappeared from the record some time before the Koh-i-nur made its appearance. Tavernier never heard of any Koh-i-nur, but his introduction to the Great Mogul is one of the most fascinating sections of his journal.

He saw it when he was visiting the court of Aurangzeb, the last of the really strong Mogul emperors of India, in 1665. He had been there for some time pursuing his calling in the normal way, buying and selling jewels, and he was about to take his leave when the Emperor invited him to stay on for a bit and witness the annual festival. According to Moslem custom, familiar to us because of the Aga Khan's publicized activities, Aurangzeb would be weighed in public and would receive presents on that occasion from the nobles of his court, the governors of his provinces, and so on. He probably invited Tavernier to stay on because he liked him. People usually did, especially when like the Emperor they made jewels their hobby. Besides extending the general invitation, Aurangzeb offered to let Tavernier see his private, special collection of choice jewels, among which was the famous Great Mogul. Tavernier of course jumped at the chance, and wrote at length in his journal about the whole thing. First he described the preparations for the great ceremony, wallowing in thoughts of how profitable it all was to the Emperor. "In diamonds, rubies, emeralds, pearls, gold, and silver, as well as rich carpets, brocades of gold and silver, and other stuffs, elephants, camels, and horses, the Emperor receives in presents on this day the value of more than 30,000,000 livres."

Apparently he was allowed to snoop around the palace very much as he liked, watching the workmen get everything ready. The courtyards were covered for the occasion with awnings "of red velvet embroidered with gold," he wrote, "and so heavy that the poles which are erected to support them are of the size of a ship's mast . . . and those near the hall are covered with plates of gold of the thickness of a ducat. . . . It should be stated that the Great Mogul has seven magnificent thrones, one wholly covered with diamonds, the others with rubies, emeralds, or pearls. . . . I counted the large balas rubies on the great throne, and there are about 108, all cabochons, the least of which weighs 100 carats, but there are some which weigh apparently 200 and more. As for the emeralds, there are plenty of good colour, but they have many flaws; the largest may weigh 60 carats, and the least 30 carats. I counted about 116; thus there are more emeralds than rubies.

"The underside of the canopy is covered with diamonds and pearls, with a fringe of pearls all round, and above the canopy, which is a quadrangular-shaped dome, there is a peacock with elevated tail made of blue sapphires and other coloured stones, the body of gold inlaid with precious stones, having a large ruby in front of the breast, whence hangs a pear-shaped pearl of 50 carats or thereabouts, and of a somewhat yellow water. On both sides of the peacock there is a large bouquet of the same height as the bird, consisting of many kinds of flowers made of gold inlaid with precious stones. On the side of the throne opposite the court there is a jewel consisting of a diamond of from 80 to 90 carats weight, with rubies and emeralds round it, and when the Emperor is seated he has this jewel in full view. But in my opinion the most costly point about this magnificent throne is that the twelve columns supporting the canopy are surrounded with beautiful rows of pearls, which are round and of fine water, and weigh from 6 to 10 carats each. At 4 feet distance from the throne two umbrellas are fixed, on either side, the sticks of which for 7 or 8 feet in height are covered with diamonds, rubies, and pearls. These umbrellas are of red velvet, and embroidered and fringed all round with pearls. . . ."

This Peacock Throne has of course been the subject of a lot of literature. Many people were privileged to see it, but never was it scrutinized by more of an expert, though according to Streeter its jewels were weighed and checked over by the palace treasurers every year. Then at last Tavernier turned his attention to the gem collection. He was vouchsafed a private viewing. It was not quite private, at that, being held in a small room at the end of the long hall where the Emperor sat on his throne and kept an eye on proceedings. Aurangzeb knew from personal experience that nobody could be trusted implicitly where big diamonds were concerned. His chief treasurer, 'Akil Khan, now commanded four of the imperial eunuchs to bring the jewels, which were carried in on trays all gilded with gold leaf and covered with embroidered velvet. All the pieces were counted over three times, and a list made on the spot by three scribes. "For the Indians do everything with great circumspection and patience," said Tavernier, "and when they see anyone who acts with precipitation, or becomes angry, they gaze at him without saying anything, and smile as if he were a madman.

"The first piece which 'Akil Khan placed in my hands was the great diamond, which is a round rose, very high at one side. [By "round rose" he meant the pattern in which it was cut. The fact that the Great Mogul was high on one side showed that like most Indian-cut stones it had been prepared with scant attention to symmetry, but much respect for size and weight.] At the basal margin it has a small notch and flaw inside. Its

water is beautiful, and it weighs 319½ ratis, which are equal to
280 of our carats. . . . When Mir Jumla, who betrayed the
King of Golkonda, his master, presented this stone to Shahja-
han [Aurangzeb's father], to whose side he attached himself,
it was then in the rough, and weighed 900 ratis, which are
equivalent to 787½ carats; and it had several flaws. If this stone
had been in Europe it would have been treated in a different
manner, for some good pieces would have been taken from it,
and it would have weighed more than it does, instead of which
it has been all ground down. It was the Sieur Hortensio Borgio,
a Venetian, who cut it, for which he was badly rewarded; for
when it was cut he was reproached with having spoilt the stone,
which ought to have retained a greater weight; and instead of
paying him for his work, the Emperor fined him 10,000 rupees,
and would have taken more if he had possessed it. If the Sieur
Hortensio had understood his trade, he would have been able to
take a large piece from this stone without doing injury to the
Emperor's jewel, and without having had so much trouble in
grinding it; but he was not a very accomplished diamond cutter."

This is the stone which, as I have said, Ball has proved to his
own satisfaction is at once the Great Mogul and the Koh-i-nur,
or Mountain of Light. Under the name of the Great Mogul it
had already seen a fair amount of treachery. Through betrayal
of his master, Mir Jumla came over to the side of Shah Jahan
and brought the diamond with him. Then Shah Jahan's son
Aurangzeb overthrew his father and confined him to prison; he
was a captive at the time of Tavernier's visit and died soon
afterward. The diamond from now on appears in history as the
Koh-i-nur. Under this name it was snatched from Aurangzeb's

descendant, a weaker prince, in 1793 by Nadir Shah, who took
it home to Persia. So it went, from one war to another, from
one conqueror to another, gathering bloodstained moss. One
of the owners of the Koh-i-nur, beaten in battle and taken pris-
oner, refused to tell where he had hidden it. His captors put
out his eyes and poured boiling oil on his head, but he remained
stubborn, and the diamond stayed in his family for a further
while. Finally, as late as the nineteenth century, it turned up
in India again, in the possession of the Sikh Ranjit Singh, ruler
of the Punjab, who lived at Lahore. He often wore the Koh-i-
nur in his turban, and many Europeans saw it there. As a sight
they considered the famous diamond definitely disappointing,
without fire and rather smaller than they had expected. Actually, it *was* smaller. Somewhere in the years that stretched
between Aurangzeb and Ranjit it had shrunk by about eighty-
three carats in weight. One of its owners in the interim, who
must have impoverished himself in times of war, had evidently
knocked a couple of pieces off the giant stone and sold them.
The two flat planes from which they had been detached were
easy to see. The famous stone did indeed look dull and flat,
though of course it was still extremely valuable. One historian
says it was worth about a million pounds at that time.

Ranjit Singh made war on the English. There were two Sikh
wars. Ranjit died, and in 1849, when the British finally won,
the Punjab was handed over to them, with the Koh-i-nur as a
part of the property. The spectacular diamond was kept in a
small tin box. It is a fact I can well believe after seeing the
strangely unsuitable containers people in the diamond industry
often use for their jewels, but still it seems odd, and that isn't
the half of the story. The box was given for safekeeping, tem-

porarily, to Mr. John Lawrence, the man who was later to be Lord Lawrence and governor general of India. No doubt he was busy administering many other details connected with the cession. At any rate he shoved it into his vest pocket and forgot all about it. Six weeks passed, and one day another administrator happened to mention to Lawrence that the authorities had decided what to do with the Koh-i-nur. They were going to give it to Queen Victoria, he said; and by the way, where was it? Lawrence suddenly remembered where it was supposed to be. He felt in his vest pocket. No, it wasn't there. He left the office somewhat abruptly and got home as quickly as he could. The box, as a matter of fact, was in his house and the diamond was quite safe. His Indian valet had found it while changing the contents of his master's pockets from one suit to another. He thought it was just a worthless piece of glass, but he never threw anything away as a matter of principle, so Victoria got her diamond after all.

There was a big fuss made about the Koh-i-nur when it arrived at Buckingham Palace. Even a tyro could see that it needed recutting, and the Prince Consort, with his deep interest in scientific matters, did not consider himself a tyro. The question immediately arose: who was to do the job? Victoria and Albert were far too patriotic a pair to consider sending it overseas when they had a perfectly good jeweler's company at hand, and that is where they made their mistake, though Mr. Atkinson would not admit any such thing. For there was evidently only one cutter in the whole country that Garrard's, the royally patronized jeweler, deemed worthy of the task, and according to later, franker writers he could have been better, even though he had been trained in the Netherlands. In fact, as At-

kinson wrote indignantly, later on the Dutch persistently tried
to snatch away the honor of having done the work.

"Any one visiting one of the largest cutting factories in Amsterdam will be shown a model of the *Koh-i-noor,* and told that
it was re-cut and polished at the factory, when it is an undis-
puted fact that in consequence of the keen interest evidenced
by Her Most Gracious Majesty the Queen and the late Prince
Consort in the manipulation of this wonderful gem, Messrs.
Garrard, the Queen's jewellers, at their instance, had a room
specially fitted up at their present establishment in the Hay-
market, where Her Majesty herself, and nearly all the members
of the royal family, personally assisted at putting on the facets,
which for perfection are unequalled; the Duke of Wellington
personally putting on the first."

If we add to this alarming picture the knowledge vouchsafed
by another writer, that the Prince Consort spent hours and
hours thus assisting in the cutting of the Koh-i-nur, it is not
surprising to reflect that the stone today is in bad shape. It's
still big, goodness knows; it still weighs more than a hundred
and six carats. But it is flat and dull, as you can see for yourself
if you like where it is on display with the other crown jewels
in the Tower of London.

It is impossible, if you are one of the many people who take
historical diamonds to heart, not to be just a bit cross with
the Prince Consort and Victoria over the Koh-i-nur. But after
all, what else were they to do? London wasn't Antwerp, and
they above all others had to Buy British. Ten years later it
would have been much easier to Buy British and still keep the
diamond in good shape, when the South African discoveries
brought new blood into the trade. Sixty-five years later would

have made even more difference, for then the Germans occupied Belgium and plenty of expert cutters came flooding into Britain for sanctuary. Like other refugees they were permitted to remain and ply their trade on condition that they return to their own country as soon as the war was over. In the meantime they taught their craft to others. Bernard Oppenheimer, late brother to Sir Ernest of Anglo American, was so active in rehabilitating disabled soldiers in his diamond-polishing works that he was rewarded by the Crown with a baronetcy, and these ex-soldiers carried on the good work.

When Germany was preparing for World War II her authorities early saw the great possibilities of industrial diamonds in armament manufacture, and they rapidly set up a strong competition to the workers of Belgium and Holland. In those days industrial diamonds hadn't been generally recognized for the important articles they later became, and Germany continued to buy rough stones from Britain as easily as if they were not very strategic material. As soon as war was declared, however, Britain put an embargo on rough diamonds. Apart from all other accusations that the diamond-cutting community of the Low Countries can justly make against the Germans, there is the one that this prewar activity of the Nazis rendered life very hard for cutters who remained in their traditional strongholds. Soon, of course, they had more tragic grievances to add to the account. When German troops invaded Belgium and Holland the Jewish cutters attempted to escape. Most of the Belgians made their way to France. Save for a few exceptions the Dutch were not so fortunate and were condemned to concentration camps or quicker means of extermination. A few refugees from both countries arrived in England, and again the Oppenheimer group found themselves helping war victims by giving them employment in their factories, but it was not a very big problem. According to Mr. Monnickendam, a cutter and himself a resident of Britain since World War I, there were only a hundred of these diamond workers who managed to reach England.

One day recently I visited the factory of Briefel & Lemer, in Clerkenwell. Like most workplaces of this most glamorous of trades, it is hidden away in a somber back street of London, in a red-brick neighborhood that the ordinary shopper would never think of penetrating because nothing is there for the ordinary shopper to buy. Mr. Briefel had sent for me in a town car of more than middling splendor, explaining with truth that otherwise I would never be able to find my way. The driver, a friendly man, laughed at my puzzled expression when he drove through a tortuous alley and turned in to a garage that was not merely a garage, but very evidently a warehouse for several factories that produced various sorts of machinery. He used practiced skill in parking the car between big stacked packing cases, discoursing as he did so. He was proud of the locality of his employer's factory. It seemed to him, as it did to me, piquant. For him the cream of the joke, evidently, was that he had to take me up to the floor occupied by Briefel & Lemer in a freight elevator. I wasn't all that much amused. I was getting used to it. An industry that carries things like the Koh-i-nur around in old cigarette tins is not likely to feel out of place upstairs over a warehouse.

The main office was a large room but pretty well filled up. Mr. Briefel was there, and his partner Mr. Lemer, and a secretary. It was more like a studio than a business sanctum, though there were desks. A long table ran along one side. There were diamond scales, and diagrams, and the usual photographs of queens inspecting jewels. There were filing cabinets, and big clean windows, because daylight is very important for diamond viewing. Mr. Briefel is a tall, thin man, full of enthusiasm and talk. Mr. Lemer is a smaller man who conceals his enthusiasm and hardly ever utters. It is Mr. Briefel who handles whatever publicity may come the way of the firm, but this isn't much. Cutters are like other people connected with diamonds: they don't seek out the public prints on purpose to make statements. Mr. Briefel, however, *has* lately appeared on television, cleaving a diamond for the edification of the audience. It was a very tense operation, as it always is. He did it because he believes in educating people on the subject of gems and he is by nature an outgoing sort of man, but it isn't a characteristic thing for a diamond cutter to have done, and some other people in the profession, possibly envious of him, have hinted that he was ill-advised. In defense of Mr. Briefel I must protest that a cannier, more secretive man never went on television. For all his bonhomie he doesn't really tell a thing. For example, it is well known in the trade that his firm a few years ago was entrusted with a wonderful pink diamond for cutting. It was common knowledge that the stone was presented by the famous mine owner, Williamson, in honor of the Coronation, to a certain *very exalted personage,* as the Victorian newspapers might have put it. The cutting was beautifully done—no Koh-i-nur business about it. Counting the thinking and the discussions and diagrams and markings and, finally, the actual deed itself, that diamond was worked on for nearly two years. Mr. Briefel showed me the work sheets; he let me heft a leaden model of the rough stone in my hand; but would he tell me who owned the stone? Would he, even though he knew I knew, and he knew I knew he knew it? No, he would not. He just shook his head when I asked (I asked just for the hell of it, of course) and severely put the papers and the lead model away again.

To change the subject he showed me an array of models designed to explain the science of cutting. Most men in the industry have a set of these. First there was a perfect pyramidal, or octagonal, or whipping-top model in quartz crystal, pretending to be a huge diamond. Next was what looked like the same model, but something less than half of it had been made separate, as if the top had been neatly sawed off: this top bit, presumably, would be cut down in its turn as another less important diamond, a by-product. Sawing is an expedient that was invented less than fifty years ago. Before it came in, the diamond had to be ground down from scratch, literally from scratch: a process that not only took practically forever, but was often a considerable waste of good stone, since the ground-down mass could only be used as abrasive dust. I asked Mr. Briefel what the difference was between sawing and cleavage, and he said they weren't the same in any respect. Cleaving means splitting along that one plane of the crystal that does split, the plane on which diamond molecules hang to each other with less persistence than they do in any other direction in the atomic framework. Using a comparison often employed by cutters, he likened the splitting to that which happens in wood. I would see cleavage being done in the factory, he assured me, and continued with his lecture.

"We will assume that the diamond we are working on is a perfect crystal like this model, though you understand it hardly ever happens in real life that you get one so symmetrical," he

said. We examined the third stage, at which some of the grinding had been done, and he called off the different facets as they
are named in the industry—the table, or flat top of the stone,
which is left comparatively big; the smaller flat bit at the bottom, which is the culet, and the girdle, where top and bottom
meet. Moving along to the more advanced model, he showed
the stars, the kites, the halves and pentagons and so on. It
looked to me purely and simply an exercise in solid geometry.
Then Mr. Briefel put the model away and brought out a few
samples of the real thing: rough diamonds. He described the
questions a trained cutter must ask himself and answer before
he begins on a stone. If there are piqués, or black spots, the
trick is to cut so that these are removable in the polishing without too much loss of weight; that is, they should be as near as
possible to the surface. An experienced man can see the spots
and recognize their position immediately, where an amateur
like me might be misled by distortion and magnification, seeing
the spot through the diamond. Moreover, the trained cutter
must be able to judge the color of his stone in the rough; he
should be able, within reasonable limits, to prophesy what
color it will be when it has been cut, which is sometimes a different one to the hue of the uncut crystal. Then there is the question of the proper angles of the facets. The ancient Indian
cutters had some inkling of the fact that facets help a stone
sparkle, but they didn't work out the angles at which the fire
would be greatest. Today it is up to the grinder and polisher to
make no mistake about that, and sacrifice no light.

We put the samples away and started our rounds of the factory. Mr. Briefel took me first to a room where a man sat alone
at a bench, a vise clamped to the edge of the table in front of

him. He was all prepared to cleave a diamond for my benefit;
it was obviously a solemn occasion, but he was a young man
with a merry, square face, and his grin kept breaking through.
The diamond he intended to operate on was a knobby stone,
embedded edge upward in reddish cement that was fixed in a
clamp, which in turn was held in the vise. He took the contraption out so that I might look at it closely, then he returned
it and picked up a small tool, a sharp-edged diamond firmly
fixed in a handle. Using this as a file he began scratching at the
other diamond, across the edge, back and forth. The scratching
made a squeaky noise of the kind that hurts the teeth.

"He must start it just so," said Mr. Briefel, "in exactly the
right place; otherwise the diamond may break into bits. This
is the hardest thing to learn." I asked if diamonds were ever
spoiled at this stage. The demonstrator laughed rather ruefully,
and Mr. Briefel said that almost every apprentice ruined a few
stones before he finished his training. Now the cutter was satisfied with the tiny impression he had made on the diamond.
He gave me his loupe so that I could examine it, and then he
picked up a piece of steel that was wedge-shaped on one edge
and blunt on the other. Fitting the wedge into the crack, he
took a small mallet and aimed carefully at the blunt edge. He
struck sharply. A part of the diamond flew off into the air.

"It's lost!" I said excitedly. But it was not: it had landed in
the cutter's lap, caught in his capacious blue apron. He gave it
to me to examine: it was sheared off neatly and presented a
glassy surface broken only by faint striations.

"Now comes the sawing," said Mr. Briefel. We walked down
a passage which, as he apologetically pointed out, was dark and
narrow. "We had to expand when we took on disabled soldiers

during the war, and our building has never caught up with it."
He flung open the door into a long, thin room completely full
of machinery that seemed to be working all on one belt. A
number of diamonds were on setups suspended in space, each
held firmly against a rotating wheel of very thin bronze. I asked
how mere copper could cut through the hardest material in the
world, and Briefel explained that each of the wheel rims was
constantly anointed with diamond dust in oil, renewed as the
wheel rotates through a small container at the back. This cuts
all right, and fairly quickly at that. He showed me the gray powdery stuff, and the tiny pestle and mortar where it was mixed.
Next we visited the grinders and polishers, where on rotating
disks or plates the diamonds were pressed down and ground
away, facet by facet, with the same diamond-dust-and-oil mixture. Each workman or workwoman watched one disk, whereon
two or three diamonds were being polished at the same time.
It was a process that involved a lot of careful inspection. The
operator would let a stone grind for a short space, lift it up and
look at it closely through his loupe, and then grind it some
more.

Returning to the office, we looked at Mr. Briefel's collection
of "fancies"—the freaks and colored gems that many dealers
love to pick out of the mass of stones that pass through their
hands. Mr. Briefel had shown a decided preference for amber
and deep yellow diamonds, but he possessed several other unusual ones. A beautiful mauve caught my eye. I remembered
that he was reputed to have a special theory as to why diamonds
should sometimes be colored, and I asked him about it. Mr.
Lemer stared noncommittally out of the window, and I recalled

what I had also been told, that Mr. Briefel's theory is not that usually accepted by scientists.

"You know how diamonds are formed?" he began.

I said that as I understood it, they occurred like other crystals in rocks of igneous origin, having solidified as the melted stuff, or magma, cooled down. Some people believe they might be formed of coal, I continued; the coal would have been subjected to such heat and pressure that it lost all trace of——

"Yes, yes, all that," said Mr. Briefel. "But what I believe is this. At certain times of the day the sky is colored. At sunrise you have what colors? Yellow, orange, and red. Suppose your diamonds take shape at these moments. They are reflecting the yellow or the red, and it becomes a part of them. Or if it is not sunrise or sunset, but the middle part of the day when the sky is blue, they reflect the blue. Just at the moment they turn hard they take on the color of the sky. If they are formed at night when there is no color for them they become pure and colorless, what we call white. That is how it happens, I am sure."

After a short pause I ventured to argue. According to the accepted theory, I said, this crystallization took place thousands of feet below the surface of the earth. That is the only way such tremendous pressure could occur. How then, if the diamonds were out of sight of the sky—but Mr. Briefel would not accept my arguments. He pointed out that nobody really knew, and I had to admit that there, at least, he was right. Nobody knows.

"So that is *my* theory," he ended happily.

Mr. Briefel comes from Austria. Unlike many of his colleagues he did not start his life's career at the diamond-worker's bench: a scholarly type, he studied at the University of Vienna for a degree in higher mathematics. As the Nazi spirit grew in strength he decided that it was time to get out, and some time before the war began he went to Belgium and there joined relatives who were in the diamond industry.

"I found no work for a mathematician, but for a diamond cutter there was always a job. So rather later than most, I set to work learning a new trade," he said. "The people who taught me were old-fashioned; you might call them traditionalist. For example, they cut facets by instinct rather than measurement. It was their pride to get the best result through experience rather than theory. They had good results, but I didn't approach the problem that way. As I saw it, the refraction of the light that gives a diamond its fire is based on certain mathematical laws and could not be otherwise. Therefore I sat down and worked out my angles mathematically, and long before anyone else used it I employed a kind of protractor that would measure these angles without possibility of a mistake. They said I couldn't do it that way; that they had done it their way for generations. But I did it my way, and I succeeded."

He happened to be in England on a business errand when the German blitz began and the Storm Troopers marched into Belgium. His family was not with him: he never saw them again. Briefel found work in England and is now a naturalized Briton.

A few days after my visit to this English factory I came upon some statistics that showed dramatically what an effect the war has had on diamond cutting. There are about five hundred cutters in England at the present time and nearly as many in France: four hundred and seventy-five. In Holland, where many of these people lived and worked before the war, there are only eight hundred. South Africa has a thousand, the States sixteen hundred, and Israel, where there has been a concerted effort among diamond men to build up the industry, there are two thousand. But what really caught my eye was the fact that Belgium has more than ten thousand, most of whom are in Antwerp. Ten thousand—the same figure quoted by Mr. Atkinson, I reflected, eighty-six years ago. It seemed to me that I would never find a place more imbued with the traditions of the trade. So I went to Antwerp.

"You were right," said Mr. Romi Goldmuntz. "It is a very old trade in Antwerp. Look at him." He pointed to a bronze statue that stood on the window sill of the board room in the Diamond Club. It was of a man in a sort of Robin Hood costume, with a jerkin and feathered hat, holding in his fingers a huge bronze diamond. Big as it was, he held it close to his eye. "That is Lodewyck van Bercken, the first diamond cutter in Antwerp," said Mr. Goldmuntz proudly.

I said, "How interesting. When did he live?" at which Mr. Goldmuntz looked stymied, and laughed a little.

"I must admit that I don't know, and furthermore I don't think anybody else does," he said. "He is a legendary figure, I suspect, but all cutters in Antwerp will tell you about him just the same."

I had found Mr. Goldmuntz in his office high up above a bank in the Rue des Fortifications, just off Pelikanstraat. It is a district almost exclusively given over to diamonds and diamond men. From Mr. Goldmuntz' office windows one can see the walls and windows of at least three of the five diamond clubs in Antwerp, and any number of diamond-cutting factories. It is quite an office, a long line of comfortably furnished rooms strung along like railway cars, each with its door leading out into a corridor that runs the length of the series. "Very convenient," he explained. "Often you don't want one dealer to meet another." The doors all had little doors set in them, like our speak-easy windows in the old days, but backed by strong steel mesh. There are framed certificates on the walls, and photographs, and a full-length portrait of Mr. Goldmuntz, who looks remarkably like a younger version of Sir Winston Churchill (he is seventy-four). There is a model of a three-masted schooner, made by the children of a home for Jewish refugee orphans which he organized. There are mineral samples, and replicas of famous diamonds, and big neat desks, and of course, here and there, a safe.

Mr. Goldmuntz and his nephew, who lives in America but comes over every year to spend several months in Europe, gave me an outline of the situation in that city. It is the clearing-house for the diamond trading of the world. A combination of circumstances has made it the most important center. To begin with there was its tradition. Then there were the laws of Belgium, which as far as diamonds are concerned are less stringent than those of Britain: to put it bluntly, diamonds licit and illicit can come in and move out, because there is no form of local control that makes it really dangerous to dispose of smuggled goods. Most important, however, is the fact that diamond cutting got under way not only as soon as World War II was over, but actually before Germany's surrender. Mr. Goldmuntz had taken refuge in England when the Germans moved in; he already had an office in London. He was the *doyen* of diamond men in Antwerp, however, and the plight of his workless colleagues was much on his mind. As soon as it was possible, therefore—perhaps even a little before it was possible—he went back to Antwerp, getting in almost as soon as the British troops did. Shot and shell were still flying about, and Germans still hid in the city when Mr. Goldmuntz approached the commanding officer.

"I want to open a diamond factory," he said.

The commanding officer, as Goldmuntz recalls it, was indignant. He said, "Don't you know there's a war on?"

Nevertheless Goldmuntz got his way, and by the time national reconstruction began, the industry was already well embarked on its new existence. Antwerp had been badly knocked about, but a lot of the old buildings remained. Today the traders are happily busy rebuilding wherever they find it possible to expand, and banks and clubs and factories are constantly on the move into roomier quarters. We visited the extensive factory of his friend Mr. Fuerstenberg, who had new-looking room after room of impressive equipment and full of busy workers.

"You have seen nothing on this scale in England," said Mr. Goldmuntz proudly and truthfully. "Notice how all the windows wherever possible face the north. The north light is best, always, for diamond viewing."

Surprised at this, I said, "But surely in a northern country like this you want all the sun you can get?"

"No," he said. "Strong sunlight makes the diamond look too good."

In my reading I had come across several statements about diamonds that exploded, or at least came to pieces, when they were being worked. Other stories told of stones that burst as they were brought out of their hiding places in deep mines. One tragic anecdote was of a big, beautiful diamond that had been carefully cut and then, as it was being shown off by its proud worker, was dropped to the floor, whereupon it burst into tiny splinters. Like most people I knew that diamond, though it is the hardest substance in the world, is brittle. Tapped sharply in the right, or rather in the wrong, direction, it is likely to break in what mineralogists call the conchoidal pattern, a series of curves that make a shallow cuplike design of cracks. Some writers hold that these miniature explosions are due to miniscule gas bubbles within the stone. I asked Mr. Fuerstenberg if such things really happen, and he readily assented. He went straight to his strong room and brought out a first-rate example of just such an accident, a white diamond between one and two carats in size that had cracked when the polisher was giving it the finishing touch. I handled it gingerly. It wasn't in pieces and its outline seemed unmarred, but it was cracked through and through like a bit of shatterproof glass after a crash. Mr. Fuerstenberg said that cracking is a well-known hazard in cutting. He puts it down to sudden extraordinary changes in temperature. Quite often he has known it to happen to a diamond, very hot from being on the polishing disk, suddenly plunged into an acid bath to remove the oil and dust.

"By the way," said Mr. Goldmuntz as we were taking our leave, "do *you* know anything definite about Lodewyck van Bercken? When did he live exactly?"

Mr. Fuerstenberg laughed heartily. "Lodewyck was just a legend," he said.

On the way to the Diamond Club, Mr. Goldmuntz gave me a short description of its part in the life of the Belgian diamond dealer. Such clubs are not social centers, except secondarily. They are really market places; "bourses," he said. Four of the five clubs in Antwerp are affiliated: the fifth is not recognized by the others because it sometimes accepts members they don't approve of. Mr. Goldmuntz, who has often been chairman of his club, *the* Diamond Club and the oldest in town, explained the system by which peace was kept among merchants: "We have our own court. If two people are disputing about some business matter, they go to court in the club. The chairman presides, and a number of other officials serve as a kind of jury. They consider the problem and make their decision. In this way the people involved don't have to pay litigation fees and all expense is avoided. Naturally, a man who is dissatisfied with the decision can then go to the civil courts if he likes, but if he does such a thing he is immediately dropped from the club, and that, believe me, is not good for his business. We arbitrate sometimes even in international affairs, and we are in communication with all the bourses in the world—in Israel, in New York, Milan, and Paris. Not Germany, though."

Arrived, we made our way through a busy short passageway to the board room, where stood the statue of Lodewyck van Bercken and his outsize gem. The room was large, and filled with a magnificent table inlaid with satinwood in a pattern of —of course—diamond-shaped lozenges. We sat at one end of this table and had a glass of port and a few bites of cheese to go with it, and then we went sight-seeing.

"Everything is here that the members can need. Anything you can think of," said Mr. Goldmuntz. "Our own post office. Cables. Telephones. Vaults. Here as you see is a board with the news of the stock market, always up to the minute. And here"—he paused and flung open a glass door—"the club!" he said. I found myself in an enormous room that stretched out ahead of me like a wing at least of Grand Central Station. There was the same effect of high ceilings and a vast amount of glass windows. Down one side of the room, which I now saw continued through more glass doors into another chamber of the same size, was a row of tables arranged like those in a plain continental restaurant, jutting out lengthwise from the wall so that four or six couples of men could sit at each, facing each other. The room was full of north light. People sat at the tables talking. Most of them possessed that peculiarly intent absorption that never accompanies ordinary social intercourse; you see it only in business or love talk. I couldn't have checked up on it by listening, though. They talked a lot of languages. I recognized French and, with less assurance, Flemish, but there were other tongues, and this seemed all the more noticeable because Antwerp in the hotel and Antwerp at the airport had been surprisingly English in speech.

"Of course you Belgians are remarkable," I said, or rather shouted, to Mr. Goldmuntz. The room reverberated with din; not only the combined conversation of uninhibited merchants, but a constant cheerful roaring from uniformed porters who marched through paging members. "You speak three languages fluently, don't you? French and Flemish and English."

"And Yiddish, in this part of town," he said. "Now then, just look." He waved to the inner side of the room, really a parallel room set off by pillars. Here and there was an indoors shop; he called my attention to the variety of things one could buy without going out of the diamond world into open air at all. There was a canteen; there was a shop where you could buy scales, loupes, and paper. There was a little room in which two men did nothing all day but weigh diamonds that were brought to them in sealed packets. That is one of the club rules, Mr. Goldmuntz explained: a selection, or parcel, of diamonds is offered to a buyer, who takes a long, careful look. Then it is sealed up so that it can't be tampered with while he makes up his mind and the two men argue about the price. During the course of the chaffering, or after it, the declared weight must of course be checked, so the parcel is brought to the weigher, who slits open the paper, pours the glittering little cascade onto his scale, writes down the proper weight on an officially stamped paper, and seals up the parcel again before handing it, with the filled-in form, back to its owner.

"It's one of the most important services we supply in the club. This, and the strong room," said Mr. Goldmuntz.

We sauntered on, past the cigar store, up to the end, and then we started back. Mr. Goldmuntz told me that though many of the men I saw sitting at the tables, or hailing each other across the room, or dashing importantly through the door, little brief case in hand, did all their business in this fashion and had no permanent offices, the biggest operators did rent offices, many of them in that building. Buyers from abroad had their choice of action. Sometimes they were quite content to make their contacts and do their talking in the big room, but the regular visitors usually went to the offices of their own firms or those of friends, and advertised their presence by means of a blackboard which he proceeded to show me.

"You get to know their names, most of them, when you've been in the business as long as I have," he said. He pointed to a message written in white chalk on the board: "v. Barsamian

. . . 'Marquises' . . . Fine silver cape de 0.35—1 ct. 713 in
Klein Bldg. Taille emeraude de 1—3 cts. extra. 8/8—60 a 100
p.c. (Single cuts.) Alle-soorten goederen."

"A mixture of languages, as you see," said Mr. Goldmuntz,
"but everybody understands it. It means this man Barsamian
is waiting in Room 713, the Klein Building—that's this one—
and is interested in buying stones of such and such description
and weight. We will now go and look at the strong room. No,
first you might like to look at the wall." He paused before a
bulletin board on which hung three forms, each with a man's
photograph affixed to it. The spaces were filled in with such
information as was requested; the man's name, nationality, age,
and experience, as well as his proposers and seconders, for these
were candidates who wished to join the club. The notices hang
there a stipulated length of time during which anyone who
might know something to the detriment of the candidate is expected to hand in his information to the club committee. If
during that time nothing of the sort transpires, the aspirant is
accepted.

Then we inspected the strong room, which looked like a safe-
deposit vault in a bank. We went back upstairs and talked to
some of the dealers. I gathered that Antwerp, though it is re-
freshingly unconfined in the matter of international business
and might fairly be described as the Tangier of the Continent,
is far from being unadulterated heaven for a diamond cutter.
Belgium is a welfare state with strong unions, and the cutters
have succeeded in jacking up their wages and welfare services,
and scaling down their hours of work, until the managers declare sorrowfully that any other country can compete dangerously. It was only recently that the cutters ended a strike that

had gone on for three months, and already they were demanding more than the advantage they gained through that maneuver.

"We get too much competition from people who don't care how long they work," said Mr. Goldmuntz. "Israel, for instance; we have asked them to cut down their working day to match ours, but they won't. They want to compete." He looked aghast at such lack of sportsmanship, and added dolefully, "And I helped set up the Israeli industry." For my part, for purely selfish reasons I was disappointed to find Belgian cutters so well off. I had understood that the cutting of really small stones, the kind we call "chips," is such fiddling work and pays so badly that nobody in England has the time or patience to take it on, whereas in Belgium there was a whole class of people who cut these tiny things at home. I found that I was mistaken. While such work is done in a lot of houses in Holland, in Belgium it isn't common. The nearest I came to finding a cottage industry was later, when I peeped through a window at a man who was obviously in his own home, wearing the familiar apron and operating a polishing disk.

A dealer expatiated on the hardships of the bosses. "People won't believe we aren't all millionaires, because we deal in parcels that run into large figures. It's true, I sometimes handle deals of seventy or eighty thousand pounds at a time, but then I've had to buy the goods before I can sell it. My own profit isn't anything like what they think it is. And then it's possible to drop a lot of money because of a sudden change in world affairs. You understand, you don't sell the same kind of goods all over the world. For instance, I had a large stock of yellow diamonds ready for the Far East. Some oriental women don't

mind a yellow tinge; it looks all right against their skin; sometimes they even prefer a yellow stone to a white one, and speaking for myself I think they're right. On some women white
stones don't look good. Well, all of a sudden down came the
Bamboo Curtain and I couldn't sell my stones there, and where
else was I to dispose of them? I lost heavily on that deal."

Antwerp and the diamond-cutting industry in general, I reflected, are a long cry from the unfortunate Koh-i-nur. I said
as much to a diamond man I had met at the club and saw again
at the airport, waiting for the same plane back to London as I
was. We had plenty of time to discuss such matters; we could
have talked thoroughly about most of the stones in Streeter's
catalogue of great gems before we got to Waterloo. Speaking by
the timetable it is a short jump from Belgium to England, but
as things worked out we were sitting in the airport all day.
There was fog over Antwerp; there was fog over London. It
was a damp, depressing day, a good day to think about fiery,
flashing diamonds.

"It's a funny thing the way these stones borrow legends from
each other," I said at last. "That story about the Sancy—or was
it the Sancy really?—having been stolen from an idol's eye.
Well, I read somewhere that Tavernier stole the Great Mogul
like that, right out of an Indian temple, which is ridiculous."

His reply was interrupted by the long-awaited summons to
our plane. We filed like sheep out of the fold, past the barrier,
out into the wet air, up the little stairs, and into our strapped
seats.

"About that idol's eye," he said, "it did happen, you know,
more than once. I don't know that particular stone, but I do
know that a maharaja brought our firm two diamonds he
wanted recut for modern setting. They were perfectly matched,

and they had, as a matter of fact, been the eyes of an Indian idol. They'd been cut to look just like it, moreover. I had them lying on my desk, and I suddenly noticed when I went across the office for something that they seemed to be looking at me wherever I went. You know what I mean? Faceted to look like eyeballs and set into some background material, they were— awfully cleverly done. Well, I didn't think he should have them recut, and I said so. It wasn't any of my business, but I couldn't help speaking out. It was a shame, I said; something really ancient like that, something you'll never see nowadays. I couldn't help thinking what it must have been like centuries ago, before they were taken out of the image's head: the priests chanting in a dark temple, and the incense, and those eyes shining in dim torchlight, really *looking* at the people. . . ." His voice trailed off. We were air-borne now, and had come out of the fog into a blaze of setting sun. Below us was a gilded floor of clouds.

"But you had to cut them?" I asked.

He said, "Oh, we had to. The Maharaja insisted. After all, he had a whole treasure house full of jewels, and this pair was a trifle to him. Those stones were terribly hard. They had come from the Golconda mines, and as you probably know Golconda diamonds are the most difficult of all to work. It took us months to grind them down."

Just then, for some reason, my mind gave a click. It had nothing to do with the Maharaja's diamonds. Lodewyck van Bercken was Louis de Berquem, the early and great diamond cutter from Paris. "Of course!" I said aloud. "Lodewyck was no legend."

"I beg your pardon?" said the diamond man.

# CHAPTER SEVEN

# The Shade of J. Ballantine Hannay

In February 1955, the General Electric Research Laboratory, in Schenectady, issued a statement that was read with great interest, and varying degrees of anxiety, by diamond people all over the world, particularly at De Beers. After four years of experimentation with "high-temperature superpressure," the laboratory announced, it had succeeded in manufacturing diamonds. These weren't imitation diamonds or diamondlike crystals, according to the statement; they were "purely and simply diamonds." A month or so later, General Electric put out a brochure entitled "Man-Made Diamonds," which explained that its research men had produced their stones in a new and powerful pressure chamber by subjecting "a carbonaceous material" to pressures of up to a million and a half pounds per square inch and to temperatures of up to five thousand degrees Fahrenheit. The stones were small—General Electric cautiously said it would be premature to suggest that the pressure chamber could produce gem diamonds—but they were perfectly adequate for use in industrial tools.

Shortly after the news came out I spent a morning visiting

the offices of Industrial Distributors—a subsidiary company, through which De Beers markets its industrial stones—and the Diamond Research Laboratory, which was set up nine years ago to conduct research into the properties and uses of diamonds. I soon saw that the officials and scientists there were highly interested, to put it mildly, in the General Electric diamonds and were eagerly awaiting more facts about them. Industrials, which are drab stones and usually small ones, constitute the less glamorous side of the diamond business, but, as the men at Industrial Distributors were quick to point out, it is a highly important side. Industrials account for 80 per cent of the diamond trade in terms of bulk and 25 per cent in terms of profit—a far from negligible sum. Some South African mines produce industrial diamonds almost exclusively, and even mines which, like the Premier, are celebrated for their gems, yield far fewer gems than industrials. Diamonds are virtually indispensable to some industries, and the United States has been stock-piling them for the last ten years; being nature's hardest substance, they are used in all sorts of cutting, grinding, and boring tools, from glass cutters to oil-well drills, and hardly a year goes by that somebody doesn't think up a new way to use them.

Upon arriving at the headquarters of Industrial Distributors, I was met by a De Beers man named White, who ushered me into a large office and introduced me to a couple of other members of the firm. After we had chatted for a few minutes, I asked them how they had felt when they heard the news of the General Electric diamonds. "Pretty bad at first," Mr. White said. "Diamond shares took a tumble right away, and for days nobody talked about anything except General Electric.

But things have quieted down a good deal since; shares are back up and business is booming. Of course, we're tremendously curious about whether—and how soon—General Electric will be able to produce industrials on a commercial basis. Mind you, we knew they were trying to do it. We've kept our eye on this kind of experiment for years, wherever it was going on in the world. A whole lot of people have tried to make diamonds, ever since J. Ballantine Hannay started the whole thing off in 1880—and, come to think of it, there must have been people trying to do it for hundreds of years before that. Did you know about Hannay?"

One of the other men said, "To tell you the truth, I've had him on my mind for weeks now."

"So have I," said Mr. White. He turned to me and continued: "Hannay was a Scottish chemist who claimed to have succeeded in an experiment he'd been working at all his life. He said he had made diamonds, and he sent a number of them to prove it, to be examined and tested by a leading authority of that day in London. Well, the specimens were diamonds all right. They were tiny specks of things you need a microscope to see with, but they were, and are, diamonds. You can go and look at them if you want to when you get back to England: they're in the British Museum of Natural History in South Kensington. Hannay said he'd manufactured them with intense heat under tremendous pressure. As I remember, he used an iron tube, a kind of bomb, and he put in powdered carbon and bone oil and various other ingredients."

"Eye of newt and toe of frog," murmured the man who had spoken before.

"Something like that," said Mr. White. "Hannay showed his

paraphernalia quite willingly and was ready to talk about the method to anybody who took it seriously; people were dubious about it nevertheless, and that was natural I suppose. They hadn't seen other accomplishments in the laboratory that would make anything seem possible, as we have today. There was a general impression that Hannay had simply got hold of some ordinary diamonds and shoved them along to the Museum as samples of his own work. Scientists did try to reproduce his experiments and his results, or alleged results, but nobody that I know of succeeded."

"What about Moissan in Paris?" put in the third man. "He had a lot of supporters to his claim."

"It's never been settled," said Mr. White. "Those arguments go on forever, but they've always been inconclusive."

The man who said he'd been thinking about Hannay was evidently still thinking about him. He said, "It's my opinion that other people beside Hannay have made diamonds but were reluctant to claim it, considering what happened to him. The question's never been resolved."

"True," said Mr. White. "I grant you that. And here's another thing that's interesting—at least it interests me. Hannay's diamonds, it now appears, are of a very special type that doesn't occur nearly so often in nature as the usual kind. It's what we now call Type 2, and you'll find out more about that at the laboratory when you go over today. For the moment, just remember that only about 5 per cent of all diamonds are Type 2. The question immediately presents itself, where would Hannay have got hold of Type 2 diamonds if he was simply looking around for something to push into his iron tubes and fool the public? Is it merely coincidence that his specimens should be

of a special kind? Well, he died discredited, and I doubt if anyone gave him much thought after the initial excitement was
forgotten. Especially as there have been a number of scoundrels
—real charlatans—since his time, who likewise claimed to have
manufactured diamonds, though always with their own secret
methods. They were exposed as fakes every time, and these
experiences helped to throw shade on Hannay's name. But
now, I wonder. I wonder, among other things, if these G.E.
diamonds are by any chance Type 2. I shall be very interested
to find out. It's just possible the world may have done Hannay
an injustice."

"I can't help but think about him," said the man who had
said it before.

The talk traveled on, to another name that was once well
known in diamond circles: Lemoine. His is a story jewel dealers love to tell. It is one of the references that always gets a
smile in the trade, because it has to do with a diamond dealer,
and diamond men like to recapitulate jokes on their competi-
tors. In this case the victim was Sir Julius Wernher, a founder
of the firm Wernher, Beit & Co., which was one of the out-
standing partnerships of old-time Kimberley. By 1905, when
the Lemoine fraud was first perpetrated, Sir Julius was one of
the leading magnates on the financial scene. The world was
still buzzing, if mildly, about Hannay, Moissan, and other
would-be alchemists.

Lemoine came to London from Paris and called on Sir Julius,
who was paying an extended visit to England, and told him he
had a new sure-fire method for making diamonds that would
be indistinguishable from natural ones. He couldn't yet divulge
the secret, of course, but he needed money to perfect the proc-

ess, and if Wernher, Beit would back him up the invention
would be under their control as soon as it was ready to put into
operation. All Lemoine wanted, he said, was a royalty on terms
to be arranged. Of course if Wernher, Beit didn't see their way
clear to backing him, some other firm doubtless would, but he
was giving them first chance.

Sir Julius listened with great interest, and it was not sheer
greed that made him do so. He was a diamond mine owner,
representing other owners, and he could see what might happen if somebody reproduced his mines' product in a factory:
the market would be ruined. If Lemoine did indeed possess the
secret of such a process the obvious thing for Sir Julius was to
acquire the exclusive rights in it. He therefore promised to
finance Lemoine if a demonstration should prove convincing
to himself and several cronies he proposed to bring along as
witnesses. Lemoine agreed to give such a demonstration. Accordingly, Sir Julius and three associates met together in a laboratory in Paris, chosen and arranged in advance by Lemoine,
who then made his appearance in a way that might justly be
called dramatic. He was stark naked. He had undressed, he explained, to reassure the gentlemen that he was up to no
skulduggery.

It was a grotesque scene, with overtones of alchemy. The
naked Lemoine made up a mixture in a crucible he had ready
and waiting, and put the concoction in an electrical furnace
to cook. They all waited until the crucible had attained
white heat, while Lemoine explained that the ingredients were
unknown to anybody but himself, and would remain so until
Sir Julius, or somebody else, paid for the secret. Half an hour
went by. Then he took a long-handled shovel and carefully re-

moved the crucible from the heater. Another long period of waiting ensued, while things cooled off. At long last Lemoine opened up the container, stirred around in the smoking, blackened mass, and started finding diamonds. One after another he lifted them out: real diamonds, small but of good color and nicely crystalline. They looked for all the world like the South African gems that the watching gentlemen knew so well, and there were twenty-five of them.

Sir Julius was much impressed, but he strove to maintain a properly skeptical attitude, especially as one of his companions, a Mr. Francis Oates, was suspicious that a trick was being played on them. The gentlemen conferred, and asked Lemoine if he could do it again then and there. Cheerfully he complied. The long process was repeated, and this time thirty stones were brought out of the ashes in the crucible. After that, however, M. Lemoine seemed tired, and he grew cross when the gentlemen asked him to give a third demonstration. Besides, he said, he simply wasn't prepared to give a third demonstration that day, and in saying this he was doubtless telling the truth.

Even now Sir Julius wasn't quite sure; not with Oates at his elbow, sniffing for rats. But he decided it was worth a try anyway, and he gave Lemoine money to carry on with—quite a lot of money, according to reports. For the next three years the Frenchman sent word at intervals as to how the research was going. He said he was working hard, and successfully, and now and then he sent over a sample diamond to Sir Julius to prove it. They were perfectly good diamonds; according to experts they were indistinguishable from those of the Jagersfontein Mine in South Africa, which is famous for the fine gems it produces. (Later, when the case came to court, it appeared that they had as a matter of fact come from Jagersfontein. Sir Julius' lawyers dug up the dealer who had sold them to Lemoine, and he appeared as a witness.) And so the months went by until, in 1908, when Lemoine had collected sixty-four thousand pounds from Wernher, Beit and was still asking for more and saying his process wasn't quite ready, Sir Julius grew suspicious enough to demand an inquiry. Lemoine, summoned to appear at trial for fraud, ran away. He was apprehended later, tried, convicted, and sent to prison. The experience saddened Sir Julius and discouraged all diamond magnates, for a long time, from investing in diamond-making adventures, until it was forgotten, along with Moissan and Hannay. The Hannay diamonds rested undisturbed in the Mineral Department of the Museum. The only people who didn't drop the subject completely were mineralogists.

"And now General Electric," I said when the men fell silent.

"And now General Electric," Mr. White repeated. "Well, all we can do is wait and see."

The turmoil I was half expecting at the Diamond Research Laboratory was not there. In fact, the place was remarkably calm, just as much so indoors as out, and that was pretty calm. It made me think of the latest addition to some new American university, with its neat brick exterior, and the broad cement staircase indoors, and the wide corridors on every floor, and the big cool rooms. I was taken in hand by a bright young guide, and the first thing he showed me was a small museum where various forms of industrials were exhibited: in wiredrawing dies, whose importance has been much enhanced since the beginning of World War II, in stonecutting saws, and glass cutters, and twist drills, lathe tools, hones, engraving pencils, grinding-wheel dressing tools, drill crowns, and the wheels themselves that are used in preparing diamonds of all sorts. For hundreds of years, ever since diamonds were first ground into facets, some version of grinding wheel has been employed in this work. In the midst of these exotic if fascinating implements it was a small shock to recognize homely, familiar things under glass, such as diamond phonograph needles and vulcanite pipestems. These last are cut and shaped with diamond tools because diamond, unlike steel, is impervious to the sulphur in vulcanite and so doesn't get spoiled in the works. It was less pleasant to spot dentist's drills, but the horrid little objects reminded me of something my dentist had said just before I left London:

"You know if the diamond traders would only release all available supplies of industrial diamonds and put them on the market where they belong, your dentistry bills would be much lower. Blame those fellows in De Beers for the high cost of good teeth. It's not only the drills; a lot of the tools our mechanics use depend on diamonds."

Now, in the Research Laboratory, I thought it a good time to bring up this matter, but my guide didn't agree at all. "He's wrong," he said flatly, "quite wrong. But it's no use saying so. We say it until we're blue in the face, but the public won't believe us. We do not hold back our industrials; it's only that the supply isn't equal to the demand."

I said, "But surely *now*, with the General Electric diamond . . ."

"Ah, that," he said. "Well, it's an interesting question, all right. Impossible to say as yet what effect it's going to have.

According to the Americans it still costs too much to produce for the thing to be a commercial proposition, but in time . . . Here's Dr. Custers: you'd better ask him."

Dr. J. F. H. Custers is what South Africans carefully call a Hollander, to distinguish him from those among themselves who are descended from Dutch settlers. In other words, he himself comes from Holland. He is joint director of the laboratory, in charge of physical research. My companion said, "We were just going to ask you what you think about the General Electric diamond. It's in your line of country, Dr. Custers, so what *do* you think?"

Dr. Custers said, speaking slowly and impressively, "I? I think—they have made a diamond." He smiled. His eyebrows lifted over his rimless spectacles. He looked attentive.

"But can they produce their diamonds in bulk?" I asked.

"That's one of many things that remain to be seen," he said, and looked attentive again.

After a pause, my guide suddenly reverted to philosophy, and said, "Well, after all, if it comes to that, what are we getting so excited about? What's the world stirred up about? A diamond is just carbon, when you come down to definitions."

"No," said Dr. Custers. "No. There are many things about it we don't understand: it is not just carbon." He spoke with great intensity. "Diamond is a *very* interesting mineral, quite apart from the qualities for which we value it. Here we are always trying to discover why it behaves as it does. We think we're on the way to finding some of the answers, and this General Electric experimentation no doubt takes us a long way on the road. Yes, it is a really exciting development."

We continued on the tour, and I was shown some of the

work they were doing on the kind of tools I had already seen in the museum. In one room a man was carefully plotting a diagram on a yard-square piece of paper. There were lines converging to the center of two concentric circles, and an irregular pattern of marks was spotted here and there around these lines. "This represents a drill crown," he explained. "I'm trying to work out the most effective places at which the diamonds should be set on it, so as to get the maximum result when it's grinding. We figure out from the wear and tear already visible on a used crown where they get the hardest treatment, and we try to set our diamonds with this knowledge in mind. Over on this table, as you see, we're resetting used diamonds. As one point wears down, the crystal can be turned so that a fresh point sticks out; that way, one diamond lasts a long time."

We moved on to another room where in the presence of three or four men in work aprons a number of diamond-pointed drills and needles were being tested on rotating disks. There were disks themselves being tested as well, solemnly turning at set speeds, round and round and round for a set number of hours, with careful microscopic examination at intervals. In this room, too, diamonds were being ground down to the various shapes needed for cutting special tools, on wheels that were saturated at their rims with oil and diamond dust. All this sounds as if it were happening in a factory or workshop, but in reality the impression given by the big clean rooms was more that of an artist's studio, even where glass cutting was being studied and an occasional glass plate was deliberately broken for the sake of testing.

When we came at length to the special laboratories devoted to Dr. Custers' studies, in the physical section, it was different.

I felt as if we were entering a hospital. Here were an X-ray unit, several high-powered microscopes, and a spectroscope. Dr. Custers explained how light is shot through a diamond crystal and analyzed on a spectrographic plate. From the width and intensity of the resulting bands of color the observer can deduce what elements are present in the crystal—elements, that is, in addition to the carbon that makes up pure diamond. One of Dr. Custers' special studies is that of color in diamond and its causes, and he said that nearly every diamond in nature does contain small amounts of foreign elements, some of which —cobalt, iron, titanium, and chromium—almost certainly affect diamond color. He added that there is still a lot to be learned on the subject and that he has his own ideas about it, but for the moment he didn't elaborate.

Quite apart from these naturally colored stones, he said, are those which have been treated in the laboratory and their color changed deliberately by irradiation in an atomic pile, which turns them green. The depth and strength of the greenness depends on the amount of irradiation, a strong dose producing such a deep bottle green that the stones look black. When a green diamond of this kind is heated, it changes color yet again, this time to amber or yellow. The greater the heat, the more the diamond reverts to its original clarity, that quality usually known as "pure white" or "blue-white," but an irradiated stone never loses all its yellow tinge. "In other words," said Dr. Custers, "some of the radiation damage is permanent. We don't know why." He added that diamonds found near uranium deposits are often green.

Speaking in what must have sounded to himself like baby talk, and looking alternately at my guide and me, he explained the reason for these reactions as far as has been figured out. The atoms of any crystal are arranged in a fixed pattern that repeats over and over one unit structure. This structure, or repetition of units, is called the "lattice," and in some crystalline substances it is a complicated arrangement but in the diamond it is quite simple. Each atom consists of a nucleus and its surrounding electrons, which ceaselessly move in fixed orbits around the nucleus like planets around a sun. Every nucleus is made up of protons and neutrons: a proton carries one unit of positive charge; an electron one of negative charge; a neutron carries neither, which is why it's called a neutron. The number of protons in the nucleus is matched by the number of electrons revolving about it.

When a diamond is irradiated, it is bombarded by more neutrons, which come along at such speed and force that they knock some of the diamond atoms out of position. This starts up a lot of excitement within the crystal. The knocked-out atoms push other atoms out of place, which in their turn crowd out yet more, until the entire lattice becomes disarranged, with atoms hanging halfway between the original positions. Thus the crystal is to some extent transformed, and some of its qualities are changed—those qualities which depend on its original atom structure, chiefly light absorption or, as we see it, color. Changes may also take place in thermal conductivity, thermal expansion, and electrical conductivity, but we don't observe these, though Dr. Custers can with his machines. The general change, or "radiation damage," appears to be permanent, and it is at ordinary temperature; it is "stable." But it's not stable when the diamond is subjected to higher temperature. Then the displaced atoms get stirred up and develop enough energy to go back to their original positions in the lattice, which is why the deep green color changes to yellow. The stronger the heat the paler the yellow, but not all the damage seems capable of being eradicated by this method, and the stone never becomes quite as clear as it was to begin with, before the irradiation. Listening, I recalled stories I had recently heard, of old-time Kimberley methods by which dishonest traders cooked badly discolored stones in various chemicals and sold them quickly while they still looked nearly clear. The cooked stones reverted to their original discolor later on. Those crooks didn't have Dr. Custers' advantages in education or equipment, but in their simple way they got there just the same.

"Do you understand so far?" asked Dr. Custers, who was just warming up. Whether or not he believed my halfhearted assurance, he continued. The irradiation method is comparatively simple because the ammunition particles, the neutrons, penetrate diamond lattices without difficulty. Because they are neutral and carry no electric charge, they aren't pulled out of their trajectory path by particles in the atoms. Bombardment by protons would be more difficult to accomplish because the positive charges already present in the atom's protons would repel them and the electrons would attract them. Moreover, the projectile proton, in shouldering the atom's electrons out of the way, loses energy because it is attracted by the opposite charge. A similar difficulty faces electron projectiles, which are deflected by the atomic electrons and are moreover much lighter than protons or neutrons and so are easily scattered. However, there is a generator that can throw electrons with such force that diamonds thus bombarded are penetrated by them to a certain depth. To that extent, such diamonds turn blue. Dr. Custers brought one out to show me.

"You will observe," he said, handing it over, "that the coloration is only a surface phenomenon. Hold it sideways and look."

I obeyed him and saw that the stone, except for a thin layer of brilliant blue on one side, was indeed clear and colorless.

"The coloration never goes more than one fiftieth of an inch deep with this method," he said, "because the bombarding electrons lose their energy and are absorbed and scattered if they get in any further. No one has yet discovered how to make this treatment any more effective: therefore, looking at it with an eye to commercial uses, I see little prospect of applying such a process to the manufacture of artificial fancy stones for the market. Any colored diamond bought for gem purposes is likely to be one that was found in a mine with that color, unless it has been temporarily doctored. Moreover, the blue of that thin layer is not the same kind of color as that of a natural blue diamond. Let us compare them."

He brought out a blue diamond that had been cut and polished in the ordinary brilliant pattern. We set them side by side. He was right; the natural blue stone had the soft color of sapphire, whereas the other was greenish blue.

"I have theories about these natural blue stones, arising from what I have observed," said Dr. Custers. "Their color may not be due to the presence of foreign elements. I find it significant that every natural blue stone we have examined in this laboratory proves to belong to Type 2-B."

I asked Dr. Custers just what was meant by 2-A and 2-B, and he elucidated. For years, researchers in his field have known that diamonds fall into the two main categories that they call

Type 1 and Type 2. Type 1 is the usual sort: Type 2 is comparatively rare. Differences exist in the spectra and also in habit of fluorescence, which is to say the manner in which the diamonds glow or do not glow under ultraviolet light rays. But after some years it was observed that Type 2 itself must be divided into subdivisions called A and B. (Type 2, incidentally, includes all naturally blue diamonds.) In ultraviolet rays the B diamonds proved themselves strongly phosphorescent; the A did not. Type 2-A diamonds, like those of Type 1, are almost non-conductive of electricity. But 2-B diamonds differ from all the others in showing that they do conduct electricity, and fairly well at that. Until recently this hadn't been suspected; it was one of the accepted facts about diamonds that the non-conductivity made them excellent insulators, though their rarity, of course, rendered such a use virtually impossible in industry.

"Let me show you an experiment proving the point, that is really dramatic," said Dr. Custers. From his collection he chose an uncut diamond of nearly two carats, roughly cubic in shape. It was a beautiful blue, but Dr. Custers didn't show it to me because of its beauty. He looked at it with fond admiration of a different sort. "A rare type of stone," he said, "a 2-B diamond. Watch now. I am placing it between two electrodes, and I will set up a very strong current through it. You must remember that an ordinary type of diamond subjected to such treatment would show no effect whatever, no matter what electrical charge I attempted to put through it. It would remain cool, for one thing: the ordinary diamond doesn't conduct. I now turn on the current. Watch."

I watched. Soon the blue diamond, wedged between its two little plates, began to change. It glowed. The blue color gradually faded in the glow. Dr. Custers stepped up the current. The diamond became a brilliant, fiery red. It glowed as angrily as a piece of coal. It was literally red-hot.

"You see?" said Dr. Custers proudly. He switched off the electricity and took out the diamond with a pair of tongs. "No, don't touch it; it will be some time before that stone is cool enough to handle."

I asked if it would still be blue after it had cooled off, or if the electric charge had altered the color. He shook his head. "It will retain its blue color. In this it is again unlike the diamonds colored by neutron bombardment. These natural blues remain unchanged at whatever heat we have yet been able to apply. Whatever the reason they are blue—and we have no idea as yet why they should be, if it isn't the presence of some other element that causes it—the possibility exists that the color owes itself to some special condition of the structure that is more permanent than the displacement of atoms in an irradiated diamond."

I looked speculatively at the blue diamond, from which the angry glow was now fading. A memory was troubling me, and then I spotted it: I was thinking about a separation method used in the diamond fields of South-West Africa, where the mines are quite different from those of Kimberley. There, the stones are obtained from rich deposits near the coast that bear no resemblance to the volcanic pipes of De Beers and Dutoitspan and the rest. At the Kimberley mines, the diamondiferous blue ground is dug out and crushed, and the diamonds are got out of the crushed material by means of grease tables over which the whole lot is washed. The method depends on the fact that diamonds from blue ground tend to stick to oil or

grease and do not get wet in plain water. But the diamonds
of the South-West deposits are water-deposited, and their surface is different. Their long immersion in the rivers that carried them such great distances across Africa has taken away
their grease-loving, water-hating property. Therefore, unless or
until they have been put through a corrective bath, grease
tables won't separate them from the gravel in which they are
scooped up. Some of the washing plant does treat them in this
manner, but a lot are recovered by a method that was specially
worked out for this purpose: electrostatic separation.

These facts seemed to have some bearing on the matter of
Dr. Custers' diamonds, and I asked him to explain the principle of electrostatic separation to me. Obligingly he did so:
"In that you have two electrodes close together, one of them
grounded and the other positively charged, between is a high-
tension electrical field. Your diamondiferous mixture has been
concentrated as far as possible by gravity methods, being
swirled about in thickened water. What you have left, the
whole lot, approaches the weight of diamond. This concentrate is fed into the separator between the electrodes, and the
high-tension field induces a charge in all its material. Most of
the gravel is made up of various different substances that conduct electricity. But diamonds do not conduct electricity.
Therefore as it enters the field . . ."

"Just a minute," I said, for we had reached the point I was
waiting for. He didn't stop: he was ahead of me.

"According to the theory on which this system is based, diamonds do not conduct electricity," he said firmly, "and so when
all the material passes through, the gravel and the diamonds
don't behave alike. The gravel falls toward the earthed electrode

and loses its charge, becoming negative, so it is pulled toward the upper electrode, which is positive. The attraction carries it past the area of the field, and it falls into the reject bin. But the diamonds, not being good conductors, don't lose their charge so quickly to the earthed electrode. They are still positive, and so they are not attracted by the positive electrode, but are repelled before they pass out of the field. Instead they fall short of that upper electrode, into another bin, and there you are."

Now he paused and waited for me to catch up. I said, "But that only works if you have non-conductive diamonds, didn't you say so?" He nodded. "And so——" I began.

He cut in and finished for me. "And so," he said, smiling, "you lose your 2-B diamonds. That is true, but we've only just found it out."

In London some weeks later, I went to the Museum of Natural History to look at the Hannay diamonds and see for myself whatever could be seen. Like that man in Mr. White's office, I couldn't stop thinking about Hannay and the excitement he caused back in 1880, compared with General Electric and the discoveries of 1955. I didn't know just what to expect: I had got the idea from what Mr. White said that the diamonds would be out on public display under glass, perhaps with Hannay's apparatus laid out next to them. But they weren't on public display. I wandered along a hall thronged with glass cases of plaster models of dinosaurs, and genuine dinosaur skeletons mounted in awesome procession down the middle of the passage, until I came to a wooden wall and a locked door and a sign saying that here was the Mineral Department Enquiries office. There was a bell next to the door which I rang. After a long wait, a young man in a smock opened it. I said I would like to see the Hannay diamonds.

"Oh yes. You telephoned yesterday for an appointment, didn't you?" he asked.

I said I hadn't telephoned: I had merely walked in. I asked if I should have telephoned.

"Oh no, it's not necessary," he said, "but somebody from Canada rang up, and I thought it must be you. A lot of people seem to be interested in those diamonds just now. Just a minute; I'll ask Dr.——" His voice trailed off as he disappeared. He had ushered me through the door into another passage full of more glass cases, but these contained rocks and minerals instead of dinosaurs. Everything looked dusty, as it should in a museum. In a little while there appeared a brisk, crew-cut, spectacled man, walking fast.

"What do you want to know about the Hannay diamonds?" he asked, a trifle aggressively.

I explained that I merely wanted to see them, and, if possible, the equipment.

"Not a trace of the equipment's left," he said, "but we've got the diamonds. Come on up to my office."

We went out of the enormous room, through the passage, out of the door in the wooden wall, and back past the dinosaurs. He talked as we went: "I'm relieved that that's all you want. For a minute I thought you intended to ask me what I think of them."

He didn't go on, so I asked, "Well, what *do* you think of them?"

He shrugged and smiled bitterly and didn't reply. For some

reason I immediately felt urged to take up the cudgels for the long-dead Hannay. "They're Type 2, aren't they?" I asked, as if I were squaring off. "And there are four, aren't there?"

"Ten," said the crew-cut man.

"A or B?" I asked.

"Why, I don't know," he said.

"Well, where would Hannay have got hold of so many rare Type 2 diamonds if he didn't make them?" I demanded. "Back in 1880, too, when he couldn't have known about the different types."

"Who said they were rare?" he asked, in the same chip-on-the-shoulder manner. "I'm not at all sure Type 2 is as hard to find as some people make out. It's an argument I'm not ready to accept until somebody does more careful sampling than I believe obtains at present. As for Hannay having made a large number of them, I have my own theory about *that*. I'll show you something. Here we are." He opened a door and let me into another large office, this one well lighted with windows: he left me there for a minute, and when he came back he was carrying, not diamonds, but a book. This he opened, found his place, and put it down on a desk in front of me.

"Read that and then see what you think," he said triumphantly.

It was an article which included an excerpt from the correspondence column of *The Times* of February 20, 1880; a letter signed by one Professor H. Story-Maskelyne at the Museum of Natural History. Professor Story-Maskelyne was taking this method, a common one even today in England, of informing the public of something he felt they ought to know. He said that a man named J. Ballantine Hannay, a Scot, "has

today sent me some small crystallized particles, presenting exactly the appearance of fragments of a broken diamond. In
lustre, in a certain lamellar structure in the surfaces of cleaving, in refractive power, they accorded so closely with that mineral that it seemed hardly rash to proclaim them even at first
sight to be diamonds."

There was a lot more to the letter, but that was the important part. "What do you think of it?" demanded the doctor
eagerly. He read aloud emphatically, in case I had missed it,
"'exactly the appearance of fragments of a broken diamond.'
. . . Isn't that quite suggestive? Isn't that enough? I never noticed it until this General Electric affair started me thinking
again about Hannay, and I read the article over. As soon as
I came across that phrase I hadn't any more doubts. That dis-
poses of part at least of your argument as to the rare type. If
they were all parts of one diamond . . ."

"Do they in fact look like parts of one smashed-up stone?"
I asked.

He said, "Oh, as to that, it's quite impossible to tell. You'll
see for yourself that they're too small for anyone to make out
to that extent. Remember, we're not sure these are the very
ones Story-Maskelyne wrote his letter about. Hannay probably
sent in several batches during the excitement; he must have
corresponded extensively with the professor, and some of his
first specimens, no doubt, were used up in tests."

I wasn't convinced. I tried to tell him something about the
Research Laboratory experiments, and he showed quick interest at the name of De Beers. "How are they taking this General
Electric news?" he asked. "Hasn't it knocked them pretty
hard?"

I said, "Oh no, I wouldn't say that. The stock went down a bit, but it's gone up again, you know." He looked disappointed. "That's probably partly because General Electric have stated they have no designs on the gem market," I added.

"I don't care about gems," he said impatiently. "They're just nonsense; that side of the industry's purely freak."

"Oh, come now," I began, but he continued rapidly:

"It's the way they hold back their industrials that's always been so bad, and now General Electric's making them. The diamond people are finished! Don't they know they're finished?"

I repeated that I hadn't noticed much perturbation at the Anglo American offices. I said, too, that nobody had been holding back production of industrials: this made him very impatient indeed. "Of course they have; it's common knowledge. There's all that undeveloped land in Sierra Leone, for instance. The General Electric diamond has changed everything, can't they understand? Of course it still costs a lot more than an industrial from the mines, but that's only a matter of time. It's only twice as costly, even now; that's a tremendous achievement." He became thoughtful, almost dreamy. "It's the fact that they've conquered the process, though, that is so exciting," he said. "To be able to attain those pressures and maintain them indefinitely! Why, there's no limit now to what we might find out. Not only about diamonds. I'm not interested in diamonds for themselves. No, the important thing about this is the *process*." He came to himself. "The Hannay specimens. I'll get them while you glance over that book," he said.

He came back carrying in his hand a shallow box about twice the width of a matchbox, with a glass top. He opened it. Two

microscopic slides lay on cotton. Mounted on one was a flat
black blob about the size of a pinhead: "I don't know what
that is," said the doctor, "but I do know it's not a diamond.
It was associated with the others." On the other slide was a
tiny group of ten specks, lined up in two rows of five each. The
whole thing was less than half an inch in width, and even less
than that in height.

"Good Lord," I said, "is that it? I mean, are those them?"

"That's it. There are your Hannay diamonds," said the doctor. He handed me a magnifying glass: "You can see them
quite well with this, if you go over to the window."

Looked at that way, the little black specks came up and
showed that they had depth and weren't black at all. They even
developed sparkle of a Lilliputian sort. They looked like diamonds all right, and the three biggest, if you can call anything
of that dimension big even in the comparative, looked like replicas of a number of diamonds I had seen and handled without
being afraid I might sneeze and disperse them. Perhaps I was
prejudiced, but I saw no signs that they were fragments of one
bigger stone. I handed the slide back to the doctor.

"And now," I said, "all we've got to do, I suppose, is figure
out if they could possibly have been made by Hannay. I already know what your private opinion is on that matter."

He had calmed down by this time and was even ready to
admit another view than his own. He said, "Not everybody
agrees with me. Only yesterday I was asked to bring these things
out to show a couple of people from Canada. They've studied
the matter for some time and they think Hannay did make
diamonds. Furthermore, they've got an idea they can repro-

duce his method. They've scraped up some money and they're going to have a try."

I said, "But if General Electric's already done it in their own way, what's the point?"

"No explaining what some people do," said the doctor. He began putting things away, clearing up his desk. The lid went on over the Hannay specks. "It's a subject that seems to fascinate a lot of people," continued the doctor, looking away from me, "especially at this moment when General Electric's put the cat among the pigeons. What I can't understand is what you say about the De Beers people not being worried. They ought to see for themselves that diamonds are finished. Finished!"

He cheered up again at the thought, and his eyes gleamed.

I thought about the doctor a good deal on the way home, even more than I thought about Hannay, and he was brought back into my mind again the very next morning when I opened *The Times*. There on an inside page under a heading that appears two or three times a week, "The Sale Room," was an interesting story. It seems that a large company of tentative bidders had gathered at Christie's, the famous London auctioneers, the previous afternoon, at just about the time I was squinting at Hannay's specimens in the window of the Museum. They were there for the purpose of making offers for a casket of jewels which had been "made up from various properties," as *The Times* reporter said in his customary discreet manner. The article continued:

"The highest price, 34,000, was given by Messrs. Biggs, of Maidenhead, for a beautiful circular-cut diamond, weighing approximately 47.85 carats, mounted in the form of a pendant with a baguette diamond and circular-cut diamond loop of

angular outline, and a single-line necklet of small diamonds."
For some reason I felt as if I'd answered back to the doctor
at the Museum. Anyway, somebody had. What's more, I reflected, I still think Hannay might have made those diamonds.

# CHAPTER EIGHT

# Staring at Stones

I've been reading Benvenuto Cellini. It seems that when he designed his masterpieces of jewelry he didn't start with a plan and a blueprint and then acquire the gems with which to work them out. A patron would produce an unset treasure, and then Cellini got to work and built up a bauble around it. I understand that Fabergé worked on much the same system: the wealthy nobles of Russia evidently kept a lot of loose jewels, and now and then they merely handed one over to the master for proper setting. It's different nowadays. Most jewelers, whether or not they consider themselves worthy to be classed with Cellini and Fabergé, don't wait around until a patron comes along with a new diamond he wants placed in suitable surroundings. They don't have to depend on commissions, not with such a large public buying their wares ready-made. They find their own material, and when the diamond supply is running low they usually go to London to replenish it. Working on this basis they mostly do well, and you will find few successful craftsmen longing for the old days. Cellini's clients were few in number. But some jewelers do feel cabined, cribbed,

and confined by the fact that they can't shop around widely for
their diamonds. To a limited extent, jewelers can shop around
for their stones, but except for a few maverick buyers the search
for diamonds ends in Kimberley or in London. And since most
of the buyers these days are Americans and Kimberley is relatively inaccessible, the search usually ends in London. If anyone should ask why the Diamond Trading Company doesn't,
under the circumstances, have a branch office in New York,
the answer would seem to be that the United States has an anti-
trust law.

Not surprisingly, the Diamond Trading Company is perhaps
the lowest-pressure selling outfit in the world, operating in an
atmosphere of serenity and almost secrecy, which isn't a matter of policy but is merely a reflection of its complete disin-
terest in publicity. Rough diamonds aren't sold as furs are, by
auction. They aren't displayed like clothes fashions against velvet curtains, to the accompaniment of soft music. What does
happen is that one week out of every month the company holds
what it calls a "sight," in Kimberley and London, during which
buyers from all over the world, if they are lucky enough, are
invited to examine and purchase an allotment of diamonds. A
few weeks before the sight, the company sends out cables to a
select list of buyers announcing the date of the sight and asking
how many pounds of diamonds the buyer is interested in pur-
chasing. When the answers are in, the company proceeds to
make up a parcel for each buyer—these days it usually weighs
less than the buyer hoped for—and the parcels, given the varia-
tions in weight, are as uniform as the company can make them,
with so many big stones, so many small ones, so many blue-
white ones, and so many off-color ones in each. (The sale of

industrials is run on a different, and simpler, basis.) Then the
buyers troop to the company's office, where they are shown
their parcels and given some time—anywhere from half a day
to a few days—to make up their minds whether to purchase
them or not. There isn't much occasion for haggling—the company's policy is usually take or leave the entire parcel—although
some large-scale, old-time buyers are permitted to bargain a bit
on the price of the largest stones in their parcels. It is a rare
buyer who turns down his parcel; these days buyers take what
they can get, knowing that their customers will take what *they*
can get.

Buyers live in a world of their own, and the headquarters
of this world are to be found in a place that always surprises
newcomers, who have been led by jewelers' advertisements to
expect something with more of an Arabian Nights setting. But
blasé old hands don't notice the contrast between the lush
shops far away, where brooches and rings and tiaras are displayed, and the London offices of the Diamond Trading Company in St. Andrew's House, Holborn Viaduct. St. Andrew's
is not far from St. Paul's. Like the land immediately around
the cathedral, this neighborhood has been badly plastered by
bombs. London was much slower than most European cities
to get around to repairing her bomb damage, and this part of
the city has been especially behindhand. There are still open
spaces near St. Andrew's, and car parks where tenements used
to stand, but repair work has begun at last. There is scaffolding
on a nearby house, and not far down the road, across the street,
something very important in the way of construction is going
on. There, the noises of riveting and general racket have rad-
ically changed what used to be a sleepy, solid, antiquely dirty

atmosphere. In spite of this, everything still seems rather grimy and worn just at the approach to St. Andrew's. The house has a narrow entrance difficult for a stranger to find, and the entrance lobby is of postage-stamp size. An elevator shaft takes up most of what space there is. The elevator attendant and one or two porters squeeze in or out, nondescript-looking and bored, among the buyers who ring the bell and wait, usually a long time, before they are carried upstairs. Not merely buyers ring the bell: the company is only one of many tenants occupying the building. One wonders, studying the directory board—most of the firms have something to do with diamonds, one way or another—where on earth they all hide themselves in such limited quarters. Once you have found the right door, however, the first impression is corrected.

It is like that old Joan Crawford movie where a large part of the action took place in a tree house that looked like a small hut from outside but turned into a vast arrangement of halls and polished floors the moment the camera peered through the door. There is a lot of space in St. Andrew's after all—roomy private offices and roomier public ones, with a spiraled iron staircase connecting it all with another, upper, floor. There isn't a lot of chi-chi about the Diamond Trading Company, but it's not shabby either, and the young men who walk swiftly back and forth through the passages with papers in their hands look as if they ought to be in the Foreign Office. Everything is comfortable, but the company isn't satisfied. One of the first things to be seen when you come in is a large model of the new building that is going up across the road behind the wooden barrier, where all the noise is coming from. That is an Oppenheimer building, and when it is finished it will occupy a full block and will shelter all the different departments of the many companies that combine under the Oppenheimer chairmanship. When the architects and builders finally sign off, Hatton Garden will be transformed. There will be a garden, or rather a small park, in front of the new building, and what with the smokeless-fuel ordinance that has already gone into effect in the city, the dingy old neighborhood won't know itself. Then at last, perhaps, it will be possible to imagine a connection between the provenance of rough diamonds and the jewels that are for sale, cosseted on their plushy beds, in Paris and along Fifth Avenue.

On a fine August day I went to the Hatton Garden district to attend a diamond sight. As I approached the Holborn Viaduct I found myself struggling to make my way in the busy streets. There was no reason they should have been more crowded that day than any other and as a matter of fact they weren't: it is always like that in London in August. According to the glossy magazines of the sort that advertise choice diamonds among other commodities, everybody leaves town in August, at any rate before the twelfth of the month, and goes to Scotland to shoot, but it is no use believing the magazines. For every person who leaves London for Scotland, there must be a replacement of a whole organized tour from the Continent or the States. Germans and Swiss and Norwegians and French flood the town. Wearing shorts and carrying great knapsacks that knock down passers-by whenever their owners turn around suddenly, they tour the most unlikely places, even the Holborn Viaduct. Sunburned and attired as if for open sandy beaches, they go shopping near Fleet Street for such things as foam-rubber dish mops and small plaster statues of guardsmen or Sir

Winston Churchill smoking an outsize cigar. I have always been mystified by the things knapsacked tourists buy, and that day their taste seemed more catholic than ever. The only things I didn't see them buying, I reflected, were diamonds, and there was good reason for that. You'd have a hard time finding diamonds in the department store and the little shops of the district. You have to go a long way to get engagement rings, far nearer to the West End. Cut stones aren't a feature of the Diamond Trading Company vicinity; American buyers aren't interested in them because there is a 10 per cent duty at the States border on all cut gems, whereas rough stones can be brought in duty free.

I had an appointment with a man high up in the company, whom I will call Mr. Bentinck because he's not named Mr. Bentinck, and like most company people he has an instinctive dislike of publicity. He met me in the passage outside his office, after I had gone past the man at the door, and the man at the desk, and the man who hangs up coats. It was early in the afternoon on Wednesday. The sights were just about half over.

"We've had a busy time and we're selling a lot of diamonds this month," he said. "It's a mystery to me why we are. *I* don't know who buys all these diamonds when they've been cut and set, but I can tell you that most of them find a market over in your country. We've sold nearly five million pounds' worth already. It's incredible."

He sounded slightly indignant about it, but I knew he wasn't really complaining. The British don't like to rejoice too openly when business is good; they seem to think, as the Romans did, that too much exaltation will bring down the wrath of the gods.

He opened a door and disclosed his office, a room that like
most of the London company's was irregularly shaped, but
spacious and well supplied with windows. Venetian blinds
were drawn against the bright sunlight, and near one of these
shrouded windows, drawn up close to a crack, sat a big man
crouched over a very small table. He held something between
thumb and forefinger which he was studying through a loupe,
and on the table close to his propped elbows was a rough pasteboard box of the shape used for filing cards. Instead of cards it
was filled with white packets like unsealed envelopes. A piece
of the white covering lay unfolded on the table; this was the
thick sort of paper in which diamonds are customarily wrapped
in the trade, lined with a smaller sheet of waxed paper.

At the sight of the stooping back Mr. Bentinck cried out in
pretended dismay, "How do you expect to see diamonds in this
kind of light?"

He stalked past the man at the table and jerked up the blind
so that the sun streamed in over the box and the hands holding
the loupe. "Sitting there in the dark!" he scolded. He turned
to me and said, "Here's the greatest expert in America. He
comes here to buy our diamonds, comes into my office for a
little peace and quiet, and then he tries to pick them out in the
dark. That's how expert he is."

The buyer looked up mildly and said, "It shows how I trust
you, doesn't it?" He spoke with an American accent superim-
posed on another accent, probably from somewhere in Central
Europe. "I trust him, all right," he added to me, and said to
Mr. Bentinck, "I can't make up my mind about this one. Nice
size but the color's against it." He was handling an enormous
crystal so regular in shape that it could have been a model for a

diamond textbook, a nearly perfect double pyramid. It was a full inch in length or more, and nearly an inch thick. He handed it to me and I was surprised, as I always am with diamonds, by the unexpected heaviness of the bit of stone. I leaned over the table and looked at the paper wrapping. Written on it in ink were the words, "Special diamond," and several figures scribbled underneath: the weight in carats and price per carat.

"It's a nice stone. You can use it," said Mr. Bentinck. "Color's against it, of course, it's a little yellow. Though how you could have seen that with the blind down is beyond my comprehension. I should have left it down and charged you more. That color's the reason you'll be paying only ninety pounds a carat instead of a hundred forty."

"I don't know," said the big man. "I'll think it over."

"Sure, you think it over," said Mr. Bentinck.

The buyer wadded the diamond carelessly in its paper and stuffed it in his pocket and picked up the pasteboard box and wandered from the room. Mr. Bentinck watched him affectionately as he went.

"He always buys a lot, that fellow," he said. "One of the biggest dealers in New York. He'll be able to use that diamond."

I said, "It was called a special diamond. Does that mean it isn't a regular part of the run-of-the-mill parcels?"

"That's right. Anything beyond a certain weight, that stands out, is sold separately," said Mr. Bentinck. "There are only a few people who'd be interested in that much of an investment, you see, so we show it to them on its own."

I asked, "And that thing like a shoe box—is that a parcel?"

He assented, and I revised my ideas accordingly. In my mind

I had always imagined a genuine parcel, a little package tied up with string, like those that hang from Christmas trees in holiday calendar pictures.

"Sit down," said Mr. Bentinck, taking his chair behind a huge desk with almost nothing on it. "I turned up an old notebook this morning that interested me, considering the figures we deal with nowadays. I happened to be totting up the week's sales as far as they've gone, and it all furnishes a striking contrast. Like I said, we've sold a lot of diamonds this week, nearly five million pounds' worth. It looks as if we might beat the year's record of '54, when we reached more than sixty-two million. That's a lot of diamonds, you know. I can easily remember when a figure like this week's wasn't considered at all bad for a whole year. Back in 1902 we weren't complaining when we sold about five and a half millions' worth. Of course that meant a good deal more than the same sum would today; money itself meant more. Nevertheless, from five to sixty-five is quite a jump. If anybody had told me in those days that we'd be doing as well as we are today, I'd have tried to have him certified. Naturally some of the increase can be explained away by the sudden jump in industrials. The more the world uses industrials, the more they figure out new ways to use them, added to which is the fact that they're stock-piling them in the States. They've been stock-piling quite a while now, and they go on doing it." He returned briefly to his anxious, indignant manner. "God knows when they plan to stop," he said. "I keep expecting a halt. We just can't keep up with the demand, the way things are just now." He grinned. "As for gem stones, that's different of course. People like gems. Looks as if they'll always like them and always buy more. I don't understand it myself. Not that I dislike them, but wouldn't you think that anyone who wants a diamond would have bought it already? Yet look at the rate the public eats them up. I can't figure how they use them all. Tiaras, collars, rings, everything you can think of has been done to death. What will they do next?"

I said, "Well, there's always something. I saw some gloves embroidered with fake jewels; we'll probably soon see gloves for sale with genuine diamond rings sewed on, all ready to wear. You could change your rings whenever you changed your gloves."

To my surprise Mr. Bentinck seemed to take the suggestion seriously. At any rate he scowled and shook his head. "Vulgar," he said. "I've seen it done."

"You haven't! Really!" I said.

"Fact," said Mr. Bentinck. "I give you my word, I saw it back in 1910 or thereabouts, in Baden I think it was. Couple of smart women were wearing gloves and rings outside, rings of every description, slipped over the glove fingers. It looked terrible. It looked definitely vulgar. Now that's a funny thing; diamond *bracelets* over gloves—you know, those long evening gloves—don't look vulgar at all, do they? Same idea really, and yet the bracelets aren't offensive; I've seen that a dozen times and I don't mind at all. You're a woman; can you tell me why there should be a difference?"

I said I couldn't, but that it must be hard to wear tight gloves over big rings and there was no other way to settle the question unless you gave up either rings or gloves. We pondered the problem for a little, Mr. Bentinck still looking unhappy at the memory of Baden. Then he glanced at the paper near his hand and said briskly, "Well, this isn't getting us any-

where; it's the past I started to talk about, not the future of
jewelry. Here, you can see for yourself in these figures just when
the bigger depressions hit the world. Depressions and wars.
Diamonds don't like war, and they're very sensitive to trade
recessions. All luxury goods are. See here where the record
went up steadily after 1902. More than six million the year
after, and the same, practically, for 1905, and a little jump
here in 1906, up to more than eight millions. I remember how
pleased we were with ourselves. Then it began slumping. Way
down in 1908, to only two and a half. It was bad here in the
City that year—bad all over. Then a sudden jump in 1909, up
to nearly eight again and so on pretty steady to the beginning
of the war, World War I that was. Three and a third million
in 1914. Less than three in '15. Then the trade recovered, right
in the middle of the war; people began investing in diamonds
the way they usually do sooner or later in times of international
stress; they figure it's better to put their cash into something
solid and valuable and small. By the Armistice we were doing
a record business; more than ten million in 1918. Let's see now
—'19 made more than fifteen million. Nineteen twenty wasn't
too bad, but then—oh, oh!—1921 was a bad slump, a very bad
slump; we didn't sell a million. That's when the place was full
of goods that couldn't find buyers. Here's a fairly good recovery
in '22. Nearly six again, and it climbed steadily until 1930 when
it tumbled from over twelve million to just over three. You can
cast your mind back to 1930, I suppose; we all can, vividly.
Lower again the year after and then a steady climb, not a rapid
one but good enough, through the years to 1938. Well, we all
remember that, too, I expect. The market fell to the 1914 level,
only by this time it seemed much lower when it hit the same

place. We'd got spoiled, and less than four millions didn't look like anything at all. But it didn't stay down. As you can see here it hit nearly six in '39 and it's gone on, up and up, ever since. In 1952 we sold nearly seventy million." He sighed. "I don't know where they all go. I often wonder. You'd think the world would be saturated. Still, it isn't, and there the buyers are now outside this door, still buying. Come on, let's look round. Let's see the sights."

This, which must be just about the oldest pun in the business, still gave Mr. Bentinck amusement which he enjoyed in his saturnine way as he led me across the passage. He talked as we went, slowing down as we came within hearing distance of the goal. "You won't see much, at that," he said. "There's nothing to look at at a sight, except a lot of men sitting near windows, staring at stones. That's all there is to diamond buying, but it's important. A man who's making a big purchase has got to chew it over in his mind. How to cut it and all that. How much will be lost, and where. He's got to soak the stone up. Some of them take a whole week over one buy, when it really mounts up to a sum. This season is always the favorite with Americans. They like coming in August, because it's a good time to be out of New York."

We went into the large room that housed the model of the new building. Along the far side was a row of tall windows stretching almost from floor to ceiling, and running along by those windows, just above sill height, was a continuous table. People were sitting there in a row like children in a library reading room, or science students doing some sort of experiment in a crowded laboratory. I had a first, and probably false, impression that they all possessed the same scholarly stoop to their shoulders, but I was not wrong in assuming that they were nearly all crouched each over his box of folded white papers like those I had seen at the big man's table in Mr. Bentinck's office. They had loupes to their eyes, at least most of them did, and they were raptly staring at diamonds, turning them slightly now and then for new focus. There were two young girls among them, working away at heaps of small diamonds, moving this stone and that from the main heap, building up little subsidiary piles on the margin. They were pretty girls in summer dresses. I couldn't quite make out what they were doing there. I know that women have taken over many jobs from the males who used to pre-empt them, but diamond dealers are conservative people, and I tried, and failed, to visualize the progressive diamond merchant who would send his young niece or daughter all the way from America on such a momentous errand as a visit to St. Andrew's House.

"Good Lord, no!" said Mr. Bentinck explosively when I asked him if the girls, too, were buyers. "Those are our own sorters. We let them sit there because we're so busy and crowded. Or, rather, we let the buyers sit there with them." His face clouded. "It's a shame," he said, with the sudden energy of one pouncing on an old and temporarily forgotten grievance. "Men like those, they're important people. Big people. A man who comes all the way to London to buy thousands of pounds' worth of goods has a right to a room by himself. That's the way it should be, theoretically: a man should be able to take his parcel into a room where he can sit alone and study as long as he wants to, all day or all week. You want to be quiet and private when you're figuring out your diamonds, but there's no way of arranging that here. When we're in the new place it'll be much better."

I pointed out that though all this was no doubt true, the buyers did not seem to mind the lack of privacy. "I never saw such concentration in my life," I said.

"Well, that's as may be," said Mr. Bentinck, slightly mollified, "but it's all wrong nevertheless. The fact is we've been overtaken by the housing shortage like everybody else, and by the diamond boom at the same time. It never used to be so bad. Place is a madhouse. Well, now, I want you to take a good look at that fellow there in the corner. You'd never think to look at him—he's a very quiet chap, isn't he?—that he's our best customer, but he is, and has been for years. Never a visit but he doesn't go back to the States with more than twenty thousand pounds' worth of diamonds. I reckon he's bought about thirty thousand this week alone. And argue! That fellow would argue day and night to save a couple of pounds: I often ask him what he thinks he's buying, anyway. Take this time, he's studying the best stone we've been able to put on the market this year, a hundred and twenty-seven carat, at a hundred forty pounds a carat. Beautiful stone. 'How much?' he asked, just as if he didn't know, as if I hadn't told him, and anyway it was written right there on the wrapping. I said, 'How much? You know how much. A hundred forty.' He said, 'What? No, no, you've forgotten; this is *me* you're talking to. I'm not spending a hundred forty on any diamond in the world. I'll give a hundred twenty.' I said, 'You're crazy.' Well, so it went. What a fellow! He pretended to think it over a while, and then he said, 'I tell you what I'll do, I'll put it up two-pun-ten.' Two-pun-ten!" Mr. Bentinck repeated, and went off into a fit of laughter. "There's a man who spends twenty, thirty thousand pounds on every buying trip, and still he says 'Two-pun-ten.' At any rate, I've had one effect on him; I've cured him of boosting the price by a couple of shillings on every bid. What a fellow!" He wagged his head admiringly and led me over to the man in the corner. He clapped the buyer on the shoulder. "Here we are," he said. "What are you going to offer me now for that diamond?"

The buyer scrambled to his feet, smiling and blinking shyly behind his glasses. He was a small, bent man. As Mr. Bentinck had said, he didn't have a prosperous appearance. He looked as if he had just been awakened or violently torn from an all-absorbing book. He put down his loupe and held out his hand: on the extended palm lay a big diamond, roughly oblong in shape, deep and clear.

"I'm getting acquainted with it," he said to me. "Every diamond is different. Just like a person, it's different. There are no two diamonds alike anywhere in the world, any more than there are two persons alike. You have to study and study them until you get to know them. I've been getting acquainted with this one for the past two days."

"It's a good one. It's a beauty," said Mr. Bentinck. "What are you offering for it now?"

"Hundred twenty," said the buyer, smiling. Like two merchants on the stage they argued for a while in broad burlesque. Mr. Bentinck turned to me and said, *sotto voce*, "In the end I'll let him have it for a hundred twenty-five, but don't tell him I said so," while the buyer listened. Mr. Bentinck winked at me, then composed his face to poker gravity and turned back. "Hundred and forty, and that's my last price," he said firmly.

The buyer laughed and looked down at the pool of light in his hand. "You like it, of course you like it," he said to me. "Women always love diamonds."

I said, "Yes. Why do you suppose?"

He seemed as startled as if someone had suddenly asked him why people breathe. "Why," he said after a pause, "it's because women love beauty." He broke off, wrinkled his brow, then dismissed the whole silly speculation. Mr. Bentinck patted his shoulder.

"Take your time," he said. "Just take your time. All the time in the world."

The buyer went back, onto his chair and into the stone. We moved off along the row of stone-gazers. It felt strange to be in a crowd so completely absorbed in what they were doing. As we walked Mr. Bentinck made comments on them, no longer troubling to keep his voice particularly low. It was quite clear that nobody was paying any attention to us; it would take a genuine physical shove to move them from their contemplations.

"Over there's a man from Holland," said Mr. Bentinck, indicating a bowed back. "He's got a big place there; I've been to see it. That man on the other side of the window is another one from the States. He's just a young fellow; doesn't know everything about the trade as yet, but he's learning. He works at it. I like to see a young fellow who's keen to learn. Let's find out how he's getting on."

The young fellow appeared to be making every opportunity that his apprenticeship offered, for he was just as motionless, just as sunk in rapt scrutiny, as any veteran diamond observer. He held a stone before his loupe that was not quite as spec-

tacularly huge as others I had seen that afternoon; even so, it
was no mere splinter. As we approached him Mr. Bentinck said
in hearty tones, "What will you bet me he's going to say he
doesn't like it?"

The young fellow stirred and turned on us the now familiar
blank gaze of a just awakened somnambulist.

"How do you like it?" asked Mr. Bentinck, indicating the
stone.

The young fellow didn't look elated. "I'm not sure," he said.

"Wouldn't you know?" Mr. Bentinck addressed me with
mock exasperation. "First thing he learns to do is grouse. Why,
boy, that's not a bad little stone. I suppose you'll be telling
me next it's got a spot on it."

"Two spots," said the young fellow.

Mr. Bentinck said sadly, "Some people grouse all day long."
We moved away, leaving the young fellow to wrestle with his
soul in solitude.

The sun glared through the high windows. Every room had
its group huddled close to the glass panes, studying; we peered
in at all of them. Even a tiny cubicle, just big enough for a
table and chair, held three American buyers concentrating
fiercely on one small crystal.

"Well, there it is," said Mr. Bentinck as we finished the
rounds and walked out past the man at the desk, the man who
takes coats, the man at the door. "That's about the extent of
it," he said, opening the door for me. "I still don't know who's
buying it all."

The corners of his mouth drooped dolefully; he looked like
a man earnestly searching for something to worry about.

# CHAPTER NINE

## Paradise—Limited

Lieutenant Fred C. Cornell, O.B.E., had to rewrite his book, *The Glamour of Prospecting,* because he didn't ready it for publication until just after World War I. He had a lot of nasty things he had long wanted to say about the Germans, but in his first, prewar draft he had held back; his interests would undoubtedly have suffered if he expressed himself frankly. Cornell's work often took him into South-West Africa, and before the war that territory, of course, was German. He was a prospector. He worked mainly in the Cape Colony, South-West Africa, and environs, and he was indefatigable. A good prospector should always have a streak of romanticism running through his practical nature, but in Cornell this streak seems to have been as wide as Park Avenue. He would hear vague rumors of a discovery hundreds of miles away, and off he would pelt. In this he was probably not as rash as he would seem today, for in the early part of our century there wasn't much future in caution, not in his line. The papers were slow to hear of and report discoveries, and there were no fast trains, no roads for cars, and certainly no commercial airlines by which a man might travel fast and get in at the head of the rush after due investigation of his chances. There was nothing else for a prospector to do except load up his gear and set off. Cornell's life during some of his explorations was definitely rugged, especially when his researches took him into desert regions. He was tough and he stood up to it, but it is impossible not to wonder sometimes, in reading his book of memoirs, if he wasn't perhaps more than usually optimistic even for a prospector. There was for instance his hopeful belief in an "Emerald Valley," in pursuit of which he nearly died in the swamps of Portuguese Africa.

"It is alleged," he wrote, "that a party of Boers, hunting on the Portuguese side of the Labombo Mountains, which form the boundary between Portuguese territory and the North-Eastern Transvaal, came upon some ancient workings which they failed to penetrate, owing to noxious gas; but that at the mouth of one they found skeletons, and with the bones a small skin bag full of rough emeralds. They got away with the stones, which fetched a large sum in Europe, but for some unexplained reason were never able to reach the spot again."

The end of that passage is typical of Cornell's most cherished stories. After a while the reader's mouth stops watering and he grows wary. Or at least he would grow wary if, like me, he had ever been indulging in dreams of following up these clues, as Cornell did, and going treasure hunting. Cornell himself never lost his enthusiasm. Where one or at most two long exhausting journeys into desert wilderness, in the vain search for fortune, might suffice for you or me, especially if the journey entailed getting lost and going without water and racing for life with leopards as seems to have happened to Cornell not infrequently, he went out again, time after time. He never stayed discouraged for long. He was, in short, a really keen prospector, and though he was quite willing to accept any sort of commission in his line of business and go looking for copper, or gold, or minerals of other sorts, his favorite private quarry was the diamond. Diamonds won every time. He didn't mind sacrificing five or six months and a good slice of health in an emerald hunt, but he'd have been really keen on the ordeal if he'd been after diamonds. He had a special feeling for them, too. "Certainly I have no love for the cut and finished article, and nothing would induce me to wear it; but for the rough stone, and the rough life entailed in searching for it, I have always had a passion," he wrote. He was introduced to this kind of search in Brazil, in the diamond fields of Diamantina and Minas Geraes that were supplying most of the world with gems before the discoveries in the Vaal, but inevitably he came to Africa, and there he stayed. It was by mere accident, in a double sense of the word, that he was to die in London.

Cornell was a fairly handy man with the pen. He published two books before he brought out the prospecting volume. One is a collection of war poems, mostly imitations of Kipling:

*We are plastered up with mud above our eyebrows,*
*Till you couldn't tell our features from our rear;*
*There is slush in every quarter, and our boots are full of water,*
    *(And there ain't no blooming beer!)*

The other is a collection of stories about Africa, under the title *A Rip Van Winkle of the Kalahari.* I do not urgently recommend that this work, which appeared in 1915, be dug up and reprinted, though it isn't a bad example of adventure writ-

ing of its kind, which is perhaps overfamiliar since Rider
Haggard. Cornell even put in a faithful Hottentot who kept referring to a Winchester repeating rifle as "the little gun that
speaks many times." But the book is definitely readable and it
adds something significant to his last publication, the memoirs
about prospecting. There he repeats a tale from the *Rip Van
Winkle* and you can see how it took hold of him: the story of
the Bushman's paradise. Or perhaps it was a Hottentot's paradise, for Cornell seemed willing to accept either theory. They
are not the same sort of person: a Bushman is a primitive native, a Pygmy who, like the Congo Pygmies, lives after the manner of the Stone Age, whereas a Hottentot is a member of an
ordinarily statured, yellow-skinned race that has been so much
intermarried with invaders, and so badly defeated, that it has
today practically disappeared. The story that so fascinated Cornell went as follows: that in a remote and inaccessible spot,
inland from the desert coast along South-West Africa between
Walfish (or Walvis) Bay and Lüderitzbucht, there was an
oasis. In that spot, well supplied with water and cattle and
game and all the rest of it, lived a tribe of Bushmen (or Hottentots) completely cut off from the world. Between the oasis
and the coast was a wide stretch of waterless country. The tribe
had taken refuge there from the Germans who were overlords
of the land. Their children customarily played with diamonds
they picked up like ordinary stones, big rough diamonds the
size of walnuts. Their elders were quite aware of the value of
these stones in the world they had renounced, and were determined that the denizens of that world should not discover their
existence and as a result come in and ruin their paradise. They
were well armed, so the Germans hesitated to attack them, and

simply let them be. "There were other versions; in fact, no two agreed exactly," Cornell confesses, "except that the oasis was situated somewhere between Lüderitzbucht, Walfish Bay, the high plateau of the interior, and the sea, and that the diamonds were as big as they were abundant."

He probably heard this story first when he went to Lüderitzbucht in 1908. (He says 1907, but the rush wasn't on then, and he probably remembered wrong.) Until diamonds were found there, South-West Africa had been an object of desire to only a few people, apart from the occasional politician. The whole coast running south from Angola, until it neared Cape Town, was unalluring—sweeps of sand dunes alternating with rocky outcrops. Down to the Orange River it was German, save for Walfish Bay, where the British had got a foothold in 1877, during the race for territory which dissatisfied Rhodes because Britain didn't grab more. From this coast inland, for distances of a hundred and fifty miles or more, the land north of the Orange River was German. Then it was truncated by a straight north-south line that marked the beginning of the desert, the British Kalahari Game Reserve and, north of that, the British protectorate of Bechuanaland. Not many people, not even the land-hungry Boers, felt like disputing the German rights of possession over the coast. The land was useless for farming; it was all, even in British territory below the Aughrabies Falls on the Orange, what Cornell rightly describes as a "terrible desolation of barren, riven rock." However, for some years before the rush on Lüderitz, rumors had been coming out of that arid country that there were diamonds somewhere about. The rumors spoke of sources not only along the coast, where diamonds were actually found ultimately, but from inland, even from the

272 DIAMOND

terrible desolation. And the more remote and inaccessible the country described by the stories, the more Cornell felt himself drawn to investigate. He had an itching foot for uncomfortable terrain. However, prospectors aren't often well enough fixed to indulge their ambitions independently, and Cornell had to take on jobs and bide his time.

He was in Kimberley, the heart of the Diamond Fields, when he got news of the definite finds at Lüderitz. For a long time diamonds had been trickling from there in the hands of natives, who found them while working on a German railroad. After a few unlucky Africans were apprehended in Cape Town for trying to sell them—the authorities would not believe they hadn't filched the stones from South African diggings and thus rendered themselves liable to prosecution under the I.D.B. laws—the boys stopped bringing them down there, but now the early victims were exonerated: there *were* diamonds at Lüderitz, outside the jurisdiction of De Beers. Cornell saw a bottle of them, very small but numerous. At about the same time, however, he was shown a big diamond which its owner declared came from elsewhere, from Prieska, near Upington in British territory, south of the Orange and in a region not usually suspected as diamondiferous. He felt tempted to take the untraveled road. Everybody else was going to Lüderitz, so Cornell went to Prieska. He drew blank. After that he bowed to public opinion and like everybody else proceeded to Lüderitz, but he didn't like it. Lüderitz was not an attractive spot. The crowd apart, he found the cold Atlantic repellent, and he was awed as well as bothered by the sandstorms that often swept the dune-filled coast. "When this prevailing wind reaches a certain violence, the whole country practically gets up and walks." Humanity had rendered nature even less appealing; his first impression on disembarking from the boat that brought him from Cape Town was of bottles, strewn on the sand as far as the eye could see— thousands of bottles that had once carried water. Nearly all the water drunk by the diggers had to be brought in and was sold exceedingly high. Even washing water was imported, because when you washed in the sea water you were immediately and painfully blistered by the pitiless sun. There was no shade at Lüderitz. The diggers invented sunglasses, smoking pieces of the omnipresent bottles and fixing them up with wire ear loops and side protectors made of screen, to keep out the sand.

"What a lot they were!" wrote Cornell in retrospect. "Only a small minority were genuine prospectors, engineers, or mining men with a legitimate interest in diamond discovering; the majority were shady 'company promoters,' bucket-shop experts, warned-off bookmakers and betting-men ['brokers' they usually styled themselves] and sharpers of all sorts, on the lookout for prey in the shape of lucky diggers or discoverers. Then, too, there were a number of self-styled 'prospectors,' runaway ship's cooks, stewards, stokers, and seamen, the bulk of whom had never seen a rough diamond in their lives, and of course a modicum of genuine men of past experience—principally ex- 'river-diggers'—men whose small capital was running away like water for bare necessities in this miserable dust-hole of creation."

The digging itself he found very strange. True, the gravel in which the diamonds were found looked familiar to his trained eye; striped ironstone, or "bantam," and agate, chalcedony, and so on, like that of the Vaal diggings. But the diamonds were neither alluvially deposited like some he had washed for in the past, nor embedded in the blue ground, or kimberlite, that formed the matrix of the crater mines. They lay scattered in the sand, on the surface of the dunes; they tended to hide in little petrified wavelets, hard little ridges of sand. Wind had sorted them out, carrying off light grains, leaving heavier particles of sand, and diamonds, behind—though sometimes the wind grew strong enough to carry off diamonds and all. The diggers crawled after this stuff on hands and knees and picked out the crystals delicately, on the points of their knives. Cornell had done most sorts of mining in his time, but this was new to him, and he was both diverted and disgusted by what seemed to him the slenderness of the pickings. Anyway, everybody else seemed to have got there ahead of him, and he saw no chance of pegging a good claim. He felt sure that these tiny grains indicated the presence somewhere, not too far away, of bigger diamonds. Surely these gem stones had been water-sorted before they were wind-sorted; the associated gravel proved that. So, where had they all come from in the first place, before the water carried them out of the matrix? He thought there was probably a pipe of diamond-bearing blue ground nearby, either inland in the bare, rocky mountains, or under the sea.

There were probably long colloquies on these questions between diggers of an evening, during which Cornell heard about the Bushman's paradise and became convinced that there was something in the story. He gathered more of the legend: he felt he had circumstantial evidence now to prove it. The place *must* exist, otherwise how explain the story of the German soldier? This man, according to the tale, had got lost in the wasteland behind the coast and was given up for dead. Months later he was found, a corpse to be sure, but a corpse only recently, slain by a Bushman poisoned arrow. His pockets had been rifled but his wallet remained, and in the wallet was a map, showing the way to the Bushman's paradise, and along with that map was one stone the murdering Bushmen had overlooked; a magnificent rough blue diamond which, sure enough, was the size of a walnut. Cornell habitually thought of diamonds in terms of walnuts, though in his more extravagant flights of fancy he visualized some the size of human heads. Well, the German officer who found the body and the map, the tale went on, kept his own counsel and later had a shot at exploring the territory himself in secret. But he failed to get very far, because he had no water and the intervening desert was impassable. Naturally, Cornell was fired with ambition to go in and try to get there where the officer had failed. Unfortunately, he didn't have the map.

In the meantime there was still the question of bigger diamonds than those offered by Lüderitz. If the direction of the prevailing wind and current was any indication, they might well have been carried along the sea edge to some place in the south, some one of the many beaches that lay between Lüderitz and Cape Town. Cornell fell in with a friend who had a friend of his own, an ex-digger now plying the trade of a sealer up and down that wild, sun-baked, yet sometimes very cold coast. The sealer was interesting. He had a ten-ton boat, and he declared that he knew a beach a hundred and fifty miles south of Lüderitz that certainly ought to yield diamonds if gravel had any significance at all. It was the exact same stuff that they had all worked so often at the Vaal River, and he had mused many a time, looking at it, that it must be diamondiferous. But he had got himself into trouble with the Lüderitz officials—

sealers were justifiably suspect of smuggling—and couldn't get a digging license for himself; he suggested, therefore, that Cornell and his friend Du Toit use his boat and his knowledge for an exploring expedition, in return for half the proceeds if they should find a fortune. They jumped at the bargain and set forth as soon as possible, loaded with supplies of food and as much water as they could get aboard, which amounted to enough for fifteen to twenty days. A very rough, slow voyage brought them to an island off the part of the coast in question. It was Hallom's Bird Island, one of a number of scraps of land under the protection of the British. It was forbidden to prospect these islets because they were valuable collecting places for guano. They are still unprospected, as a matter of fact, still forbidden territory, and thus a great tantalization to fortune hunters who maintain that they are possibly the source of all the South-West coast diamonds. Anyway, Cornell didn't waste time or break the law by looking around or disputing possession with the hundreds of seafowl and seals that scrabbled on the rocks for foothold. He and his companions were in a hurry, and soon they stood on their beach.

At first sight of this, Cornell was sure they had made the strike of their lives. The pebbles were indeed exactly like those of the Vaal. Before starting to dig he climbed a high dune to look round. "And east, and north, and south there was nothing but sand; not a tree anywhere, only here and there a stunted bush struggling forlornly against adversity; nothing but bare waves, mounds, and ridges of desolate dunes as far as the eye could reach, and to the west the equally (but not more) desolate ocean." No sign of life but a few gulls, and a jackal that followed him a few paces behind, too wild to be afraid. He supposed that jackals and hyenas managed to exist on the fish cast up and stranded by the sea. He never saw the track of any other beast.

"And all along that most disappointing beach we searched day after day, always hoping and expecting to find, and always in vain. We tried the larger-graded pebbles farther from the water first, hoping for Cullinans or at least Koh-i-noors, and by degrees we worked down to the water's edge, where the grit was but little coarser than that of Lüderitzbucht; but all to no avail." The search was arduous, involving the digging every few paces of prospecting pits five or six feet deep. The men had to work furiously fast, too, in order to get as much done as possible while their water supply held out. Ten days they allowed for all this toil, and then they were forced to give up because of the water. Before they left, however, Cornell and Du Toit went inland four miles and climbed the highest dune they could find and got a good view of the country round about. It was, said Cornell, a "terrible waterless waste surrounding us, treeless, bare, and horrible in the glaring sun, awful in its featureless monotony of huge wave after wave of verdureless sand." Yet, still further inland, the faintest shadow against the glaring sky, were mountains.

He and Du Toit went separate ways and did a little exploring. Cornell climbed a series of steep ridges straight across: it was like walking across a city by climbing up and down the houses of the streets one crossed, instead of going through them. He found an ancient river course, dry and choked with sand, now forming a "pan." Du Toit reported, when they were together again, that he had seen more than that—a far-off place that appeared to be thickly wooded; he had even made out

figures moving about among the woods that might have been
gemsbok but could also have been cattle. In any case the place
was certainly an oasis, he said, and Cornell's heart leaped as he
thought of the Bushman's paradise. But . . . they had no water. It was at least a day and a half's travel. The Bushmen or
Hottentots were armed, perhaps—and anyway they had no water. They sailed away instead with their sealer.

During the following years, until the important date of 1914,
Cornell went on a lot of prospecting trips that need not interest
us. One does, however. In 1910 he traveled to Namaqualand,
the British territory just south of German South-West Africa,
to the lonely district where the Orange River emptied into the
sea. It is still called by the German name, Oranjemund, meaning the mouth of the Orange. Cornell was not aiming for
Oranjemund itself, but merely making his way to the Richtersveld territory inland from that spot, enclosed in a wide
bend of the river. In earlier days Richtersveld had been the
scene of a certain amount of copper mining, and Cornell's employers wanted to know if it was worth recommencing; he was
to find the copper if possible and estimate its potentialities.
The nearest settlement to the region was Port Nolloth, fifty-
five miles south of the river mouth, a desolate place. Cornell
spoke feelingly of the fog that spread over the land early
in the morning and the sticky heat that supplanted it when the
sun had driven all moisture away. Leaving Port Nolloth, his
party traveled up to Alexander Bay, and camped there. A short
trek brought them to the Orange. The river mouth was simply
a wide expanse of mud flats interspersed with low islands and
haunted by an abundance of wild fowl. He mentioned flamingos standing in military formation. The men plodded upriver,

observing a number of handsome horses that ran wild on the
riverbanks and islands where there was plenty of vegetation:
they were bred, he was told, by a Boer farmer who lived at the
one farm on the river and sold the horses to German officers.
Though all the country at a distance from the river was desolate, Cornell was refreshed and charmed by the land close to
the water, where grew willows and mimosa thorn and a number
of other trees, as well as smaller plants—a strip of paradise, he
said, running through a desert. The party came upon the old
pegs of an almost forgotten diamond rush, on a flat, sandy
stretch of riverbank: the quest had been quickly abandoned,
Cornell reflected, and the place had probably not been searched
as well as it might have been. Cornell was not the man to give
up hope easily, even on behalf of other people, but he was not
on this journey to prospect for diamonds, and he continued inland, not knowing he had already crossed over land worth millions of pounds.

Making their way through country that now grew broken and
hilly, they found a "deserted and dreary expanse of flat, barren
land" called the Aries drift, composed of silt brought from the
mountains by floods, laid down and built up, and later slashed
by deep canyons made by more floods. Later they crossed much
granite debris: here the canyons were full of boulders of foreign-
type rock, and then at last they reached the Kubos range of
mountains, which looked like a great granite wall. At this point
in his reminiscences Cornell indulges in a gentle joke. It was a
barrier "so formidable that a careful inspection . . . made us
wonder whether, instead of a wagon, we ought not to have
brought an aeroplane!"

Joking apart, it was strangely depressing. Cornell had never

before seen mountains that didn't have some sort of vegetation
no matter how stunted, "but these queer peaks were stark and
bare and of the most startling colours. In serrated lines they
stretched out like the teeth of a saw, and their crumbling slopes
of rotten schist were every shade of red, of brick-red, of flaring
vermillion, of bright orange-red, in fact of every gradation of
colour. And across their flaming flanks, in startling contrast,
were drawn long broad bands of intense black, sharply defined
in huge zigzags, and looking as though they had been scrawled
across the scorching landscape by an enormous pencil. Between
these strange peaks 'ran' rivers of glaring white and yellow sand.
. . . The whole land seemed dead, burnt up, absolutely devoid
of life; not a bird or other living creature was to be seen anywhere. . . ."

The prospectors spent quite a time working their way
through that blasted region, until they felt conscientiously sure
that there was plenty of copper. They saw great rounded boulders "the size of cottages" piled on one another, and a formation of conglomerate and pudding stone exactly like that of the
Johannesburg gold-bearing rock. There were mountains of
pink and white marble, and then at last they had got through
and came out on the other side, to Upington north of the river,
where the Orange no longer ran between German and British
territory but marked the lower limits of Gordonia, south of the
Kalahari, the "Great Thirst." There they made a special journey to the Great Falls, called by their discoverer Thompson,
in 1824, the "Falls of King George" but better known today by
their native name, the Aughrabies. These are higher than the
Victoria Falls and more than twice the height of Niagara. Cornell was suitably awed by the sight, and gives a vivid description

of it, pointing out that the falls' peculiarity, which sets it apart
from the other great waterfalls even more than height, is that
it exists in such a bare, tumbled waste of rock. It was nearly
impossible to reach the edge, as there were several smaller channels to cross first: "And then came chaos: huge monoliths of
riven rock . . . strewn and heaped about in the wildest con-
fusion, piled on each other, balanced and tottering, a maze of
bare stone without a vestige of vegetation. And now the dull
murmur that had scarcely been noticeable became a muttering
thunder of appalling depth: and emerging from a rift in the
labyrinth of granite, we stood suddenly on the edge of a pro-
found chasm. . . . On all sides nothing but riven, shattered
rock, sheer precipice, and great buttress, a nightmare of bar-
renness, of desolation so appalling that one might well be standing in some other planet, some dead world from which all sign
of life had long since vanished."

His commitments as to the copper had been fulfilled, but
this further journey was not taken for the sheer love of sight-
seeing. Cornell was investigating another report, this time by
a man named Brydone, who claimed to have found diamonds
in the mountains near the falls. Cornell had a good try but
found nothing. In fact, in the whole book he never gives himself credit for finding anything, and after a long while one begins to get just a bit suspicious. Soon after this expedition he
joined up with a friend and obtained a sort of permit from
the Cape Government to go into the Kalahari Game Reserve
for a look round. The government was not enthusiastic about
the project. They took the word "Reserve" seriously, and before he could get right of entry Cornell had to promise not to do
any mining. He was so sure, however, that he would find some-

thing—perhaps a gigantic kimberlite pipe, the mother of all the other pipes that were making South Africa rich—that he managed to overcome some at least of their objections, and won permission to travel and look in the forbidden ground. It is doubtful if very many other prospectors, hard-bitten crew though they are, would have been eager to make a similar trip. Cornell had to take an oxcart for the white party's gear. Oxcarts mean oxen, and oxen mean food and water which they were unable to carry with them. For the livestock's maintenance Cornell and his friends meant to depend on t'samma, a desert melon that secretes a lot of juice. Desert-wise oxen and horses simply crunch the fruit: Hottentots baked it in hot ashes overnight and drank the water that collected. Hard-boiled specimens like Cornell chewed the melons without bothering to bake them. T'samma never took away the sensation of thirst, says Cornell, but it seemed to supply the necessary moisture. The main trouble was finding the stuff once you were in the desert, and there was another drawback to depending on t'samma—it destroys the teeth. Cornell seemed slightly discomforted by losing half his teeth on this journey, but he didn't make an untoward fuss about the mishap. He was much more bothered when the party couldn't find t'samma. For a few days desert oxen are able to get on without drinking or eating melons; after that they are in a bad way, and on several occasions water or t'samma was found only just in time. Then, too, the white men sometimes came down with fever, and the scorpions weren't too pleasant, nor were the snakes, but one gets the impression that Cornell didn't really take all this too hard. He was used to it. What *was* annoying was that they didn't find any diamonds. They came upon indications of this and that, especially gold, but when they got back to civilization the government refused to let them follow it all up.

As I said, the continuing failure of all Cornell's treasure hunting becomes not only suspect but almost incredible. How did he keep going so long without the slightest encouragement? Gamblers have stamina, but even gamblers must get the occasional windfall, otherwise they run out of resources—other people's as well as their own. Yet Cornell must have found backing somehow, when he couldn't back himself. In all the book there is only one passage that isn't clear and doesn't tally with the long cheerful record of failure. It comes near the end, just before he starts his account of the beginning of the war. He was again near the Aughrabies Falls, between them and Upington, prospecting at the German border and probably sometimes across it. He refers to "the end of May, when after six weeks of systematic work and exhaustive search in all directions, I was in possession of data that made a trip to the nearest telegraph station imperative." There is no more mention of the data, and then came the war, and after the war Britain took over German South-West Africa. In 1920 Cornell for some reason went to England. It was generally supposed that he had gone to see a man about a deal. He may have had a valuable secret, but he kept his own counsel. He wasn't used to London traffic. Crossing the street soon after arriving in the big city, this seasoned survivor of a hundred close shaves was knocked down and killed.

It was a geologist named Hans Merensky who with a prospecting party found the diamonds of Alexander Bay in 1926, sixteen years after Cornell camped there. Like Cornell,

Merensky was accustomed to study and figure and wonder what he would do if he were a diamond being carried down the Orange River. Unlike Cornell he already had some data to build on, garnered from the discoveries made in the north. Whether or not his reasoning was correct—and scientists are still thrashing the question out—he arrived at the right result. He selected the coast south of the river mouth as the reasonable location for the droppings of an overloaded stream suddenly released into sea water, with the tide flowing south. The question still remains, was there a river about where the Orange is now? Was the tide flowing south then, and were the diamonds brought by river, anyway? . . . But the important point is, the diamonds *were* there. With the first few potholes Merensky sank, he found them. He came upon a number of big stones lying all together, like a clutch of eggs in a nest. He began to pick them up and realized he would need a container. He had a water bottle; he emptied out the water and started to drop the stones into it, but many of them wouldn't go: they were too big to pass through the neck. He stopped to think about what to do; as he told a friend later, he was trembling with excitement. Then he hit on a solution to the agreeable problem. He was not far from the tent where they were camping, and among his possessions was an Eno's Fruit Salts bottle, which as most of the civilized world knows has a big, roomy neck. He ran back and got the bottle and poured out the salts and poured in the diamonds; into that vessel, big as they were, the stones went easily. So far so good; Dr. Merensky emptied the nest and went on to find more, and at least on that day the Eno's bottle sufficed. However, as time passed he found himself getting notional. He trusted his party not to talk—they were as happily busy as he was, picking up diamonds and making their observations—but he still felt nervous, with diamonds like that contained, but not hidden, in a glass bottle. Anybody could see them; it was foolish to leave them unshrouded. Merensky made a trip into town, to the general store, and told the storekeeper that he had suddenly developed a raging sweet tooth and that no mere paper bag would hold the amount of candy he wanted. Storekeepers in the colonies kept their candy in big square tin boxes: it was one of these that he bought. He carried it back to camp, the candy was sent to join the fruit salts, and the party stowed their diamonds in the tin from that time on.

Fred Cornell at Alexander Bay had noticed what he described as a number of middens of oyster shells, which he decided had been left by Bushmen or Strandloopers of long ago, eating enormous meals of shellfish and leaving the remains. "We soon recognized," wrote Dr. Merensky in his report, "that the gravel carrying diamonds invariably contained shells and valves of a large fossil oyster, so that in a sense this particular oyster is an indicator of diamonds." In time the fossiliferous strata became known to diamond hunters as the "oyster line," and prospectors always brightened up when they came upon similar oyster beds and terraces. Sometimes these beds have proved rich in gem stones and sometimes they are barren, but those first discoveries have never been matched for treasure trove.

"Amongst the stones so far discovered," said Merensky, "is one of 81 carats and another—a magnificent specimen—of 70 carats. When shown to experts they acclaimed the parcel as the best they had ever seen recovered in such a short space of time."

Dr. Merensky made a million pounds out of his Namaqualand discovery, for the government could not afford to let this new cache remain outside their control, and he was bought out. Dr. Merensky was happy, but it would be false to say that the Syndicate was. Things were not humming just then in the diamond industry, though the war had made it possible at last to apply control in South-West Africa, where before 1914 the "Diamond Régie," Germany's counterpart of the Syndicate, had sold the diamonds produced throughout South-West Africa at whatever price offered. Fortunately for traders everywhere, the flush of Lüderitz production had coincided with a period of world affluence when nothing, not even this policy of underselling, could have spoiled the diamond market. Since the war and the opening up of South-West Africa the German mining companies had been amalgamated, on the urgent advice of the Syndicate, into the "Consolidated Diamond Mines of South-West Africa," financed by Sir Ernest Oppenheimer's Anglo American Corporation, and Anglo American acquired a controlling interest. C.D.M., as people call it when they are in a hurry, reigned over the large area which the Germans had declared *Sperrgebiet*, or forbidden ground; about sixty by two hundred and twenty miles, from Oranjemund to a point north of Lüderitz. Alexander Bay where Merensky made his find was thus just south of the area. Unfortunately 1920, when the amalgamation was completed, was also the time of a world depression, and C.D.M. didn't get around to starting things going until 1926. Just as they were getting under way the Lichtenburg discoveries were made, and while the Syndicate was still wondering how to cope with this new and unwelcome flood of wealth, Merensky made his strike. It is straining metaphor to call those thumping great beautiful stones that wouldn't go into a water bottle ugly ducklings, but sometimes one's got to strain metaphors.

Besides, it was hard for some of the older Syndicate directors to alter their methods of thinking. They had watched the industry grow up as the original South African mines deepened into great craters, and in their minds the *real* diamonds, the diamonds that counted, came out of those holes in the ground. They felt that alluvials were only an annoying flash in the pan. As things were to turn out, they were wrong, and very glad to be wrong at that, but for the time being it looked bad. Hardly had they swallowed the bitter fact of Merensky's great windfall, when yet more diamonds were found not far from his area.

"The Consolidated Diamond Mines again found it necessary to restrict production," as a short company history in *Optima*, the Anglo American house organ, glumly put it, "but, at the same time, it directed its attention to geological formations north of the Orange River, similar to those at Alexander Bay, and in 1928 found diamond-bearing, marine terraces only a few hundred yards from the prospecting pits unsuccessfully dug in 1912. A careful geological survey showed that, under a blanket of sand, often 30 feet deep, these diamond terraces extend northwards for many miles. By 1930 it was estimated that 2,500,000 carats of gem stones of exceptional quality lay waiting to be mined in a strip stretching 25 miles north of the Orange River. Similar terraces were found round Bogenfels, 106 miles from the Orange River."

Then came the depression of 1929, which demanded a reorganization of the whole diamond industry. Some of the old-timers were badly frightened and they were relieved to pass over the responsibility for saving the diamond trade to the fresh and far-seeing Ernest Oppenheimer, who was so strong-minded that he wasn't afraid of anything, even new diamond discoveries. The Syndicate was replaced by the Diamond Corporation, and so one way or another the traders managed to struggle along until the worst of the depression was over. Production started again in 1935. Nowadays the main part of C.D.M.'s output comes not from the Lüderitz area, which is almost worked out, but Oranjemund, from the terraces that correspond roughly to Merensky's strike. Nowadays, also, nobody is complaining about that strike. As production in the Union wanes and demand steps up, the diamonds of South-West Africa have come to the rescue of the industry.

Like Cornell I started out for South-West Africa from Kimberley. Unlike him I went by plane, thus bringing to reality the joke he made in 1910. True, I was going the other way, but the principle was the same. It was Anglo American's own private plane, and I went in company with a couple of their people. It was just as well for me that I got the lift, for the territory managed by C.D.M., though nothing like as rugged as it was in the old days, is still hardly as easy to get into as Central Park. Both the terrain and the authorities tend to be forbidding to casual tourists. However, it used to be a lot worse. People in Cape Town will tell you stories of how it was at Alexander Bay, when wire surrounded the diggings and everybody working on them, white or black, had to stay put for the duration of their contracts, and there were few mitigations of the climate. In Cape Town they naturally heard about all this because it was only from there that the miners could get to and from

Alexander Bay. There were no roads from Kimberley or Johannesburg and no bridge over the Orange River. Today there are roads and a bridge; there are planes, and a certain amount of railway lines at the coast, and no wire, but even with all this it is still quite a trip.

Right from the take-off the terrain was different; it didn't look at all like the land between Johannesburg and Kimberley, with which I was familiar. I had thought the veld empty-looking and dry, but it wasn't as parched as the land we were soon flying over. For miles we flew past formations that looked like the dried puddles I have seen in gutters in hot weather; there were long gullies down the middle and veinlike tributaries spread out on either side, all dry. Here and there as we approached the river we saw new towns that looked as sharp and empty as blueprints, and then we crossed the water itself with its startlingly green belt of irrigated, growing crops—vineyards and lucerne and orchards and mealies—and found ourselves again over tan-and-brown country. It was not all flat; here and there was a little cone-shaped hill. The land grew more and more somber, though I was assured by the men that the landscape was unusually green and flourishing after a protracted rainy season. The Orange was in flood, they said, and the Aughrabies Falls should present a fine sight.

We didn't have to stop at Upington, the pilot decided; we had enough fuel to go straight through, and so, without coming down, we crossed the lower edge of Gordonia, where Cornell got lost in the sand dunes and nearly died of thirst. Then suddenly—far more suddenly than any earthbound prospector ever came upon them—we were over mountains. From this height I couldn't see details of the rock. I wish I had, for Cornell wrote of huge *kopjes* of rose and amethyst quartz. Then we saw the river, seemingly meandering in slit ribbons over a wide bed, and then it didn't meander any more but ran in a deep channel. The pilot pointed ahead wonderingly; at our height what we saw looked like a mass of smoke from a fire. It was spray coming off the Aughrabies. We flew around and around the falls, the pilot and the other veterans as fascinated as I, for it was in full spate and they had never seen it like that before. A great roaring mass of deep chocolate-colored water tore along like an express train and threw itself over the cliff and disappeared in water smoke: it was amply overflowing its channel. One of our men pointed out that it had broken through and made itself a new subsidiary falls over to one side, but there were already so many smaller channels of angry water and so much outlying activity that I didn't see how he could be sure.

"Some day . . . mankind will be given an opportunity of seeing what no man yet can possibly have seen at close quarters and live, the Orange River in flood, filling not only its self-worn channel, but spreading all over the lip of that nightmare of an abyss in one appalling maelstrom," wrote Cornell.

There were miles of scorched granite and tumbled rocks, and I had long since given up trying to spot any sort of living thing, animal or vegetable, on the landscape. It was the sort of thing I would never have believed could exist in nature, though Doré often pictured it: pure Death. Then the Kubos Mountains suddenly dropped off to a plateau, and the plateau grew less deathlike, and in its turn it dropped off, and then we saw wide spaces of sand and the sea. The plane turned and flew over the river's mouth. There were the mud flats, the sand bars, the bright ribbon of vegetation, and there as we came lower was a flight of flamingos heading upstream just beneath us.

"The bridge. Look at the bridge," said one of the men. He was not speaking to me but I looked too, without seeing anything at first. The men were all staring down and making shocked noises. The bridge was under water—I saw it now, or anyway I saw a line of posts, the tops of posts, around which swirled chocolate water and logs and broken bits of things.

"Looks as if she's holding," said the pilot doubtfully. Everyone agreed that if the Sir Ernest Oppenheimer Bridge stood up to that, it was a pretty good bridge. It was a new type, and the first ever built in that place. We circled and came down at the airport, where people were waiting for us. They had brought Land Rovers specially fitted, like nearly all the cars in the township, with sandproof tops. We drove toward the town across low-lying dunes.

Like everything built by the Oppenheimer group, the town is carefully planned. Every single thing that has gone into it, wood and metal and cement, furniture and paint, animals and plants with which to stock the farms and gardens that supply food, has had to be brought in, by sea or road or air. This being so, it is as well that expense was no object, for it had been an expensive proposition. The "boys" are imported mostly from Ovamboland, in the northern portion of South-West Africa, and to a lesser extent from Portuguese West Africa. They used to travel overland and it took three weeks, but now they are flown in, and flown back when their eighteen-month contracts are expired. White workers and their families are compensated for their lonely lives by high wages, good houses ("You'll find 'Housing' engraved on my heart after I'm dead," said a disgruntled manager), and as much in the way of recreation as can be supplied: organized sports, movies, a clubhouse, company parties. There were about two thousand Europeans when I was there, which makes a respectable town. The general store is kept by a man whose pride it is that many of the women have lately abandoned their old custom of ordering direct from mail houses in Cape Town because they like his stock better. "Only one piece of each pattern for dresses," he assured me. "That way you avoid trouble." There are also an abattoir and butcher's shop, all run by the company on a non-profit basis. There is, of course, all the electricity you can use. As for wire fencing, they don't use it. Where would you go to, even if you managed to elope with a sack of rough diamonds? Desert surrounds Oranjemund, and without a caravan of camels or a plane the theft wouldn't be feasible.

The men who used to swelter and suffer behind the fences of Alexander Bay might wonder why anybody should mind living at Oranjemund, but there are drawbacks, chief of which is the climate. Though it's not true that it never rains—in fact there were fine showers in the morning during my stay—the endless stretches of sand, the occasional fog, and the glaring, metallic sun that drives away the fog can become nerve-racking. Worst of all are the sandstorms, "whirling and driving in all directions," if I may again revert to Cornell, "penetrating every house, every room, every orifice, choking and blinding one." A resident told me that he once started out from Lüderitz for Oranjemund in a brand-new car. He ran into a sandstorm and took shelter until it was over. When he came back he found that there wasn't a scrap of paint left on the front of the car; it was all naked metal, including the front license plate.

When Merensky found diamonds in his test pit he was luckier than he knew, as were the prospectors who first turned up gem stones on the Lüderitz beaches. They might have stumbled instead on the beaches near Oranjemund where sand dunes lie on top of the diamondiferous gravel, and a test pit would have to be sunk thirty or forty feet to reach it. The diamonds of Oranjemund, in gravel which has sometimes been cemented into a conglomerate in the course of time, lie buried under sandy mountains. Moreover, because dunes are dunes and shift their position with every sandstorm, it is impossible to guess, going from one location to another, how deep pay dirt may lie.

Small wonder that the gentlemen on the board of the Syndicate found it hard to readjust their ideas back in 1929 and accept the terraces of South-West Africa as bona fide mines. They are in no way similar to the conventional blue-ground pipes of Kimberley, because they are opencast mines and no tunneling is required to reach the deposit. An average of twenty feet, and sometimes as much as forty feet of sand must be stripped off before the rock is reached. When production first started up in 1935 the sand was taken off by the sort of steam shovels that are used in building operations: dredgers and scoops. Today these scoops have vastly increased in size and elevation. I saw them at work, mounted on Sherman tanks that serve both for foundation and transport: as the ground is stripped the machinery moves forward, and all the while the sand is being run off by conveyer belt. Two million tons a month are shifted in this manner, and for every two million tons of sand, thirty pounds of diamonds are recovered.

Some of the land when it has been stripped looks extraordinary; cut and carved like old clay roads in the country that have been deeply rutted in wet weather and then hardened in the sun, all this magnified as if seen by Lilliputian eyes. This gray, dead, grooved earth was once the floor of the sea. In the deep grooves, boulders and heavy pebbles collected, and some of the heaviest of these pebbles were diamonds that had been rolled along river bottom for many years, emptied into the sea, and finally deposited on the terraces by wave action in shallow water. Laid down in long beds along the grooves, this mixture of pebbles filled up the irregularities of the sea floor and the chinks between the boulders. Flat beds of gravel then covered the whole system, sorted and re-sorted by underwater action of the waves. When the terraced surface of the sea bottom was brought up and exposed to air, it soon became covered by sand, blown about into dunes, and ultimately stripped off by C.D.M.'s scoops. Now the bottom is laid bare, and native workers follow in the wake of the scoops, scraping the last of the gravel from the crevices and leaving the rock as naked to the wind as it was eons ago.

A large stretch of this stripped earth gave me one of the strangest impressions I have ever had. It recalled feelings I used to get when I looked at a picture in a geology textbook, by some imaginative artist portraying the Jurassic period. He had got the same vast, gray, empty feeling into his picture. The palm trees he had sketched sparsely in the distance and the dinosaurs feeding on them did nothing to change the atmosphere of lonely space, and slow, inevitable time, and massive moving water over the gray ground.

The miners dig trenches, occasionally pausing to blast the gravel where it is cemented too strongly for simple digging. In the trenches I was taken to see there were natives carefully digging out gravel, which may have been diamondiferous, from between the great boulders exposed in the slit, and throwing it into small cars that took it up to an extempore washing plant rigged up nearby. The washing process for the test was the primitive method used by the early Vaal River diggers, rather like "panning" for gold. The gravel was sieved and put into a rotary separator. Everything was done by hand, though the largest and most elaborate plant money could supply was within a few miles of the site. This was a simple trench, dug to prove whether or not it was in diamondiferous land, and in hunting for diamonds nothing can take the place of the human eye. Where a trench is already known to be productive, special precautions are taken; every bit of gravel must be got out of the crevices. When the bulk of it has been shoveled out the rest is swept up with small brooms, and every tiny pothole, too, must be emptied and swept clean. Workers who come across diamonds during this delicate process are given bonuses *pour encourager les autres*. C.D.M. are not overly fussy about searching their boys at that stage, but when the time comes for them to leave the compound it is different. I saw a contingent of workers preparing to be flown home to Ovamboland after their tour of duty. Their persons and their luggage were fluoroscoped just in case they were trying to take diamonds out, but nobody was caught. White workers, too, are fluoroscoped when they take their leave of Oranjemund. It is not easy to smuggle diamonds out of that town. Nobody takes furniture out; the furniture in Oranjemund is all company property and stays there, so there isn't much chance to bring out gem stones in the overstuffed sofa. Evidently some people have tried, one way or another.

"We don't have smuggling trouble here," said one of the officials to me. "That is, never with natives." He did not elaborate.

Once you have got over the first impression that it is all the same, you see many kinds of landscape in the dune country, and all spacious. There are stretches of sand and nothing but sand, where scoops are at work or a bevy of fast-moving, jiggling, noisy Le Tourneau machines working away toward the same end. (I remember the Le Tourneaus especially because one of the engineers showed me a small screw that came out of one of them—just a stubby little screw—and told me it costs three dollars to replace, counting transport and tax.) Then there are the flayed ribs of hard rock. There is the township itself, with neat roofs and club and the valiant green of a few plots of grass, and the hospital garden where tortoises swarm and lay eggs in sandy spots and forget about them. The houses and the farm have a temporary look in spite of their solidity and the hard gravel roads between them, like bathhouses on a beach. There is too much sand; they are too easily hidden by the dunes, flat though these seem. A few minutes' drive toward the screening and washing plant, for instance, and they have disappeared.

To look quite right a desert should have camels on it, and as a matter of fact this one used to. The Germans patrolled on camels, and the first prospectors used them because they were so well fitted to the climate; they were brought specially from North Africa, but they have long since been supplanted. There are still horses running wild near the farm at Oranjemund, but they are really wild now; the farmer who bred them and the Germans who bought them are gone. Out of sight of the horses or the town, it is as if all human endeavor on that coast had never been; it seems as quiet and lifeless as Cornell thought it when he landed on the sealer's beach higher up. I didn't even see a jackal. Most melodramatic of all Oranjemund landscapes, however, is that around the washing plant. In other surroundings the plant would probably be just another group of houses full of machinery, roaring away. Here, its roar seems small stuff compared with the wind and the waves, but it looks heroic. It is located at the edge of the sea, and below the sand cliffs the Atlantic pounds the beach for mile on mile of sandy waste. In the brass sunlight it looked wonderfully green and cool the day I saw it.

"Cool is right," said the man who was showing us around. "It's the coldest water in the world, I sometimes think—too cold to swim in at any rate, no matter how hot the air is. The Atlantic's always a cold sea. Pity. But then the current would be too strong anyway."

Back of us the plant was crashing and banging and sending out an endless beltful of washed sand and gravel, shooting it over the edge of the cliff, building up a mountain as it worked. The sea below kept eating away at this mountain, undermining it, receiving tons of it in great splashes, carrying it off, spreading it again on the beach farther down, and there was always more piling up on top; it was a struggle that never ended. Inside the buildings the gravel was being sieved and washed and jiggled about and concentrated by weight. It was a shorter process than the crushing and washing at the kimberlite mines. The heavy concentrate of gravel and diamonds was passed along at last to a brightly lit, studiolike room where men sat behind broad tables, taking small scoops of the concentrate at a time, and sorting out diamonds with tweezers.

"These alluvial diamonds aren't hydrophobic," said the guide, "and they don't stick to grease tables until they have been treated in a solution that makes diamonds unwettable again. And then of course there's the electrostatic separator, which has been a great help in the final stages of concentrating the smaller diamonds."

The men at Oranjemund like to show visitors diamonds in bulk when all the washing and sorting is done—diamonds heaped up like gravel, displayed on trays. I was shown a glittering heap of considerable extent, and told it was one week's output. Dutifully I looked at the crystals, and admired them, and observed as dutifully that they were indeed, as I had been told they would be, unusually clear and beautiful and large. Just the same, my mind kept straying to walnuts. Not many of them could honestly have been declared as big as walnuts.

I was taken back to the town in a carefully caulked Land Rover, all enclosed in glass and rubber-filled crevices, and I strained my eyes to the horizon, over miles of dunes. I asked the driver about Bushmen. He said there were still Bushmen to be found, very occasionally, in the clumps of rocks and mountains inland. He said:

"I've heard that when our fellows were first prospecting and making things ready here, they came across a few Bushmen in the hills, nearly dead. A man or two, a couple of women, a few children—they'd evidently settled into a place where there must have been some water and growth, just about enough to keep alive on, you know. They probably lived there until the water dried up completely, and then I suppose they hadn't got the strength to get away. Our fellows moved them out, and they were fed and all that, and ultimately went to live somewhere else. On a really clear day you can see the mountains."

A long way north and northwest of Oranjemund, there have been enough diamond strikes since Cornell's death to send his ghost into a frenzy. He probably would not have minded so much about missing out on the Tanganyika discovery, when John Thorburn Williamson found his incredibly rich mine: Cornell never even thought about East Africa. But there are so very many diamonds in the Belgian Congo and Sierra Leone that a prospector like Cornell might wonder how it happened that they lay unknown for as long as they did. Of these places, the British colony of Sierra Leone is the smallest, yet it has made history in a big way, only recently. It has given a headache to the Selection Trust, a mammoth concern that has subsidiaries almost everywhere: more than that, Sierra Leone has flouted the Rhodes tradition and got away with it.

The colony is not naturally divided from the rest of the west bulge of the continent, where it occupies a bit of the extreme point: it is a political creation. During the time of the first nationalist urge that swept Africa, in the twenties, some of the less ignorant of the local chieftains demanded that Britain give the country independence. The British Colonial Office retorted, truthfully enough, that Sierra Leone was in no shape for independence; it is, or at any rate was then, a poor place, with only a few tin mines and some agricultural activity on which to support itself. This argument gave signs of wearing out when, in 1930, geologists who had been industriously prospecting West Africa found diamonds there. They were good diamonds, too, occurring alluvially like those of the Congo and the Gold Coast, but whereas most Congo diamonds are small and fit only for industrials, Sierra Leone stones are often of gem quality. However, the colony didn't become wealthy overnight. Nineteen thirty was a bad year for finance. But conditions improved, and in a short time—settling the matter in 1933—the Sierra Leone Selection Trust, a subsidiary of the aforementioned Selection Trust, which I shall refer to from now on as the S.L.S.T., moved in on the strength of a far-reaching monopoly. The government agreed to terms whereby the company owned all rights to diamond prospecting and mining, anywhere in Sierra Leone, until 2033.

The S.L.S.T. set to work and hired local labor. Getting out the diamonds was nothing like so costly and difficult as it is in South Africa. It was not a question of underground mining; it was more like Nooitgedacht. The diamonds lie scattered very widely in topsoil. The ground is dug up and washed in the good old way. "It's easier to find diamonds in Sierra Leone than not," a man told me, exaggerating slightly. "They're all over the place. They lie around on the ground. All you have to do is pick them up and slip them into your pocket." It isn't really as easy as that, but he made his point, which was that such conditions rendered it just about impossible to protect the company's interests. Strangely, however, the African workers were a very long time discovering the benefits of I.D.B. For a long time the legal system worked well, and the S.L.S.T. profited. Europeans taught the brighter boys how to manage the rest of the work gangs, and appointed these leaders to be foremen, and paid them higher wages. The few natives who did make off with diamonds had to run the risk of the occasional company guard—but there were not many guards, it being difficult to know just where to station them—and then discover some way to sell their hot goods. Before the war this wasn't so easy.

It was not until after the end of the war, in 1945, that the situation changed, both as to diamonds and Britain's political attitude toward colonies. It was now understood that Sierra Leone was on the way to independence, and the Colonial Office began training Africans to hold posts in the government. At the same time, diamonds suddenly became more valuable on the black market. The Iron Curtain countries desperately needed industrials, and as relations worsened between Russia with her satellites and the West, industrials were placed on the "forbidden" list: not for export. Among the sparse foreign population were a number of Lebanese, known locally as "Syrians," who provided outlets for illicit stones by buying them and then reselling at a handsome profit to messengers from the Iron Curtain countries. Then at last it dawned on the ordinary Sierra Leone native that for a small outlay—enough for a pick, a shovel, and a sieve—a man could go into business for himself and make a nice living with a minimum of effort. The idea caught on.

People were not impressed when S.L.S.T. officials lectured them about dishonesty. Just over the border, on the Gold Coast, Africans were free to dig for diamonds; all they had to do was buy a license and thereafter they could sell their diamonds straight to the authorities. Sierra Leoneans may have been told about the S.L.S.T. hundred-year agreement, but this did not impress them. They continued to dig for diamonds, no doubt reflecting that in one way, at least, they were better off than the Gold Coast public—they didn't have to pay for licenses. Diamonds poured into the hands of the black marketers, and from there to far-off factories. Conveniently, just about that time a diamond mine was discovered in Kuwait. At least that is what diamond dealers in Kuwait claimed. And though geologists say that this is very unlikely, considering the nature of the territory, nothing could be done about it. The Syrians prospered, and so in their more humble way did the black diggers. For the first time in their lives they learned how nice it was to own bicycles and to buy all the liquor and other luxuries that they wanted. The company campaigned more and more vigorously for law and order, but it was no use. More and more Africans went into the digging business. Whatever jobs they may have held before, they abandoned them. Sierra Leone was beset by a labor shortage; ricegrowers couldn't hire the hands they needed, and even the government went short of help, though in earlier days a government job had been the average African's highest ambition. Thousands of men wandered about the company leases with their pickaxes, almost at will. Inevitably these lone wolves joined up together, and men who had been regular foremen for the company now became leaders of these illicit gangs. Some of them had stayed just long enough at their S.L.S.T. jobs to learn the technique and to find out where the best pickings were likely to be before they set off on their own. So fast was the company turnover in foremen that officials claimed bitterly to be running the best mining school in Africa.

From 1945 to 1955, the S.L.S.T. struggled against mounting disorder. They hired more guards, but the guards ran away and went digging. They called on the government for more police, and the policemen, as soon as they reached the fields, grabbed picks and shovels and went digging. Now and then a malefactor was caught, in spite of all his advantages, but the new government was reluctant to flout public opinion by being harsh, and he usually got off with a light sentence. By the time the company called a halt, it was estimated that at least two million pounds' worth of diamonds were being smuggled out of Sierra Leone in one year—more than the company was exporting on the legal market. Then, too, the situation was growing acutely dangerous. The gangs had become strong and self-confident, and resented being disturbed at their work. Once or twice, when policemen or company personnel attacked them and tried to drive them off the diggings, they simply showed fight and hit back, using their knives. Now and then a shot was fired.

Finally, in 1955, the directors of the S.L.S.T. held a meeting and talked things over frankly. There was no doubt in the minds of most of them that the battle was lost. "We had to give in. There was simply no other way to cope," an official told me after the decision had been made. "And it wasn't a matter of having handled it particularly badly, either. Other colonies were up against the same thing—at any rate the Gold Coast was, and still is. Those people don't want to pay for licenses, and sometimes they go out digging without. Well, one day lately on the Gold Coast a white policeman with two native assistants came upon a gang digging illicitly on the banks of a river. He tried to arrest them and they drove all three into the river. The white man swam across and escaped, but the two natives haven't been seen since; they must have drowned. No, it's not so easy nowadays. . . . We had to decide between complete disappropriation, which was going on every day no matter how we fought it, or negotiation. So we negotiated."

The result of these negotiations, which went on for months between Sierra Leone government ministers and the company, was that the agreement of 1933 has been set aside. The S.L.S.T. has given up all ordinary prospecting rights, retaining only some special leases. In return it has accepted compensation of slightly more than a million and a half pounds. From now on the land will be open to Africans under ordinary mining law, and they will be able to stake out claims with the usual paraphernalia of pegs and so forth. Also, of course, they will have to pay for their licenses. "They won't like that," said my informant, with a certain grim relish. No doubt he is right, and the Sierra Leone Government will find it hard to combat I.D.B. But the interesting fact remains that history has not repeated itself. Sierra Leone's diamonds now belong to the natives of Sierra Leone. Cecil Rhodes wouldn't have cared for that.

# Bibliography

BALL, VALENTINE
>The Diamonds, Coal and Gold of India, London, 1881
>Jean-Baptiste Tavernier's Travels in India (Transl. by), London, 1925

BATEMAN, A. M.
>Economic Mineral Deposits, New York, 1950

CHILVERS, HEDLEY A.
>The Story of De Beers, London, 1939

COHEN, LOUIS
>Reminiscences of Kimberley, London, 1911

COLVIN, IAN DUNCAN
>Life of Jameson, London, 1922

CORNELL, F. E.
>The Glamour of Prospecting, London, 1920

IDRIESS, IAN L.
>Stone of Destiny, London, 1953

JEFFRIES, D.
>A Treatise on Diamonds and Pearls, 1750

DE KIEWIET, C. W.
>A History of South Africa, London, 1942

LEWINSOHN, RICHARD
>Barney Barnato, London, 1937

MANDEVILLE, SIR JOHN
>Travels (Hakluyt Society, Series II, Vol. CI, 1953)

MAWE, J.
>A Treatise on Diamonds and Precious Stones, London, 1813

MILLIN, SARAH GERTRUDE
        Rhodes, London, 1952
        The South Africans, London, 1934
MONNICKENDAM, A.
        Secrets of the Diamond, London, 1941
PLOMER, WILLIAM
        Cecil Rhodes, London, 1933
RAYMOND, HARRY
        B. I. Barnato, London, 1897
ROSENTHAL, ERIC
        Here Are Diamonds, London, 1950
SAUER, HANS
        Ex Africa . . . , London, 1937
SIEVIER, R. S.
        The Autobiography of R. S. Sievier, London, 1906
STREETER, E. W.
        A Short History of Diamond Cutting, London, 1888
        Precious Stones and Gems, London, 1898
        The Great Diamonds of the World, London, 1882
VEBLEN, THORSTEIN BUNDE
        The Theory of the Leisure Class, London, 1924
WILLIAMS, BASIL
        Cecil Rhodes, London, 1921
WILLIAMS, GARDNER F.
        The Diamond Mines of South Africa, New York, 1902

# Index

Oppenheimer, Frank Leslie, 158
Oppenheimer, Gustav, 158
Oppenheimer, Harry Frederick, 105, 150, 151, 158, 170
role in politics, 172–86
Oppenheimer, Mrs. Harry Frederick, 175, 178–80
Oppenheimer, Louis, 158
Oppenheimer, Lady Mary, 149
Oppenheimer, Mary, 178
Oppenheimer, Sir Michael, 170
Oppenheimer, Nicholas, 176, 178
Oppenheimer, Otto, 158
Orange Free State, 29–30, 35
Orange River, 19–20, 25, 271–72, 278–81, 284–87
Oranjemund diamond field, 286–99
O'Reilly, Jack, 18, 21–22

Paris
diamond industry in, 192–93, 210
Peacock Throne, 196–97
Pniel, South Africa, 25–26, 33, 36
Premier Mine, 110, 123, 125, 127–29, 134–42
Pretoria, 131–32
Prinsloo, Joachim, 125–26

Rawstorne, Fleetwood (diamond prospector), 40–41
Raymond, Harry, 103
Red-Cap Company (diamond miners), 40–41
Regent diamond, 194
Rhodes, Cecil John, 43, 98, 146–48
creates first diamond monopoly, 92–97

death of, 104
gains control of De Beers, 83, 85, 89–91
gold-mining interests, 101, 103
role in mechanizing diamond mining, 81–82
role in politics, 100, 104
Rhodesia Broken Hill Development Company, Limited, 145
Rhodesia Copper Refineries, Limited, 145
Rhodesian Anglo-America, Limited, 145
Rhokana Corporation, Limited, 146
Richards, Bishop, 21–22
*Rip Van Winkle of the Kalahari, A*, by Lieutenant Fred C. Cornell, O.B.E., cited, 269–70
Robinson, Sir Joseph B., 107–9
Rothschild (banking house), 92, 94
Rudd, Charles D., 82

Schultz, Wilhelm, 33
Selection Trust, 299–300
Sierra Leone diamond fields, 299–304
Sierra Leone Selection Trust, 300–4
Singh, Sikh Ranjit, 199
Société Minière du Beceka, 146
Star of Africa diamond, 25
Stewart, Mr. (diamond digger), 88
Story-Maskelyne, Professor H., 243
Streeter, Edwin W., 194, 197, cited, 191–2